About the Editors

Boris Korsunsky holds graduate degrees in physics and physical chemistry from colleges in Russia, and a doctorate in learning and teaching from the Harvard Graduate School of Education. His dissertation focuses on cognition as it relates to solving non-trivial physics problems.

In the past 10 years, Dr. Korsunsky has written several thousand original physics problems for various college-level textbooks. He has also published two books of original problems and several articles on physics education. He has conducted numerous workshops for teachers, presented at AAPT (American Association of Physics Teachers) conferences, and participated in developing online teaching materials for physics and mathematics. In 1996 and 1997, Dr. Korsunsky was one of the coaches for the U.S. Physics Team. In 2002, he traveled to Japan as a Fulbright Memorial Fund Scholar.

Dr. Korsunsky has been teaching physics since 1986 and is currently teaching at Weston High School in Weston, Massachusetts.

James L. Love teaches part-time at Richland College, Dallas, Texas, and runs a tutoring service. He has taught Advanced Placement- and International Baccalaureate-level physics in Texas secondary schools and holds two advanced degrees from the University of Texas at Dallas.

In the course of his distinguished teaching career, Mr. Love, now semi-retired, won a number of National Science Foundation and U.S. Department of Energy awards for advanced study and training at national labs, including Kitt Peak Observatory, the Fermi Laboratory, and the Thomas Jefferson Laboratory. He continues a seven-year association with International Baccalaureate as an examiner for extended essays in physics.

About Research & Education Association

Founded in 1959, Research & Education Association is dedicated to publishing the finest and most effective educational materials—including software, study guides, and test preps—for students in middle school, high school, college, graduate school, and beyond.

REA's Test Preparation series includes study guides for all academic levels in almost all disciplines. Research & Education Association publishes test preps for students who have not yet completed high school, as well as high school students preparing to enter college. Students from countries around the world seeking to attend college in the United States will find the assistance they need in REA's publications. For college students seeking advanced degrees, REA publishes test preps for many major graduate school admission examinations in a wide variety of disciplines, including engineering, law, and medicine. Students at every level, in every field, with every ambition can find what they are looking for among REA's publications.

Unlike most test preparation books—which present only a few practice tests that bear little resemblance to the actual exams—REA's series presents tests that accurately depict the official exams in both degree of difficulty and types of questions. REA's practice tests are always based upon the most recently administered exams, and include every type of question that can be expected on the actual exams.

REA's publications and educational materials are highly regarded and continually receive an unprecedented amount of praise from professionals, instructors, librarians, parents, and students. Our authors are as diverse as the subject matter represented in the books we publish. They are well-known in their respective fields and serve on the faculties of prestigious high schools, colleges, and universities throughout the United States and Canada.

Acknowledgments

In addition to our authors and technical editors, we would like to thank Larry B. Kling, Manager, Editorial Services, for his overall guidance and supervision of editorial development; Gianfranco Origliato, Project Manager, for coordinating revisions; Christine Saul, Senior Graphic Designer, for designing the cover; Jeff LoBalbo, Senior Graphic Designer, for coordinating pre-press electronic-file mapping; Network Typesetting, Inc., for typesetting the manuscript; and Pam Weston, Production Manager, for ensuring press readiness.

THE BEST TEST PREPARATION FOR THE

ADVANCED PLACEMENT EXAMINATIONS

AP PHYSICS B & C

Fifth Edition

Edited and Revised by

Boris Korsunsky, Ed.D.
Instructor of Physics
Weston High School
Weston, MA

James L. Love, M.S.
Instructor of Physics
Richland College
Dallas, TX

Larry Dale Brown
Instructor of Physics
Lake Mary High School
Lake Mary, FL

Steven Brehmer
Instructor of Physics
Mayo High School
Mayo, MN

Michael L. Lemley
Instructor of Physics
Buckhannon–Upshur High School
Buckhannon, WV

Research & Education Association, Inc.
61 Ethel Road West • Piscataway, New Jersey 08854

The Best Test Preparation for the
AP PHYSICS B & C EXAMS

Printed in the United States of America

Library of Congress Control Number 2004101374

International Standard Book Number 0-7386-0042-3

REA supports the effort to conserve and protect environmental resources by printing on recycled papers.

G04

CONTENTS

AP PHYSICS B REVIEW

AP PHYSICS C REVIEW

AP PHYSICS PRACTICE TESTS

ABOUT THIS BOOK

This book provides an accurate and complete representation of the AP Physics Exam for both the B & C exams. It includes a completely revised and expanded AP Physics Course Review and four complete Advanced Placement Physics Exams: two AP Physics B and two AP Physics C exams. Each exam is composed of every type of question that can be expected on the AP Physics Exam. In addition, each exam is followed by an answer key and detailed explanations to every question. By completing the exams that correspond to the test you are taking (B or C) and by studying the explanations of answers and our AP Physics Review, you can discover your strengths and weaknesses and thereby become well prepared for the actual exam.

ABOUT THE TEST

The Advanced Placement (AP) Physics B and C Exams are given each May by the Educational Testing Service under the direction of the Advanced Placement Board. The Advanced Placement program is designed to allow high school students pursue college-level studies while still attending high school. The AP exam is administered to high school students who have completed a year's study in a college-level physics course. The exam is taken by students in an attempt to earn college credit. At many colleges, if the student scores high enough on the exam, he/she will earn college credits, and will be granted appropriate academic placement. Thus the student may enter higher level classes while still a freshman.

There are two AP Physics examinations:

- the Physics B exam, and
- the Physics C exam

The Physics B exam primarily tests mechanics, heat, kinetic theory and thermodynamics, and electricity and magnetism, as well as wave theory and modern particle physics. Knowledge of algebra and trigonometry is necessary. The more difficult Physics C exam consists of two tests. One concentrates on mechanics, and the other concentrates on electricity and magnetism. Physics C requires a strong knowledge of calculus.

The Physics B exam consists of two sections.

- Section One — 70 multiple-choice questions
  90 minutes (calculators not allowed)
- Section Two — about 7 free-response questions
  90 minutes (calculators allowed)

The Physics C exam consists of two individual tests that are each divided into multiple-choice questions and free-response questions. The student may choose to take both tests, or, if it is preferred, the student can take either test individually. Each test consists of multiple-choice questions and free-response questions on one topic. Whether you choose to take one or both tests, you must take both the multiple-choice and the free-response questions for that test.

- Test One-Mechanics — 35 multiple-choice questions dealing only with mechanics
  45 minutes (calculators not allowed)

  3 free-response questions
  45 minutes (calculators allowed)

- Test Two-Electricity and Magnetism — 35 multiple-choice questions dealing only with electricity and magnetism
  45 minutes (calculators not allowed)

  3 free-response questions
  45 minutes (calculators allowed)

WHICH EXAM SHOULD YOU TAKE?

You can either take the Physics B or the Physics C exam (which, as we've said, actually comprises two tests), but you cannot take both. There are two ways to determine which exam you should take: *1*. If your school is offering only the Physics B course, then take the B exam. If your school is offering only the Physics C course, then take the C exam. If you are taking the C exam, then you can choose to take only the Mechanics test, only the Electricity and Magnetism test, or both. It is your option depending on which subject areas are more comfortable for you. 2. If your school only offers a general AP Physics course and does not specify B or C, speak to your teacher regarding which exam you should take. Your teacher will be able to review your abilities and knowledge, and help you pick the appropriate exam.

The C exams are more difficult and require more preparation time than the B exam; however, a good grade on either exam may earn you college credit. Keep in mind that you cannot take both exams, and that you cannot change your mind once you have signed up to take one of the exams, so think carefully about which exam you wish to take.

ABOUT THE REVIEW

Our AP Physics B and C Reviews provide a comprehensive summary of the main areas tested on each of the AP Physics Exams, and are written to help you understand these topics. The review chapters have been developed based on the topical outline given by the test administrator.

By studying our review, your chances of scoring well on the actual exam will be greatly increased. After thoroughly studying the material presented in the Physics Review, you should go on to take the appropriate practice tests. Used in conjunction, the review and the practice tests will enhance your skills and give you the added confidence needed to obtain a high score.

TAKING THE PRACTICE EXAMS

Make sure to take the practice exam(s) that correspond(s) to the exam you are taking. When taking the practice exams, you should try to simulate your testing conditions.

- Work in a quiet place where you will not be interrupted.
- Time yourself!
- Do not use books, or similar articles, since these materials will not be permitted in the test center.

By following these tips, you will become accustomed to the time constraints you will face when taking the exam, and you will also be able to develop speed in answering the questions as the test format becomes more familiar.

SCORING THE EXAM

The multiple-choice section of the exam is scored by crediting each correct answer with one point, and by deducting one-fourth of a point for each incorrect answer. Questions omitted receive neither a credit nor a deduction, so it is to your advantage to utilize the process of elimination if you are unsure of an answer. The free-response section is scored by a group of "chief readers" who read your response and assign it a grade. Then both grades, the raw score on the multiple-choice section, and the grade on the free-response section, are combined and converted to the program's five-point scale:

5—extremely qualified

4—well-qualified

3—qualified

2—possibly qualified

1—no recommendation.

Colleges participating in the Advanced Placement Program usually recognize grades of three or higher.

CONTACTING THE AP PROGRAM

For more information on the exams, contact Educational Testing Service or the College Board:

AP Services – Educational Testing Service
P.O. Box 6671
Princeton, NJ 08541-6671
Phone: (609) 771-7300
Fax: (609) 530-0482
E-mail: apexams@ets.org
Web site: http://www.collegeboard.com

AP PHYSICS STUDY SCHEDULES

It is important for you to discover the time and place for studying that works best for you. Some students may set aside a certain number of hours every morning to study, while others may choose to study at night before going to sleep. Other students may study during the day, while still others may study while waiting in line. Only you will be able to know when and where your studying is most effective. Use your time wisely. Work out a study routine and stick to it.

For those students taking one of the two AP Physics C exams, either Magnetics or Electricity and Magnetism, you only have to study the appropriate chapter and take that test. For those taking both tests, be sure to study both subjects.

AP PHYSICS B

You will find below a suggested four week study schedule. You may want to follow a schedule similar to this one. (Depending on the amount of study time before the exam, you may want to add to this schedule, condense it, or reorganize it.)

Week	Activity
1	Study chapters 1 through 3 of the Physics B review. As you study, notice that the bolded words are defined in the text. Because there are so many of them, you may want to design a flashcard study system. Write the word on one side and the definition on the other. You can test yourself or study with a friend. This will help you to remember key terms and refresh your memory as you learn more and more terms throughout the chapters.
2	Study chapters 4 through 6 of the Physics B review in the same manner. Draw up flashcards to test your retention of key definitions and concepts. Take the quiz at the end of each chapter.
3	Take Practice Test 1 and score yourself. Study the detailed explanations of answers to understand why you may have chosen incorrect answers. Go back and re-study any material with which you feel uncomfortable.
4	Take Practice Test 2 and score yourself. Has your score improved? If not, you may want to re-study the review once again in order to fully grasp the more difficult concepts. For extra confidence, you might want to re-work some of the problems of the test to make sure you fully grasp their concepts. You may also want to re-take test 1 or 2 to feel more comfortable with the time constraints of this test.

AP PHYSICS C

This is a suggested six-week study schedule. If you have more time to prepare for the exam, you can add to the schedule, you can change which subject you study first, or, if your time is restricted, you can condense the schedule by combining two weeks into one.

Week	Activity
1	Begin to study chapter 7, Classical Mechanics. For those students who have opted to take only the Electricity and Magnetism exam, you should begin to study chapter 8. If you are taking both Physics C exams, start with chapter 7.
2	Complete your study of chapter 7, Classical Mechanics, or, if you have opted not to take the Mechanics exam, complete your study of chapter 8, Electricity and Magnetism.
3	Take either Test 3 or Test 4. If you are taking only the Mechanics exam, or both Physics C exams, answer questions 1–35 of Test 3 now. If you are taking only the Electricity and Magnetism exam, answer questions 1-35 of Test 4 now. Score yourself and study the detailed explanations of answers to determine your strengths and weaknesses. If you are still weak in certain areas, restudy them.
4	If you are taking only the Mechanics exam, or both Physics C exams, complete Section II of Test 3. Complete Section II of Test 4 if you are only taking the Electricity and Magnetism exam. If you are not satisfied with your score, re-study the appropriate material, and retake the exam. If you are taking both Physics C exams, you should now start studying Electricity and Magnetism, chapter 8.
5	If you are studying for both exams, finish studying the Electricity and Magnetism chapter.
6	Take the Electricity and Magnetism exam (Test 4). Score yourself and read the detailed explanations of answers. Restudy any area in which you still are weak.

AP PHYSICS B

Chapter 1
Vectors & Scalars

Chapter 1

VECTORS AND SCALARS

BASIC DEFINITIONS OF VECTORS AND SCALARS

A **vector** is a quantity that has both magnitude and direction. Some typical vector quantities are displacement, velocity, force, acceleration, momentum, electric field strength, and magnetic field strength.

A **scalar** is a quantity that has magnitude but no direction. Some typical scalar quantities are mass, length, time, density, energy, and temperature.

Note: In this book, vectors are indicated by bold type.

The distinction between vectors and scalars is an important one because different rules of mathematical operations apply to the two. The rules of vector addition and subtraction are the most important ones for AP Physics B.

ADDITION OF VECTORS — GEOMETRIC METHODS

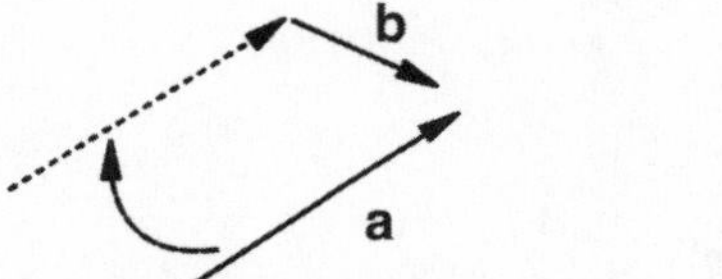

(i) Attach head of **a** to the tail of **b**.

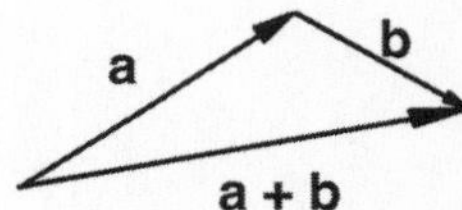

(ii) By connecting the head of **a** to the tail of **b**, the vector **a + b** is defined.

Figure 1 — Triangle Method of Adding Vectors (Head-to-Tail)

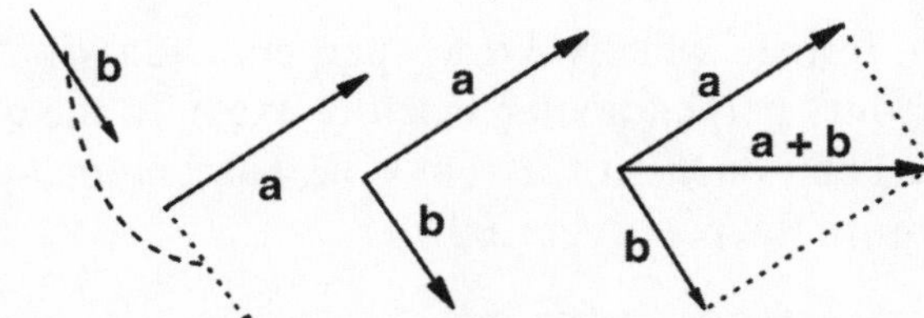

(i) Join the tails of the two vectors

(ii) Construct a parallelogram having **a** and **b** as two of its sides. The long diagonal of the parallelogram represents the vector **a + b**.

Figure 2 — The Parallelogram Method of Adding Vectors (Tail-to-Tail)

SUBTRACTION OF VECTORS

In mathematics, the opposite vector to a given vector **F** has the same length as **F**, but opposite direction. The subtraction of a vector is defined as the addition of the corresponding negative vector. Therefore, the vector (**P** – **F**) can be obtained by adding vector (– **F**) to vector **P**, i.e., **P** + (– **F**). See the following figure.

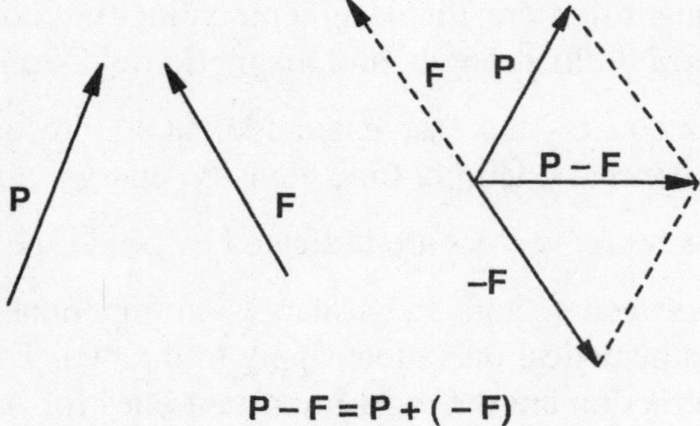

Figure 3 — The Subtraction of a Vector

THE COMPONENTS OF A VECTOR

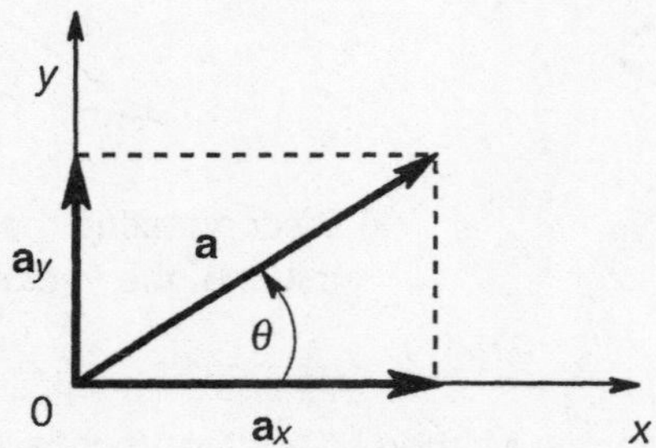

Figure 4 — Vector Components on the Positive *x*– *y* Axes

The components are formed when we draw perpendicular lines to the chosen axes (most commonly perpendicular *x*- and *y*-axes). In the diagram above, a_x and a_y are the components of a vector **a**. The angle θ is measured counterclockwise from the positive *x* axis.

The components of a vector are given by

$\mathbf{a}_x = |\mathbf{a}| \cos \theta$ and

$\mathbf{a}_y = |\mathbf{a}| \sin \theta.$

A component is equal to the product of the magnitude of vector **a** and the cosine of the angle between the positive axis and the vector. Note that the component of a vector can be positive, negative, or zero, depending on the direction of the vector.

The magnitude of a vector can be expressed in terms of its components:

$$a = \sqrt{a_x^2 + a_y^2}\,.$$

For the angle θ,

$$\tan\theta = \frac{a_y}{a_x}.$$

The concept of components is quite useful in solving problems involving vectors. As shown above, given the magnitude and the direction of a vector, one can easily determine its components—and vice versa. Instead of the expression "to find the components of a vector," we often say, "to resolve a vector into its components."

ADDING VECTORS ANALYTICALLY

Very often, we can use vector components to quickly add vectors and to determine the magnitude and direction of the resulting vector. Analytical addition involves adding the components of the individual vectors to produce the sum, expressed in terms of its components.

To find $\mathbf{a} + \mathbf{b} = \mathbf{c}$ analytically:

i) Find the x- and y-components of $\mathbf{a}$:

$$\mathbf{a}_x = |\mathbf{a}| \cos\theta$$

$$\mathbf{a}_y = |\mathbf{a}| \sin\theta$$

ii) Find the x- and y-components of $\mathbf{b}$:

$$\mathbf{b}_x = |\mathbf{b}| \cos\theta$$

$$\mathbf{b}_y = |\mathbf{b}| \sin\theta$$

iii) The components of $\mathbf{c}$ equal the sum of the corresponding components of $\mathbf{a}$ and $\mathbf{b}$:

$$c_x = (a_x + b_x)$$

$$c_y = (a_y + b_y)$$

iv) The magnitude and direction of $\mathbf{c}$ can now be found:

$$|c| = \sqrt{c_x^2 + c_y^2} \qquad \tan\theta = \frac{c_y}{c_x}$$

MULTIPLICATION OF VECTORS

For some physics applications, multiplication of vectors is important.

Multiplication of a Vector by a Scalar

The product of a vector **a** and a scalar k, written as k**a**, is a new vector whose magnitude is k times the magnitude of **a**; if k is positive, the new vector has the same direction as **a**; if k is negative, the new vector has a direction opposite that of **a**.

The **dot product** (scalar product) of two vectors yields a scalar:

$\mathbf{a} \bullet \mathbf{b} = ab \cos \theta.$

The **cross product** (vector product) of two vectors yields a vector:

$\mathbf{a} \times \mathbf{b} = \mathbf{c}$ and $|\,\mathbf{c}\,| = \mathbf{ab} \sin \theta.$

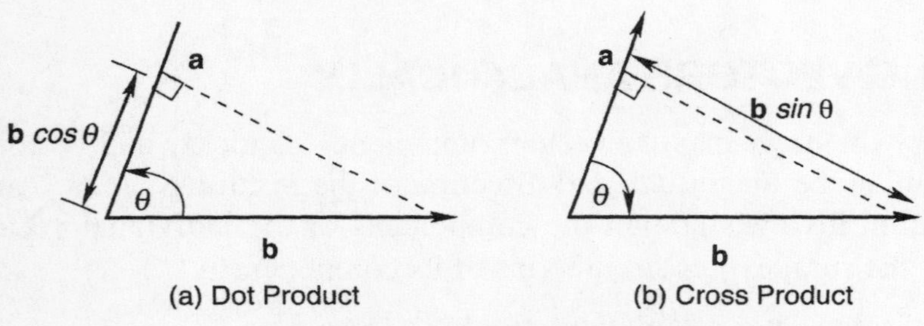

(a) Dot Product (b) Cross Product

Figure 5 — Vector Multiplication

The direction of the Vector Product $\mathbf{a} \times \mathbf{b} = \mathbf{c}$ is given by the "Right-Hand Rule":

i) With **a** and **b** tail-to-tail, draw the angle θ from **a** to **b**.

ii) With your right hand, curl your fingers in the direction of the angle drawn. The extended thumb points in the direction of **c**.

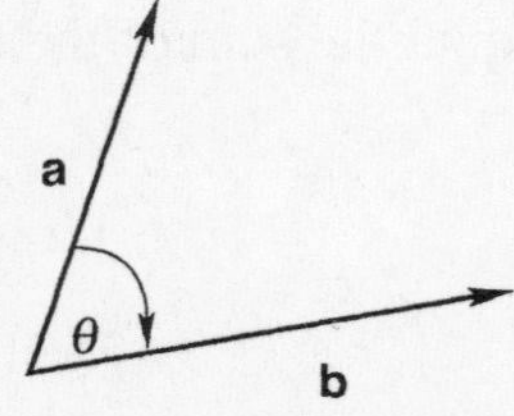

Figure 6 — The Direction of the Vector Product, $\mathbf{c} = \mathbf{a} \times \mathbf{b}$ ($|\,\mathbf{c}\,| = \mathbf{ab} \sin \theta$), is into the page.

AP PHYSICS B

Chapter 2
Mechanics

Chapter 2

MECHANICS

KINEMATICS

Kinematics is a branch of mechanics in which motion is described mathematically without any concern for the reasons that cause motion. Kinematics deals with such concepts as trajectory, displacement, distance, speed, velocity, and acceleration—but not force.

Trajectory is the path followed by a moving object.

Distance is the length of the trajectory.

Displacement is a vector with a tail at the starting point of motion and a head at the ending point of motion.*

Speed is the rate at which distance is being covered.

Average speed can be calculated as

$$v_{av} = d/t,$$

where v is the speed, d is the distance traveled, and t is the time to travel the distance. If, for example, a member of a track team were to run 100 meters in a time of 11.5 seconds, his speed would be 100 m/11.5 s, which is 8.7 m/s.

The understanding of speed leads to a more complex concept known as **velocity**. Unlike speed, velocity is a vector; it has magnitude (speed) *and* direction. The numeric speed value is called the magnitude of velocity and the direction must be specified in order to define velocity. Examples of velocity values are 250 m/s south, or 50 m/s 10° north of west. When calculating velocity values, the equation is similar to the speed equation:

$$\mathbf{v} = \Delta\mathbf{x}/\Delta t$$

where $\mathbf{v}$ is the average velocity, $\mathbf{x}$ is the displacement, and t is the time. The magnitude of velocity can also be represented graphically.

Let us consider an example. Graph A shows the distance covered by a moving object as a function of the travel time. The velocity is represented by the slope of the line. Since the slope of the line is constant, the magnitude of the velocity is constant. However, if the slope of the repre-

* Note: distance and displacement can only be equal if the object is moving in a straight line without ever reversing direction.

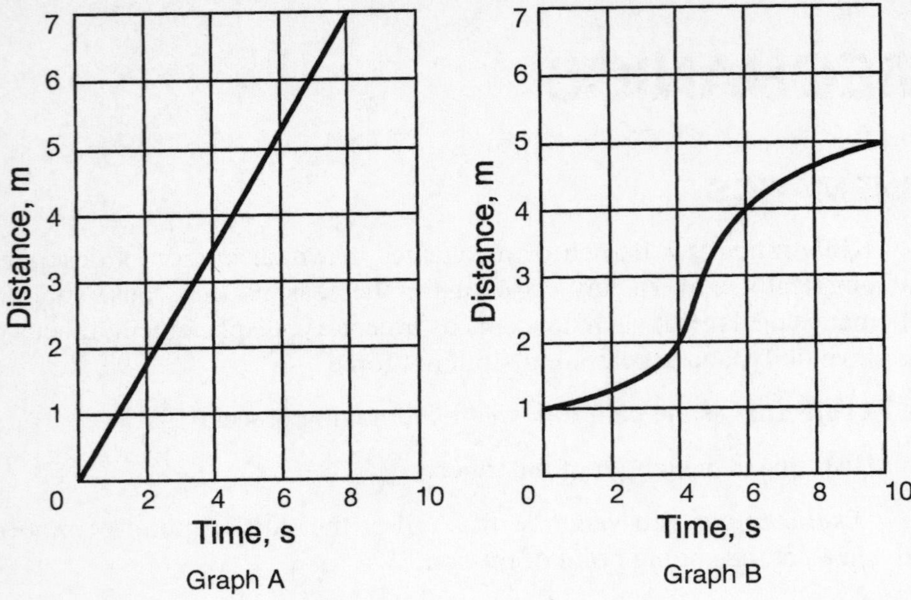

Graph A

Graph B

sentative line changes during the time period, then the velocity is variable. Motion with variable velocity is shown illustrated in Graph B. The velocity increases between 0-5 s, and then decreases between 5-10 s.

The following example shows the importance of the vector nature of velocity.

PROBLEM

An airplane flies due east with a velocity of 150 km/hr. The wind has a constant velocity of 45 km/hr due south. What is the plane's resultant velocity with respect to the ground?

SOLUTION

To solve the problem, a graphic representation is made using vectors (see Figure 7). By adding the vectors representing the plane's velocity and that of the wind, we find the resultant vector, **v***r*, at some angle south of east.

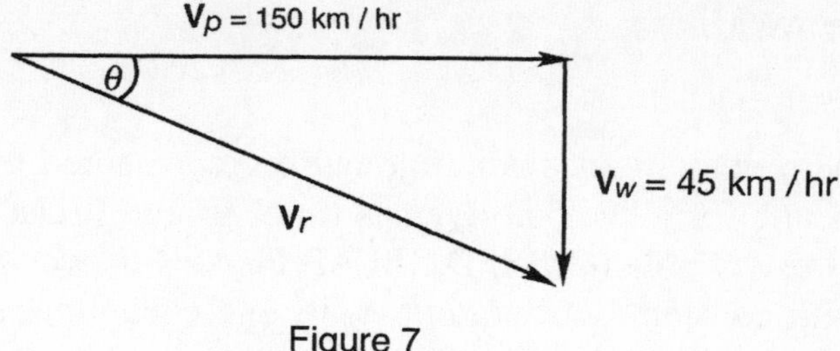

Figure 7

The angle, showing the direction of $\mathbf{v}_r$, can be measured with a protractor. Alternatively, we can solve the problem trigonometrically, using the tangent function:

$$\tan\theta = 45/150 = 0.3$$

$$\theta = \arctan 0.3 = 16.7° \text{ S of E}$$

$$\sin\theta = 45/\mathbf{v}_r$$

$$\mathbf{v}_r = 45/\sin 16.7° = 156.6 \text{ km/hr}$$

Accelerated Motion

When an object changes velocity, it is said to be accelerating. **Acceleration** is the rate of change of velocity within a given time period. Acceleration, a, is defined as the change in velocity Δv divided by the time interval Δt required for the change. The equation is

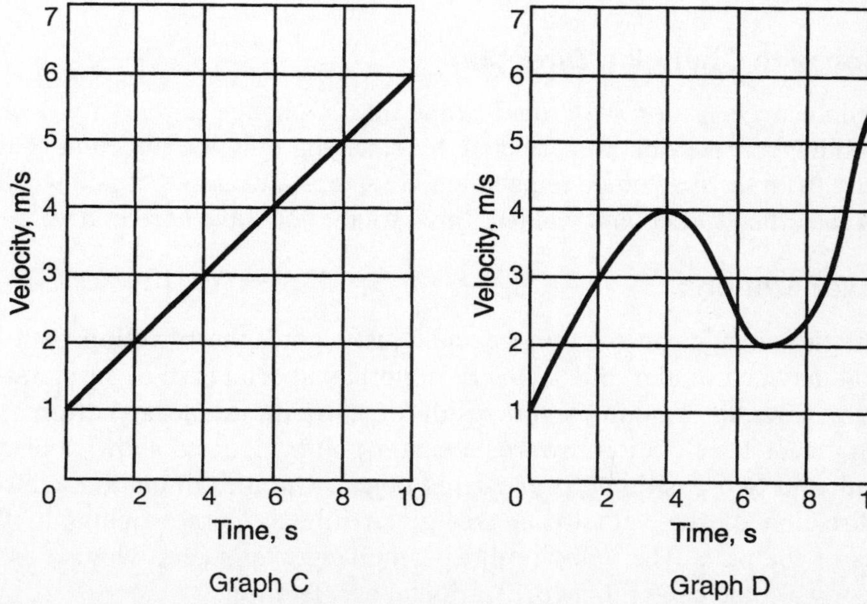

Graph C

Graph D

$$a = \Delta v/\Delta t,$$

where $\Delta v = v_f - v_i$.

As with velocity, acceleration can be represented graphically as the slope of a line for a "velocity versus time" graph. It can also be constant (Graph C) or variable (Graph D). In AP Physics B, we will only consider motion with constant acceleration (with one exception, simple harmonic motion, which will be discussed later).

Let us consider an example. If a car is traveling in a straight line at 36 km/hr, then accelerates to 90 km/hr in 15 seconds, the acceleration would be (90 – 36)/15 = 54/15 = 3.6 km/hr/s. This means that for each of the 15 seconds, the velocity increases by 3.6 km/hr. Usually, the units of acceleration are m/s^2 (meters per second squared). To solve the problem above in m/s^2, one must first convert both velocities into m/s. Calculations show that acceleration is then 1.0 m/s^2.

Motion at Constant Acceleration along a Straight Line

The acceleration equation $a = (v_f - v_i)/t$ can be solved for final velocity so that

$$v_f = v_i + at.$$

Combining this equation with the velocity equation, $v = d/t$, we can produce an equation for the displacement of an accelerating object:

$$d = v_i t + \frac{1}{2}at^2.$$

Motion with Changing Direction

Since acceleration is defined as the rate of change in velocity over a given time, it is possible to accelerate by changing only the direction of the velocity, with the magnitude remaining the same. An example: if you walked 3 m/s east, then turned and walked 3 m/s south, you have accelerated.

Circular Motion

If the changes in direction occur "just right," the resulting path of motion may be circular; this is a very important special case of accelerated motion. Circular motion is the result of **centripetal acceleration**, a_c, which means acceleration towards a center point. Figure 8 shows a circular path and two positions for the same object. Upon examination, we see the direction of the velocity at any given time is perpendicular to the radius of the path. The velocity direction changes in such a way so as to move toward the center, hence, centripetal acceleration.

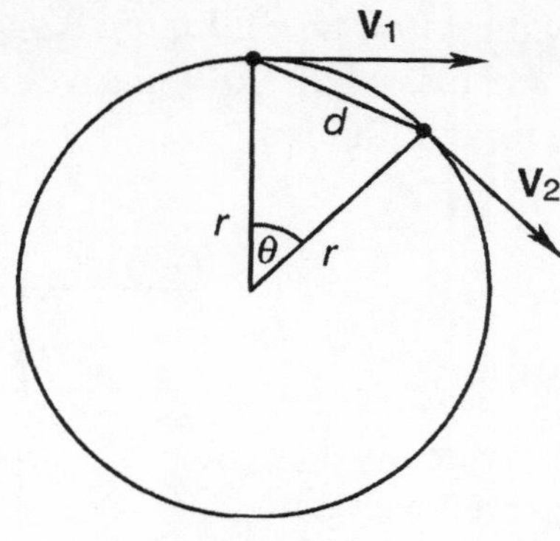

Figure 8

Centripetal acceleration can be calculated as

$$a_c = v^2/r,$$

where v is the linear speed of motion (defined, as usual, $v = d/t$) and r is the radius of motion.

Uniform circular motion is also described by angular quantities. Since the angular displacement for circular motion can be measured by angles (in radians, rad), velocity about a circular path is known as **angular velocity** (ω) so that

$$\omega = \Delta\theta/\Delta t,$$

where $\Delta\theta$ is the angular displacement in rad and Δt is the time interval corresponding to that displacement.

In terms of ω, centripetal acceleration can be expressed as

$$a_c = v^2/R = (R\omega)^2/R = \omega^2 R.$$

Angular acceleration, α, is related to angular velocity by

$$\alpha = \Delta\omega/\Delta t,$$

where $\Delta\omega$ is the change in angular velocity, and Δt is the time interval corresponding to that change.

Falling Objects

On earth, gravity pulls masses toward the center of the earth. Gravity accelerates all masses at 9.8 m/s^2. This means that objects with smaller masses fall at the same rate as larger ones. However, the air around the earth can cause objects to fall more slowly. If we consider objects falling in a vacuum, then we can make predictions about their motion. Any equation involving acceleration, a, can be adapted for gravitation acceleration by replacing a with g (9.8 m/s^2). Figure 9 shows the fall of a mass starting from rest. As the mass falls, it gains velocity at 9.8 m/s^2. The velocity after any given time of fall is

$$v = gt.$$

The velocity after 3 s is

$$v = (9.8)(3) = 29.4 \text{ m/s}.$$

We see that as the velocity increases, the distance traveled per second also increases. The distance an object falls in a given time is given by

$d = {}^1/_2 gt^2$ (note that the term $v_i t$ disappears since $v_i = 0$).

During a three second fall, the distance traveled is

$$d = {}^1/_2(9.8)3^2 = 44.1 \text{ m}.$$

An additional application of free falling objects is the motion of a projectile. Projectiles, such as a bullet, baseball, etc., are objects given an initial velocity that then move under the influence of gravity alone. Air resistance is usually neglected in projectile problems.

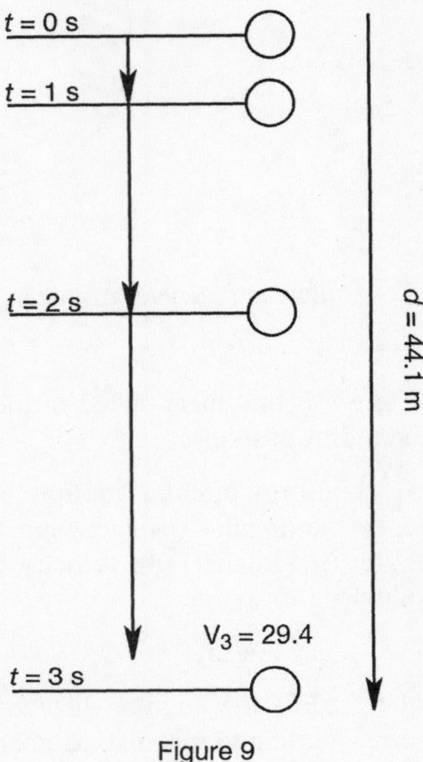

Figure 9

Projectiles have motion characteristics in two dimensions simultaneously. However, these horizontal and vertical motions are independent of one another. Figure 10 shows the path of a projectile with an initial velocity of 100 m/s directed at 30° above horizontal.

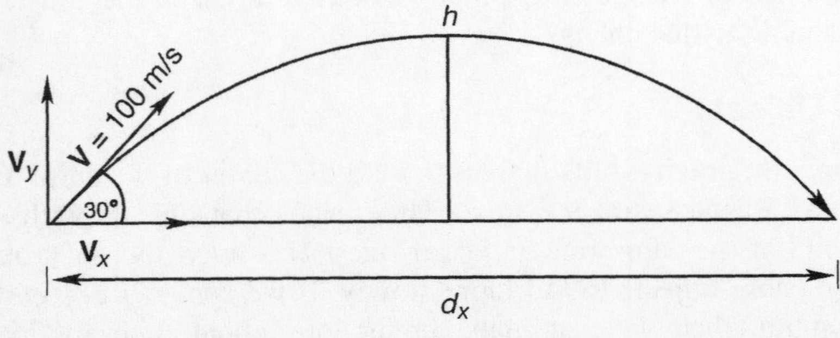

Figure 10

Since v is directed at an angle, the horizontal motion of the object depends only on the horizontal component of v, $v_x = v \cos 30°$. The vertical motion results from the vertical component, $v_y = v \sin 30°$. The horizontal motion is analyzed with a linear equation (the x-component of acceleration is zero), and the vertical motion is analyzed with falling object equations (the y-component of acceleration is 9.8 m/s^2). The maximum height of a projectile, h, is the point at which $v_y = 0$. The time to reach maximum height is half the time of total flight, and can be found since the initial vertical component of the velocity is

$$v_i = v \sin \theta$$

$$v_f = 0$$

$$v_f = v_i - gt.$$

Therefore,

$$t = v \sin \theta / g.$$

For our example,

$$t = (100)\sin 30°/9.8 = 5.1 \text{ s}.$$

The maximum height can be found using the formula

$$h = v \sin \theta t - 0.5gt^2,$$

where t is the value found above. By substitution,

$$h = v^2 \sin^2 \theta / 2g.$$

Thus, $h = (100)^2 \sin^2 30°/(2)(9.8) = 127.55$ m.

Since the total time (t_{total}) is twice the time to maximum height, or 10.2 s, the horizontal distance can be found by $d_x = v_x t_{total}$.

$$d_x = v_x t_{total} = v \cos \theta t_{total} = (100)(\cos 30°)(10.2) = 883.3 \text{ m}.$$

DYNAMICS

The central concepts in the study of dynamics are inertia, mass, and force.

Inertia is an object's tendency to retain its velocity constant unless an external influence changes it. Inertia is the platform for Newton's First Law of Motion. The first law states that for any object, inertia tends to keep the mass moving with a constant velocity (possibly, zero). Once the motion is established, it will not change unless some external force acts upon it.

Mass is the quantity of matter in an object; mass is the measure of inertia.

Force is defined as "push or pull" or, more specifically, "an action that causes acceleration of objects." Examples of forces are gravity (or weight), friction, tension, and the normal force.

The relationship between the applied force and the acceleration of an object is given by Newton's Second Law of Motion. Mathematically,

$$\mathbf{F} = m\mathbf{a},$$

where **F** is the force applied in a particular direction, *m* is the mass to which the force is applied, and **a** is the acceleration resulting from the force. The acceleration is in the same direction as the applied force. The unit of a force is

$$\mathbf{F} = (\text{kg})(\text{m/s}^2),$$

which is called a Newton (N).

If more than one force is applied to an object, the concept of net force is useful in analyzing its motion. **Net force** is the resultant of the forces and it can be found as the vector sum of the individual forces. For instance, a 20 N force east and a 13 N force east will result in a net force of 33 N east. Conversely, a 400 N force north added to a 150 N force south results in a net force of 250 N north. Finding the net force when the individual forces act at angles other than 0° or 180° requires a vector diagram and the use of trigonometric functions to calculate. The determination of net forces from force combinations is known as **force composition**.

PROBLEM

Suppose a race car has a mass of 2000 kg. What force must be applied to the car to accelerate it in a straight line at 5.0 m/s^2?

SOLUTION

Since

$$\mathbf{F} = m\mathbf{a},$$

$$\mathbf{F} = (2000 \text{ kg})(5.0 \text{ m/s}^2) = 10{,}000 \text{ N}.$$

PROBLEM

> Two forces act on an object. One is 10 N east and the other is 30 N 30° south of west. What is the magnitude and direction of the resultant net force?

SOLUTION

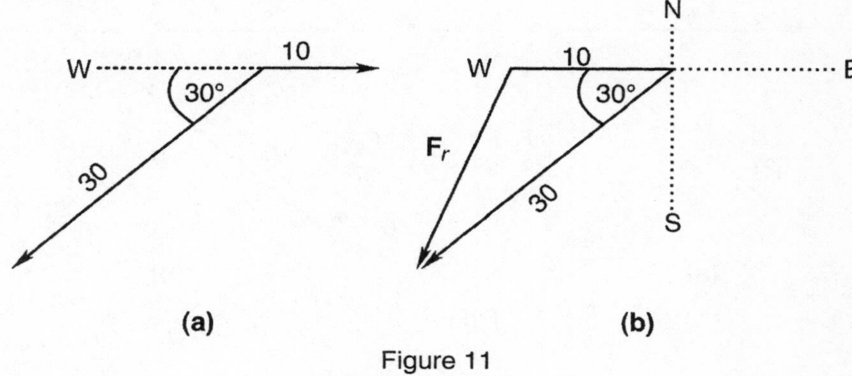

Figure 11

To solve, a diagram is necessary. Figure 11 shows the proper position and proportion of the forces. If we now diagram the addition of the 30 N force to the 10 N force, we create a triangle that shows the resultant force, $\mathbf{F}_r$. Since $\mathbf{F}_r$ is opposite the known angle, the law of cosines is applied to find its magnitude.

$$F_r = \sqrt{F_1^2 + F_2^2 - 2(F_1)(F_2)(\cos\theta)}$$

$$F_r = \sqrt{10^2 + 30^2 - 2(10)(30)(\cos 30°)}$$

$$F_r = 21.9 \text{ N}$$

To find the direction of $\mathbf{F}_r$, the law of sines is applied. Solving for θ_2,

$$\sin \theta_2 = (\sin 30°)(30)/21.9 = 0.685$$

$$\theta_2 = \arcsin 0.685 = 136.8°$$

This is the angle in question, but not considered the proper direction for $\mathbf{F}_r$. $\mathbf{F}_r$ is 136.8° from east, but the west reference is closer. In this case,

$$\theta = 180° - \theta_2 = 180° - 136.8° = 43.2° \text{ S of W}$$

$$\mathbf{F}_r = 21.9 \text{ N, } 43.2° \text{ S of W}$$

Alternatively, one can solve vector problems using components. Components use right-triangle relationships and the sine and cosine to resolve forces into their *x* and *y* (orthogonal) components. Law of cosines and law of sines are used, typically, when the forces involved do not exhibit themselves as a right triangle. Examine Figure 12 below.

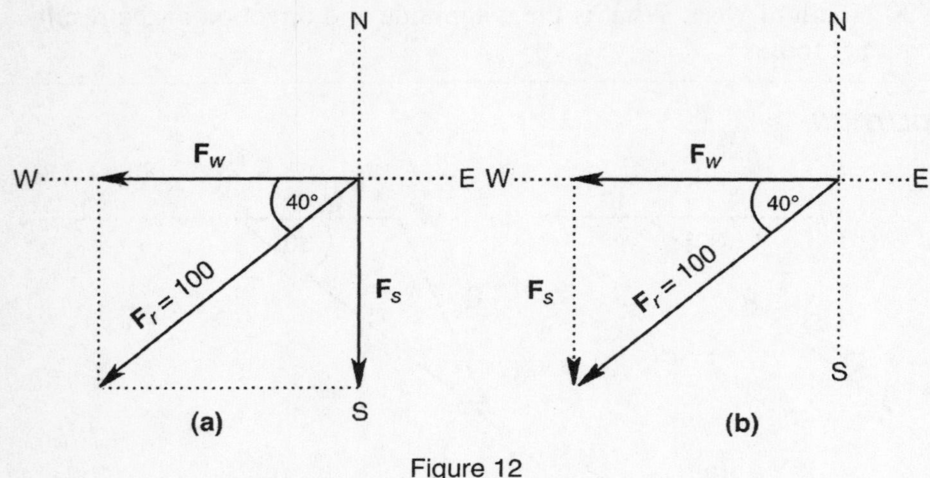

Figure 12

Shown here is a force of 100 N, directed 40° S of W. What amount of the force is south and what amount is west? Adding the forces in triangular form, shown in Figure 12(b), shows $\mathbf{F}_s$ as the sine of 40° and $\mathbf{F}_w$ as the cosine of 40°.

$\sin 40° = \mathbf{F}_s/100$

$\mathbf{F}_s = \sin 40° \, (100) = 64.3$ N south

$\cos 40° = \mathbf{F}_w/100$

$\mathbf{F}_w = \cos 40° \, (100) = 76.6$ N west

If the net force acting on an object is zero, the object has zero acceleration. It is either at rest or moving at a constant velocity. Such an object is said to be in equilibrium. For instance, a car moving straight at 100 mph is in equilibrium despite having a velocity.

Newton's Third Law of Motion establishes forces as reciprocal interactions. This law states that when one mass exerts a force on another, the second mass will exert a reaction force equal in magnitude and opposite in direction to the first. For example, if you stand on the floor, your feet press down on the floor—as a result, the floor presses upward on your feet with a force of the same magnitude and opposite in direction.

Universal Gravity

As stated earlier, the force of gravity pulls masses toward the earth. Newton developed a gravity relationship known as the Universal Law of

Gravitation. The idea is that all masses exert a pulling force on all other masses. The attraction between two masses is directly proportional to the product of their masses, and inversely proportional to the square of the distance between their centers. The equation describing the attraction between two masses m and m', located a distance d from each other is

$$\mathbf{F} = \frac{Gmm'}{d^2},$$

where G is the universal gravitational constant. The value of G is 6.67×10^{-11} Nm^2/kg^2.

The motion of planets and satellites can be approximated by considering their orbits as circular. The gravitational force between the masses is the centripetal force that maintains circular motion. From the Law of Gravitation,

$$\mathbf{F} = \frac{Gmm'}{d^2}$$

and the centripetal force is given by

$$\mathbf{F}_c = m\omega^2 r.$$

Since $\mathbf{F} = \mathbf{F}_c$ and d can be considered the radius of the orbit,

$$Gmm'/r^2 = m\omega^2 r$$

$$\omega^2 = Gm'/r^3$$

This equation is the determination of the angular velocity for planetary or satellite orbits where m' is the larger mass that holds the planet or satellite. This equation also shows that the mass of the orbiting satellite, m, does not affect its velocity. If we wish to place a satellite in orbit 75,000 km from the center of the earth, the velocity required to maintain this orbit is

$$\omega^2 = Gm'/r^3,$$

where G is 6.67×10^{-11} Nm^2/kg^2, m' is the mass of the earth, equal to 5.96×10^{24} kg, and r is the radius, 7.5×10^7 m.

$$\omega^2 = (6.67 \times 10^{-11})(5.96 \times 10^{24})/(7.5 \times 10^7)^3$$

$$\omega^2 = 3.97532 \times 10^{14}/4.21875 \times 10^{23}$$

$$\omega^2 = 9.4229807 \times 10^{-10}$$

$$= 3.07 \times 10^{-5} \text{ rad/s}$$

Since one radian is the angle at which the circumference traveled equals the radius, the linear velocity is

$$v = (3.07 \times 10^{-5} \text{ rad/s})(7.5 \times 10^{7} \text{ m/rad})$$

$$= 2302.5 \text{ m/s} = 2.3 \text{ km/s}.$$

In most problems, planets and satellites are assumed to have circular orbits. In reality, the orbits are always elliptical. The object that serves as the center of gravitational attraction (the sun, in the case of the earth) is always located in one of the two foci of the ellipse (foci is the plural form of the Latin word focus). Figure 13 shows the orbit of the earth around the sun. The earth is shown at the farthest point of the orbit (called the apogee). The closest to the sun point is called perigee. Note that, in reality, the earth's orbit is nearly circular; the separation from the sun varies from 149,000,000 km to 151,000,000 km.

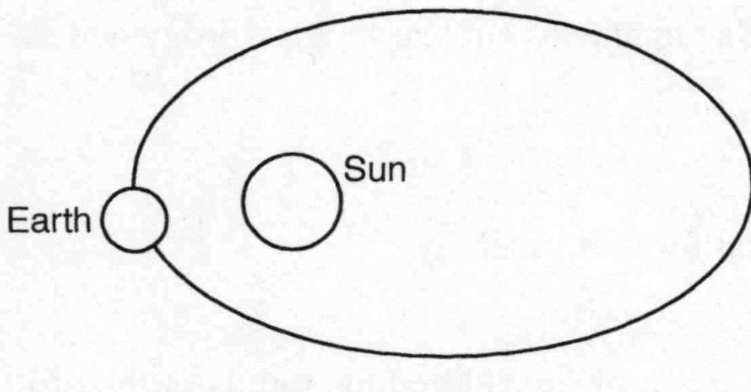

Figure 13

Friction

Sometimes, one object must slide over another to move. When this occurs, a new force must be considered, **friction**. Frictional forces resist the sliding motion of objects by acting parallel to the sliding surfaces in the direction opposite the motion. The magnitude of friction depends upon certain situations, one of which is the nature of the surfaces that are in contact. Smooth surfaces have less friction than rough surfaces. Also, friction depends on the magnitude of the force pressing the surfaces together. Looking at Figure 14, we see a block on an incline.

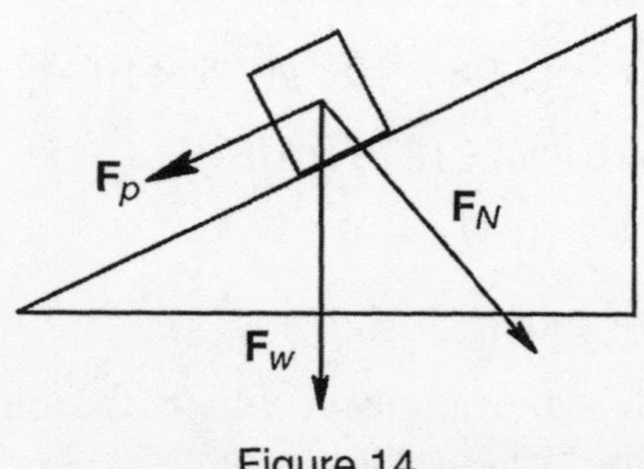

Figure 14

The weight of the block is shown as force $\mathbf{F}_w$. If $\mathbf{F}_w$ is resolved into its components, we see that component $\mathbf{F}_p$ is parallel to the surface and could cause motion. Component $\mathbf{F}_N$ is the pressing force perpendicular to the surface. This force is known as the normal force, hence, $\mathbf{F}_N$. Figures 15(a) and 15(b) show the friction force, $\mathbf{F}_f$, which is parallel to the surface.

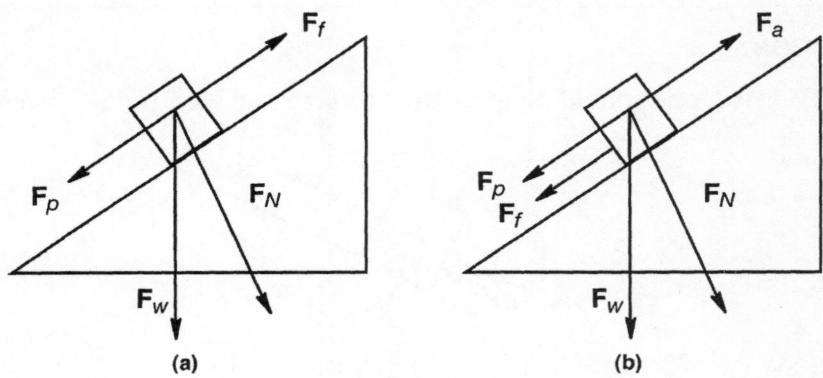

Figure 15

In Figure 15(a), $\mathbf{F}_f$ is opposite $\mathbf{F}_p$. If the block is at rest or sliding down the incline with a constant velocity, then $\mathbf{F}_f$ will equal $\mathbf{F}_p$. If $\mathbf{F}_p$ is larger than $\mathbf{F}_f$, the block must accelerate down the incline because of the net force in that direction. If a force, $\mathbf{F}_a$, is applied to the block, parallel to the surface and up the incline, as shown in Figure 15(b), then $\mathbf{F}_f$ will be in the direction of $\mathbf{F}_p$. For $\mathbf{F}_a$ to cause upward motion, it must be at least as large as the sum of $\mathbf{F}_p$ and $\mathbf{F}_f$:

$$\mathbf{F}_a \geq \mathbf{F}_p + \mathbf{F}_f.$$

For motion up the plane, $\mathbf{F}_f$ is determined by $\mathbf{F}_N$ and the contact surfaces. The surface factor can be incorporated using the ratio of $| F_f |$ to $| F_N |$, which is unique to each case. This value is the coefficient of kinetic friction μ_k. In this ratio,

$$\mu_k = | F_f | / | F_N |,$$

where μ_k is the numeric value related to the types of surfaces in contact.

In cases of the surfaces not moving to each other, the coefficient of static friction is defined,

$$\mu_s = | F_f | / | F_N |,$$

where $\mathbf{F}_f$ is the maximum force of static friction.

PROBLEM

> The coefficient of kinetic friction between a metal block and an inclined surface is 0.20. If the surface makes a 20° angle with the horizontal, and the mass of the block is 80 kg, what force is required to slide the block up the incline at a constant velocity?

SOLUTION

To solve, one should diagram the problem and identify all forces.

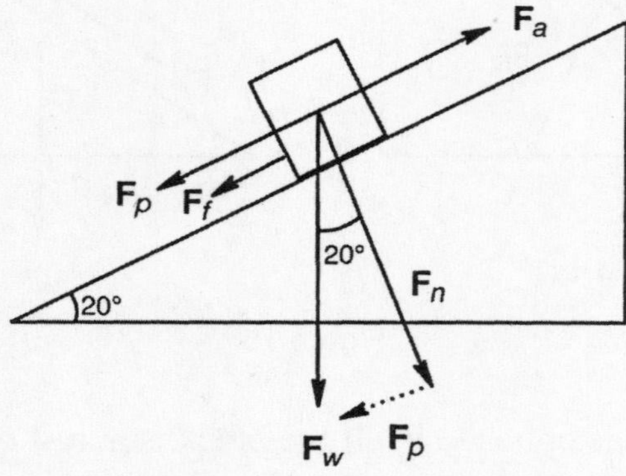

Figure 16

The weight of the block, $\mathbf{F}_w$, would be 80 kg times the gravitational acceleration for earth, $g = 9.8 \text{ m/s}^2$.

$$\mathbf{F}_w = (80)(9.8) = 784 \text{ N}$$

To resolve $\mathbf{F}_p$ and $\mathbf{F}_N$,

$$\mathbf{F}_p = \sin 20°(\mathbf{F}_w)$$
$$= \sin 20°(784) = 268 \text{ N}$$
$$\mathbf{F}_N = \cos 20°(\mathbf{F}_w)$$
$$= \cos 20°(784) = 737 \text{ N}.$$

Since the block is moving up the incline, $\mathbf{F}_f$ is in the direction of $\mathbf{F}_p$. To produce constant velocity up the incline, the net force must be zero:

$$\mathbf{F}_a = \mathbf{F}_p + \mathbf{F}_f.$$

Because μ is given as 0.20, $\mu = \mathbf{F}_f / \mathbf{F}_N$ becomes $\mathbf{F}_f = \mu\mathbf{F}_N$.

$$\mathbf{F}_f = \mu\mathbf{F}_N = (0.20)(737) = 147 \text{ N}.$$

Solving for $\mathbf{F}_a$,

$$\mathbf{F}_a = \mathbf{F}_p + \mathbf{F}_f = 268 + 147 = 415 \text{ N}.$$

TORQUE AND ROTATIONAL STATICS

Until now, we have viewed forces acting on objects as if they were acting on a single point. However, sometimes the object cannot be approximated as a point. To analyze the motion of such objects, it is helpful to know that every object has a special point, called the center of mass. The center of mass (center of gravity) is the point within an object where all the mass is considered to be concentrated. If all forces act on the center of mass, the object's motion is the same as the point objects we have examined. If, however, forces act on points other than the center of mass, a new situation occurs: an object may begin to rotate. **Torque** is the term used to describe an action that causes rotation of an object about a fixed pivot point.

Torque is defined as

$\tau = Fd\sin\theta$ (for AP Physics B)

or

$\boldsymbol{\tau} = \mathbf{r} \times \mathbf{F}$ (for AP Physics C),

the cross product of displacement, **r**, and force, **F**. A force applied to a rigid body a distance **r** from a certain pivot point will produce a torque at the pivot point (see Figure 17).

The displacement vector **r** extends from the pivot point to the point where the force **F** is being applied. The torque vector $\boldsymbol{\tau}$ is perpendicular to **r** and **F**, since the cross product of the two vectors is always perpendicular to each one. The direction of $\boldsymbol{\tau}$ is given by the right-hand rule. In the

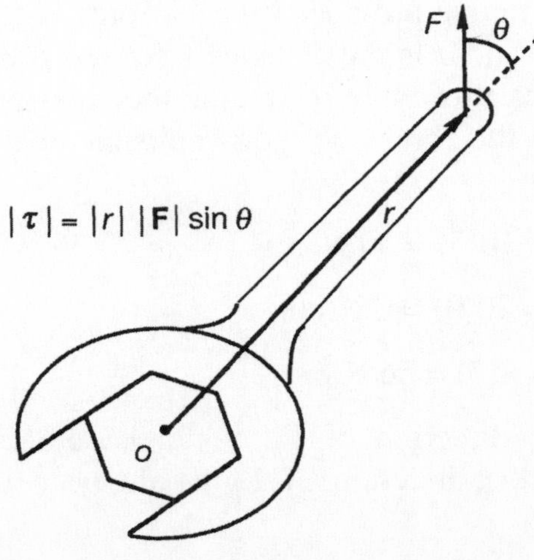

Figure 17

diagram on the previous page, the torque vector extends upward, out of the paper, from point O. If the torques applied cancel out each other, the net torque is zero. This condition is known as **rotational equilibrium**, and no rotation will occur. If the net torque is not zero, the object will rotate about the pivot point. In order for an object to be in equilibrium with respect to both straight line and rotational motion, two conditions must be satisfied:

1) The net force must be zero.

2) The net torque must be zero.

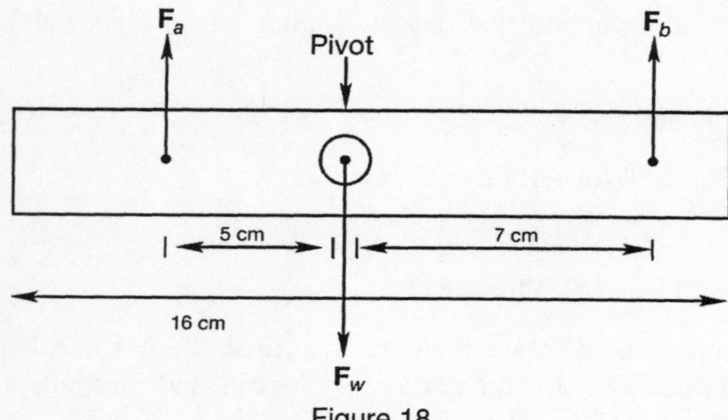

Figure 18

Consider the example, illustrated in Figure 18, of a uniform bar, pivoted at the geometric center, which is also the location of the center of gravity. The weight of the bar, 20 N, acts downward at the center of gravity. $\mathbf{F}_a$ is a force of 10 N (directed upward) acting 5 cm left of the pivot point, and $\mathbf{F}_b$ is an 8 N force (directed upward) acting 7 cm right of the pivot point. The torque provided by each force is found using $\boldsymbol{\tau} = \mathbf{F}d$, where **F** is the force and d is the distance from the pivot point. Note that the relatively complex procedure of finding the cross product can be simplified here because the forces act perpendicular to their corresponding displacement vectors.

$\boldsymbol{\tau}$ for $\mathbf{F}_a$ is $\boldsymbol{\tau} = 10(5) = 50$ N(cm)

$\boldsymbol{\tau}$ for $\mathbf{F}_w$ is $\boldsymbol{\tau} = 20(0) = 0$ N(cm)

$\boldsymbol{\tau}$ for $\mathbf{F}_b$ is $\boldsymbol{\tau} = 8(7) = 56$ N(cm)

Rotation in the direction of $\mathbf{F}_a$ would be clockwise, or negative torque. Rotation in the direction of $\mathbf{F}_b$ would be counterclockwise, or positive torque.

$$\boldsymbol{\tau}_{net} = \boldsymbol{\tau}_{clockwise} + \boldsymbol{\tau}_{counterclockwise}$$

$\tau_{net} = -50 + 56 = 6$ N(cm)

This means the net torque is 6 N(cm) counterclockwise, and the bar will rotate counterclockwise. It is important to realize that forces applied at the pivot point do not create torque.

However, in AP Physics B, all problems will deal with the case of rotational equilibrium. In solving such problems, you may be asked to find the magnitude or the point of application of an unknown force that would provide for the condition of equilibrium.

WORK AND ENERGY

When forces move objects through some distance, it is said that work has been done on the object. **Work** done by a force is the product of the force (F or $\mathbf{F}$) and the distance (r or $\mathbf{r}$) through which the object is moved:

$W = F\Delta r \cos \theta$ (for AP Physics B)

or

$W = \mathbf{F} \bullet \Delta\mathbf{r}$ (for AP Physics C).

Energy is defined as the ability to do work. All objects possess energy in one form or another. Energy can take a variety of forms, and can change forms at any given time.

The unit used to measure both work and energy is the *joule* (J). 1 J = 1 N × 1 m.

Kinetic energy is energy due to motion. For an object of mass m moving at a speed v, the kinetic energy is defined as

$K = (^1/_2)mv^2$.

If a 2000 kg automobile is traveling at 12 m/s, then its kinetic energy is

$K = {}^1/_2(2000)(12)^2 = 144{,}000$ J.

Potential energy is energy due to interactions between objects. The most common forms of potential energy are caused by gravity or elasticity. Lifting an object to some height through which gravity may accelerate it produces gravitational potential energy. To calculate the gravitational potential energy for an object, we use the equation

$\Delta U_g = mgh$,

where m is the mass, g is gravitational acceleration, and h is the height through which the object may be accelerated. Thus, we can find the potential energy of a 100 kg boulder at the top of a 25 meter high cliff:

$$\Delta U_g = (100)(9.8)(25) = 24{,}500 \text{ J.}$$

A second type of potential energy is produced by elasticity, such as the compression of a spring. When a spring is stretched or compressed beyond its equilibrium position, it applies a force with which to return to equilibrium. The energy that applies the force is the elastic potential energy. To calculate the elastic potential energy, use the formula

$$U_s = {}^1/_2 kx^2,$$

where x is the distance from the equilibrium position and k is the force constant for the spring. The value of k depends upon the nature of the spring. The force constant is defined by the equation called Hooke's law:

$$F_t = kx,$$

where F_t is the tension in the spring, k is the force constant, and x is the elongation or compression of the spring.

The study of energy leads to a very important concept known as the Law of Conservation of Energy. This law states that the sum of all energy of all forms is equal to the total amount of energy within a system. Furthermore, the total energy in a closed system has a constant value. Although the energy may (and does) change its form in such a system, the sum of the energies will always equal the same constant total.

Conservative systems have zero frictional energy losses and, therefore, the sum of kinetic and potential energy is constant.

MOMENTUM AND IMPULSE

Laws of conservation also apply to other areas of motion study. Another motion-related quantity that is conserved is called **momentum** (**p**), the product of an object's mass and velocity:

$$\mathbf{p} = m\mathbf{v}.$$

Momentum is a vector quantity. For the motion of an object to change, its momentum must change. For example, a train and a car may be traveling with the same velocity, but the train will require a larger force to stop because its mass is much larger, thus having a greater momentum to overcome. Momentum is involved in another idea regarding motion called impulse. **Impulse** (**J**) is the product of a force and the time interval over which it acts.

$$\mathbf{J} = \mathbf{F}\Delta t = m\Delta v = \Delta \mathbf{p}$$

Hence, an impulse is equal to a change in momentum.

The Law of Conservation of Momentum states that the sum of all momenta in a closed system remains constant. If an object in a system loses momentum, another object somewhere in that system must gain momentum to preserve the total amount of momentum. This idea can be better understood by studying collisions. Objects transfer momentum between one another when they collide. If momentum is conserved, the total momentum before and after the collision is equal. An equation,

$$m_1v_1 + m_2v_2 \text{ (before)} = m_1v_1' + m_2v_2' \text{ (after)},$$

is used to calculate momentum magnitudes for a two object collision in one dimension. The sum of momentum before the collision is equal to the sum of momentum after the collision. Remember that momentum is a vector quantity and if collisions occur in two or three dimensions, momentum must be calculated in the same manner as force and velocity vectors.

SIMPLE HARMONIC MOTION

Any object that moves over the same path repeatedly in equal time intervals has periodic motion. When the mass on the spring in Figure 19 is stretched and released, a special type of periodic motion occurs.

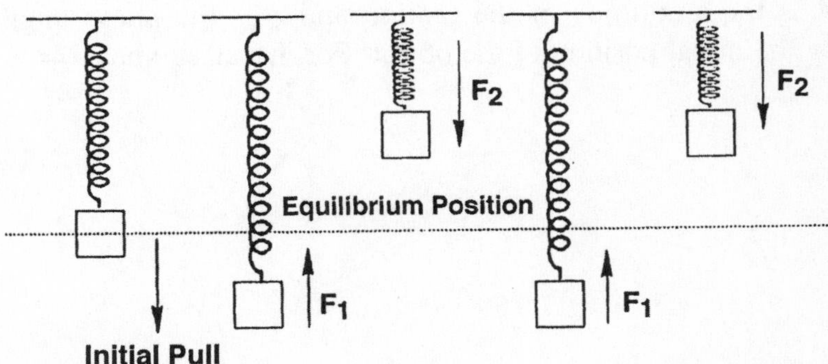

Figure 19

The mass is accelerated with a force proportional to the displacement from equilibrium and acting to restore the mass to a certain equilibrium position. The motion under such conditions is known as Simple Harmonic Motion (SHM). When the mass moves back towards equilibrium, it accelerates past it. This causes compression of the spring, which applies a force in the opposite direction with the same result. The motion of the mass continues in a periodic fashion. A period (T) is defined as the time it takes to complete one cycle of oscillations; frequency (f) is defined as the number of cycles completed per second. (Frequency is measured in units of reciprocal seconds, or Hz.) The relationship between T and f is

$$T = 1/f.$$

Many other systems, including a small mass hung from a long strip (simple pendulum), exhibit SHM. Interestingly, the period of SHM does not depend on the maximum displacement from equilibrium (called amplitude); it only depends on the properties of the system. For a mass m on a spring with force constant k,

$$T_s = 2\pi\sqrt{\frac{m}{k}},$$

and for a simple pendulum of length ℓ,

$$T_p = 2\pi\sqrt{\frac{\ell}{g}}$$

(note that T does not depend on the mass of the simple pendulum).

The coordinate of any object undergoing SHM can be found as

$$x(t) = A\cos(2\pi ft + \phi),$$

where A is the amplitude of the motion and ϕ is the phase angle determined by the initial position of the object. For instance, when $x_i = A$, $\phi = 0$.

AP PHYSICS B

Chapter 3
Electricity & Magnetism

Chapter 3

ELECTRICITY AND MAGNETISM

ELECTROSTATICS

Electrostatics is the study of stationary (static) electrical charges. Electric charges are of two kinds, commonly known as positive and negative. The Basic Law of Electrostatics states that like charges repel one another, while opposite charges attract each other. Electric charge is measured in a unit known as a coulomb (C). One **coulomb** of charge is equivalent to the total charge of 6.25×10^{18} electrons, which means that one electron holds a (negative) charge of 1.6×10^{-19} coulombs. (A proton holds a positive charge of the same magnitude.)

The forces of repulsion and attraction acting on point charges are proportional in the same manner as gravitation between two masses. The magnitude of the force of interaction between two **point charges** (charged objects of minute size) located in vacuum is given by Coulomb's law, which can be expressed mathematically as

$$F = kq_1q_2/r^2,$$

where F is force, k is a constant, q_1 and q_2 are the magnitudes of the charges, and r is the distance between the centers of q_1 and q_2. The value of constant k is

$$k = 1/(4\pi\epsilon_0) = 8.987 \times 10^9 \text{ Nm}^2/\text{C}^2 \approx 9 \times 10^9 \text{ Nm}^2/\text{C}^2.$$

Figure 20 shows two sets of charges that are separated by a distance (r). In Figure 20(a), the opposite charges produce attraction forces, and in Figure 20(b), the similar charges produce repulsion forces. Note that, in both cases, the size of each charged object must actually be much smaller than r, in order for Coulomb's law to apply in its simple form.

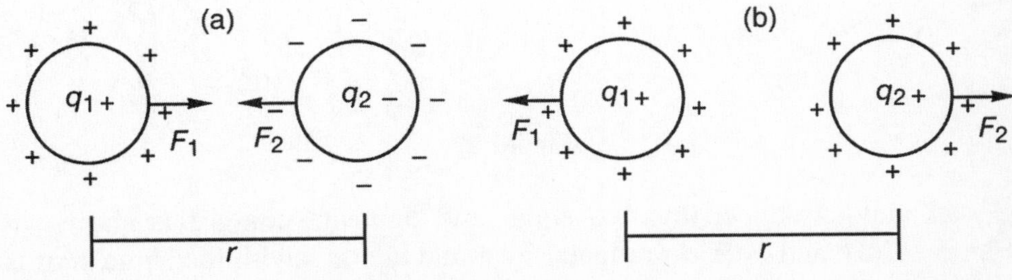

Figure 20

For example, for the force between a 3-nC charge and a 7-nC charge located 0.60 m apart in vacuum, Coulomb's law yields

$$F = kq_1q_2/r^2 = (9 \times 10^9)(3 \times 10^{-9})(7 \times 10^{-9})/(0.60)^2$$

$$F = 5.25 \times 10^{-7}\ \text{N}.$$

Since both charges have the same sign, the charges repel each other.

Forces between charges occur because each charge generates an electric field. An **electric field** is the region in space surrounding each electric charge. Any other charge placed in the field experiences an electric force. Electric fields can be shown graphically through lines of electric forces, as in Figures 21 and 22. These lines indicate the direction of the force that would act upon a positive charge placed at any point in space.

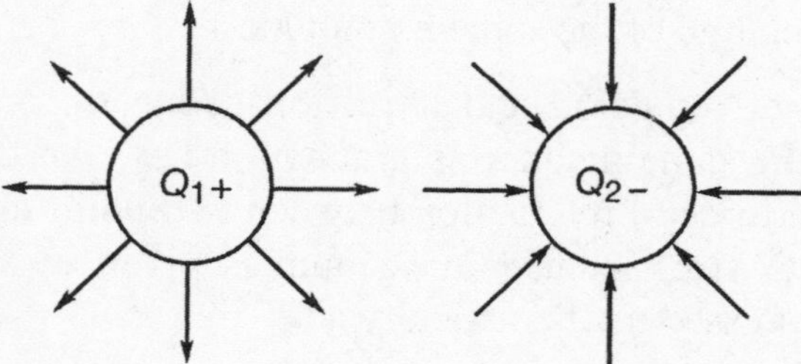

Figure 21

For instance, positive charge Q_1 has lines of force directed outward. If another positive charge is placed in space near charge Q_1, that charge would experience a force away from charge Q_1, as expected. On the other hand, negative charge Q_2 shows force lines directed inward, so a positive charge would be attracted to charge Q_2.

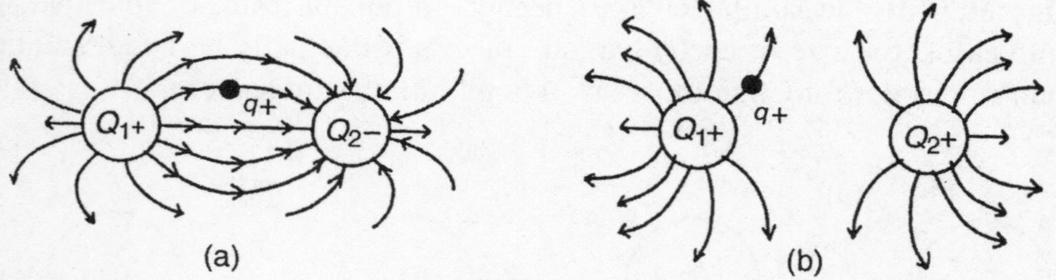

Figure 22

A field produced by two equal and opposite charges is shown in Figure 22(a), and a field produced by equal charges with the same sign is shown in Figure 22(b). In Figure 22(a), the force lines complement each other, flowing out of one charge and into the other. In Figure 22(b), the force lines oppose each other, causing a repulsion effect. Any charged particle, such as $q+$, which enters an electric field would experience a force according to Coulomb's law and the direction of the force would be tangent to a given force line.

Electric Field Intensity (**E**), at any point in the field, is defined as the ratio of the force acting upon a positive charge at that point to the magnitude of that charge. Thus,

$$\mathbf{E} = \mathbf{F}/q,$$

where **F** is the force acting upon charge q. For instance, if a charge of 0.75 C in an electric field experiences a 0.5 N force, the field intensity would be

$$\mathbf{E} = \mathbf{F}/q = 0.5/0.75 = 0.67 \text{ N/C}.$$

The electric field of a point charge (q) is given by the formula

$$E = kq/r^2.$$

If an electric field acts on and moves a charge from one point in a field to another, then these points are said to differ in **electric potential**. By moving the charge, the field does work on the charge. The **potential difference** (V) between two points in an electric field is the ratio of work done by the field on a charge to the magnitude of that charge:

$$V = W/q$$

Potential difference, or **voltage**, is measured in volts (V). One volt is the potential difference between two points such that the electric field does 1 J of work on a charge of 1 C to move it from one point to another. In problem solving, it is useful to remember that, if the field does positive work on a charge, the charge is moving from higher to lower potential.

The potential of the field due to a point charge is given by

$$V = kq/r = \frac{1}{f} = \frac{1}{d_o} + \frac{1}{d_i}$$

A uniformly charged infinite charged plane creates a uniform electric field: its intensity is the same at any point. That intensity equals

$$E = 2\pi k\sigma,$$

where σ is the surface charge density, equal to (q/A). Here, q is the charge residing on an area A of the plane. The electric field lines are perpendicular to the plane.

If a charge is moved in a uniform field, the potential difference is found through

$$V = Er,$$

where E is the field intensity and r is the distance the charge is moved along the electric field lines.

ELECTROSTATICS WITH CONDUCTORS

Conductors are materials with movable charged particles inside—usually these particles are electrons. Metals are the most common conductors. When placed in an electrostatic field, conductors change the field.

1. *The electric field* (E) *inside a conductor is zero.* If this were not the case, a free electron inside the conductor would feel a force and accelerate because of it. Since this goes against the assumption of electrostatic equilibrium, which requires no set force or any change, the electric field inside must be zero.

2. *The electric field at the surface of the conductor must be perpendicular to the surface.* If it is not perpendicular (i.e., the field has a nonzero component parallel to the surface), any free electron at the surface would experience a force and start accelerating.

3. *Any net change on a conductor resides on the surface.* If there is any net change inside the conductor, there must be an electric field inside the conductor, which is impossible since $E = 0$ inside.

PARALLEL PLATE CAPACITORS

An important device used in electric circuits is a **capacitor**. A capacitor is a combination of conducting plates that are separated by some insulating material. Such a device can be used to store electric energy within a system, or for some other purpose. By connecting the capacitor to a voltage source, the plates are given a potential difference that causes a buildup of equal and opposite charges on each plate. The ratio of the charge on either plate to the potential difference is called **capacitance**:

$$C = Q/V,$$

where C is the capacitance, Q is the magnitude of the charge on each plate, and V is the voltage between the plates. Capacitance is measured in farads (F). When one coulomb of charge on a capacitor results in a potential difference of one volt between plates, capacitance equals one farad (1 F).

A parallel-plate capacitor consists of two conducting plates of area A separated by distance r. The area between the plates is occupied by a vacuum, or air (or possibly a dielectric material). The capacitance is given by the formula

$$C = A\epsilon_0/r,$$

where ϵ_0 is the permittivity constant ($\epsilon_0 = 8.85 \times 10^{-12}$ F/m).

A capacitor of capacitance C F can be charged to any particular voltage V. The charge of each plate is then $Q = CV$.

The charge on a capacitor can be increased by using dielectric materials for insulators rather than air. The magnitude of the capacitance increase differs depending on the material used. Dielectric materials do not conduct electricity. When placed within an electric field, they do not reduce it to zero (as a conductor would), but decrease it by a certain factor k, which depends on the material. Factor k is called the dielectric constant. If the vacuum inside a capacitor is replaced by a material with a certain value of k, the capacitance also increases by a factor k.

The capacitance value of capacitors in combination depends upon the connections within the circuit. Figure 23(a) shows capacitors in parallel (they all have the same voltage across them). When capacitors are in parallel, the total capacitance (C_t) is given by

$$C_t = C_1 + C_2 + C_3 \ldots + C_n.$$

For the capacitors in series (same charge on each capacitor), C_t can be found through

$$1/C_t = (1/C_1) + (1/C_2) + (1/C_3) \ldots + (1/C_n).$$

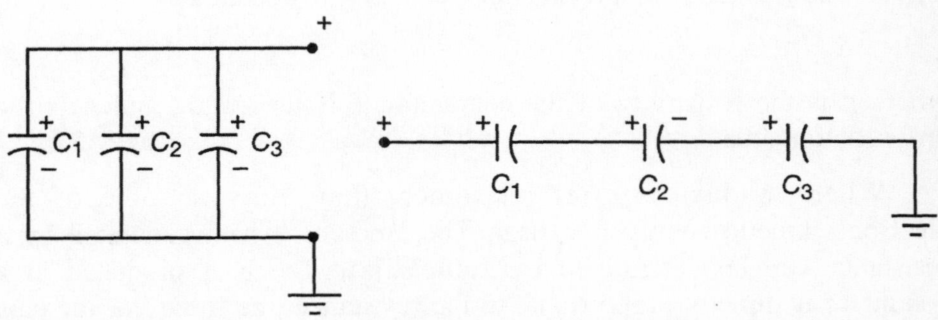

(a) Capacitors in parallel (b) Capacitors in series

Figure 23

ELECTRIC CIRCUITS

The existence of a potential difference within a conductor makes electric charges move. When many charges are moving through a conductor, the rate at which they flow is referred to as **electric current** (I). More specifically,

$$I_{avg} = \Delta Q/\Delta t,$$

illustrating that current is a measure of the amount of charge (Q) that passes a given point within a given time (t). The unit of current is the ampere (A):

$$1 \text{ A} = 1 \text{ C}/1 \text{ s}.$$

As current flows, conductors resist the movement of charges. This opposition to the current flow is called **resistance** (R). The resistance within a conductor depends on the nature and material of that conductor. Mathematically, resistance is given by

$$R = V/I,$$

where R is the resistance of a conductor, V is the potential difference across it, and I is the current flowing through the conductor. The unit of resistance is the ohm (Ω):

$$1\ \Omega = 1 \text{ V}/1 \text{ A}.$$

According to **Ohm's law**, the resistance of many conductors remains constant, and the formula

$$I = V/R$$

is often used to find the current if the voltage and the resistance are known. The resistance of a conductor can also be calculated as

$$R = \rho\ell/A,$$

where ρ is the resistivity of the conductor, ℓ is its length, and A is the cross-section area.

When conductors offer resistance, they convert some of the electron's kinetic energy into heat. The amount of heat generated by a resistance can be determined by **Joule's law**; the heat produced in a conductor is directly proportional to the resistance, the square of the current, and the time the current is maintained:

$$H = I^2Rt,$$

where H is the heat in joules, I is the current, R is resistance, and t is the time.

PROBLEM

What amount of heat is generated in a 10-Ω resistor that carries 0.3 A of current for 3 minutes?

SOLUTION

Since t must be expressed as seconds, $t = 3$ min = 180 s. Therefore,

$$H = I^2Rt = (0.3)^2(10)(180) = 162 \text{ J}.$$

Ohm's law is essential in the analysis of direct current (DC) electric circuits. These circuits contain batteries and constant resistors.

Figure 24 presents an example of a simple DC circuit.

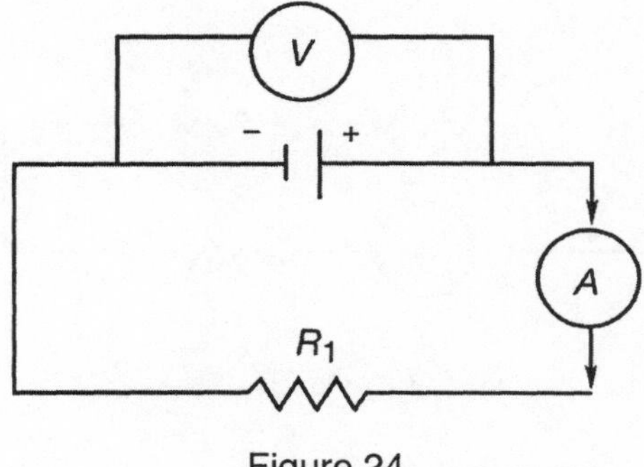

Figure 24

The potential difference in this circuit is provided by a battery, and can be measured with a voltmeter, connected in parallel with the battery:

.

Assuming the resistance of the wire to be insignificant, the circuit resistance is equal to the resistance R_1. Let us assume that $R_1 = 3\ \Omega$. If our ammeter,

,

reads a current of 0.5 A, what is our voltmeter reading? By Ohm's law,

$$V = IR = (0.5)(3) = 1.5 \text{ V}.$$

Electrical circuits can be connected in series or parallel configurations. In a series connection, the electrical devices are connected such that the current must go from one device to the next. Parallel connections provide different paths for current flow.

Figure 25 shows the difference between a series and a parallel connection. Between points *A* and *B*, there are three resistors. The set of resistors between *C* and *D* shows two paths for the current. Some current will pass through R_1 and R_2, and some current will pass through R_3. R_1 and R_2 are in series; the current must go through both in that path. The resistor R_3 is parallel to the R_1-R_2 set because both are connected to the same two points (*C* and *D*). Therefore, for a series connection, the currents through all resistors are the same, whereas for a parallel connection, the voltages across the resistors are the same.

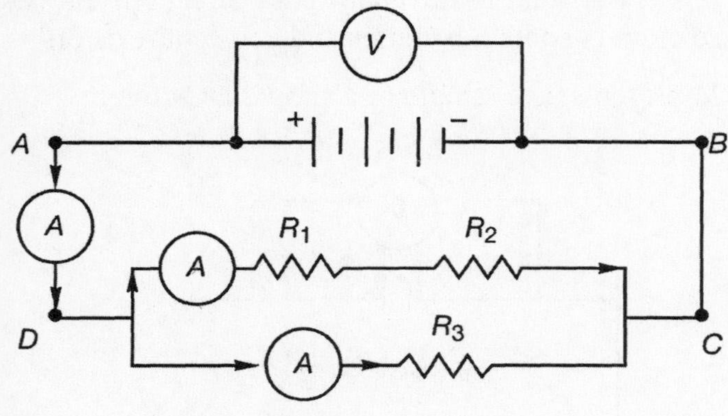

Figure 25

To obtain the total voltage for a group of resistors connected in series, the voltages across each resistor are added, as in Figure 26. Thus, for resistors in series,

$$V_t = V_1 + V_2 + V_3 \ldots + V_n.$$

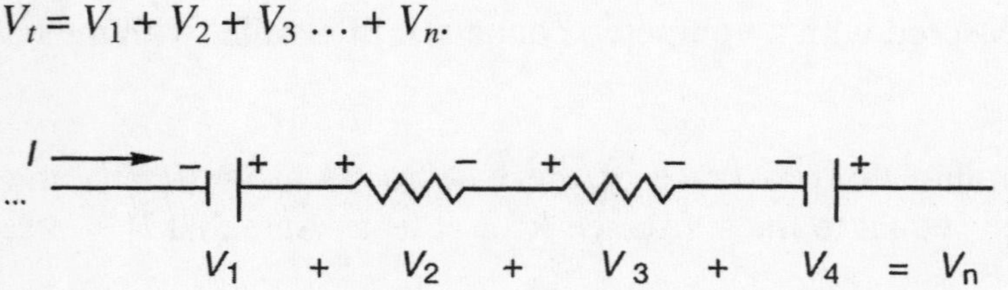

$V_1 + V_2 + V_3 + V_4 = V_n$

Figure 26

For parallel connections, each device is essentially connected to the same two points, as in Figure 27. This means that the voltage for each device is equal. Thus, for voltages in parallel,

$$V_t = V_1 = V_2 = V_3 \ldots = V_n.$$

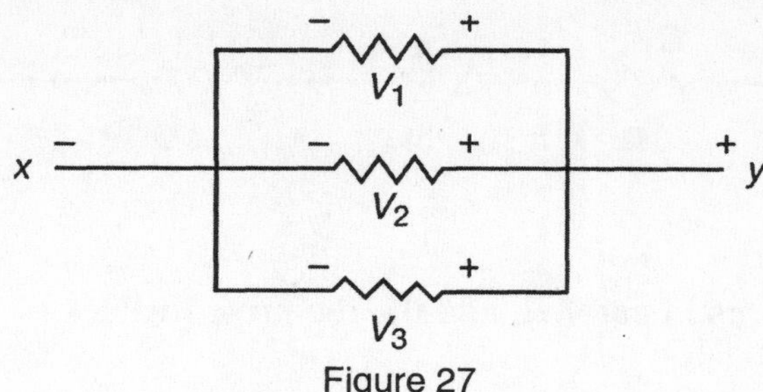

Figure 27

What about the currents? When considering current through a series, we find that the same current passes through each device, as in Figure 28.

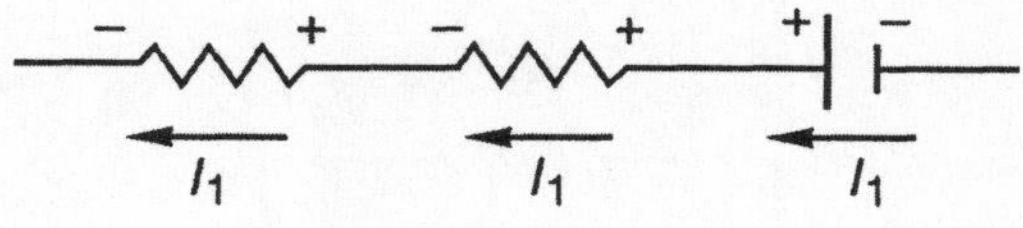

Figure 28

Thus, for currents through a series circuit,

$$I_t = I_1 = I_2 = I_3 \dots = I_n,$$

which is logical because the current has no other path. For parallel branches, we find that current which reaches a divided path must divide so as to send some current through all branches. The amount of current through a branch depends upon the resistances encountered in that branch. Thus, for parallel circuits,

$$I_t = I_1 + I_2 + I_3 \dots + I_n,$$

as illustrated in Figure 29.

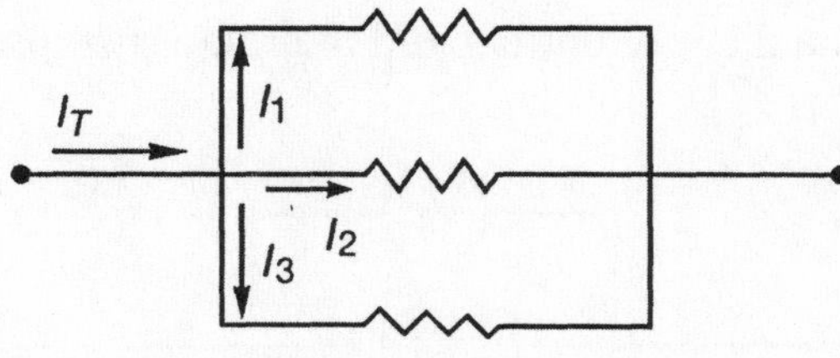

Figure 29

To calculate the total resistance for resistors in series, the individual resistances are added. Thus, for resistances in series,

$$R_t = R_1 + R_2 + R_3 \dots + R_n,$$

as illustrated by Figure 30, where only three resistors are considered.

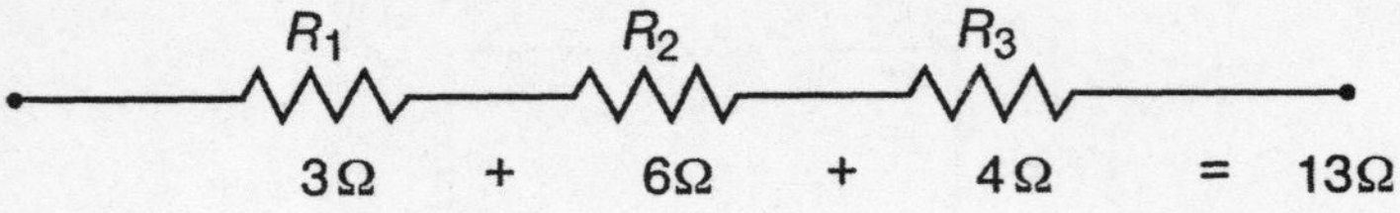

R_1 R_2 R_3

$3\Omega + 6\Omega + 4\Omega = 13\Omega$

Figure 30

For resistances in parallel, add the reciprocal values,

$$\frac{1}{R_{eq}} = \frac{1}{R_1} + \frac{1}{R_2} + \frac{1}{R_3} ... + \frac{1}{R_n},$$

as shown in Figure 31.

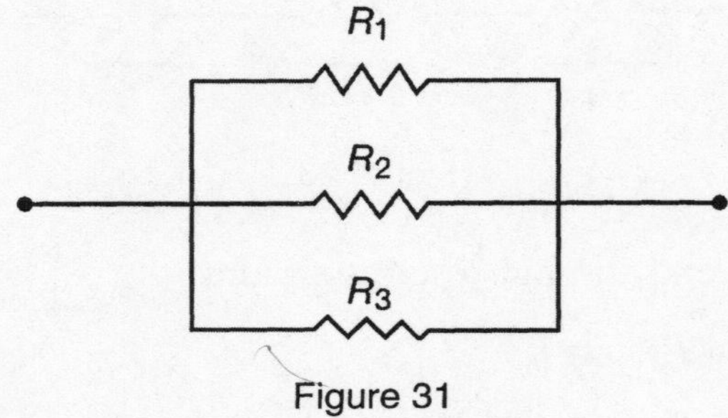

Figure 31

Here, if $R_1 = 4\ \Omega$, $R_2 = 6\ \Omega$, and $R_3 = 12\ \Omega$, the total resistance can be found:

$$(1/R_t) = (1/R_1) + (1/R_2) + (1/R_3) = (1/4) + (1/6) + (1/12) = 1/2 = 0.5.$$

$$R_t = 2\ \Omega.$$

Note that R_t is less than any one resistance, since there is more than one path for the current to take.

We can now apply these ideas to the circuit in Figure 32 both to analyze the circuit and better understand the relationships.

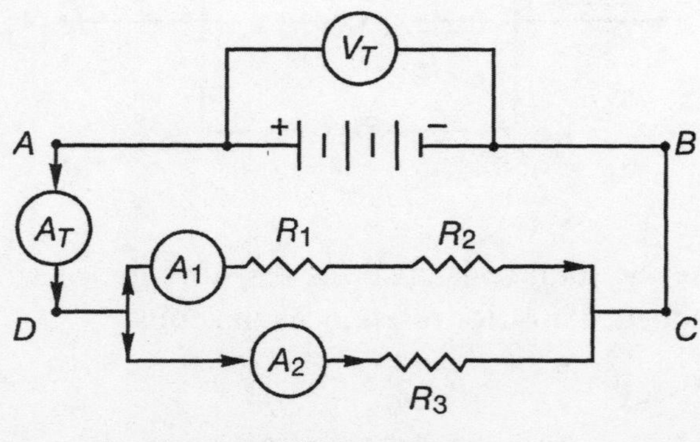

Figure 32

PROBLEM

Given that the voltage for each battery is 3 V and $R_1 = 2\ \Omega$, $R_2 = 3\ \Omega$, and $R_3 = 7\ \Omega$, find the total current (I_t), the current through R_1-R_2 (I_1), and the current through R_3 (I_2).

SOLUTION

To begin, we must realize that Ohm's law can be applied to the total circuit, any section of the circuit, or any device within the circuit. The reading on the voltmeter will be the total for 3 batteries in series:

$$V_t = V_1 + V_2 + V_3 = 3 + 3 + 3 = 9\text{ V}.$$

Since point *C* is connected to *A* and *D* is connected to *B*, the voltage across the parallel resistor set must be 9 V. If we calculate the total resistance of our set, we could calculate the total current by

$$I_t = V_t/R_t.$$

To calculate R_t, we must apply the rules for the series and parallel resistors. Since R_1 and R_2 are in series, their resistances are added together. Also, their series combination is parallel to R_3. Since there are no other resistances to consider, R_t will equal R_{eq} for our set. Thus,

$$\frac{1}{R_t} = \frac{1}{R_1 + R_2} + \frac{1}{R_3}$$

$$\frac{1}{R_t} = \frac{1}{5} + \frac{1}{7}$$

$$\frac{1}{R_t} = 0.2 + 0.143 = 0.343$$

$$R_t = 1/0.343 = 2.9\ \Omega.$$

Now we can calculate the current (I_t):

$$I_t = \frac{V_t}{R_t} = \frac{9}{2.9} = 3.1\text{ A}.$$

This means that 3.1 A of current flow through point *C*. The current is then divided among the branches according to Ohm's law. Since the voltage for both branches is 9 V,

$$I_1 = \frac{V}{R_1 + R_2} = \frac{9}{5} = 1.8 \text{ A and}$$

$$I_2 = \frac{V}{R_3} = \frac{9}{7} = 1.3 \text{ A.}$$

Note that 1.8 + 1.3 = 3.1 A. The sum of the divided currents must equal the total current.

ELECTROMAGNETISM

Magnetism is a concept closely related to electricity, and shows many similarities to electrical phenomena. Magnetism is a property of electric charge in motion.

Just as electrical charges produce electric fields, magnets produce magnetic fields. Magnetic fields flow out of the north pole and into the south pole of a magnet, as shown in Figure 33.

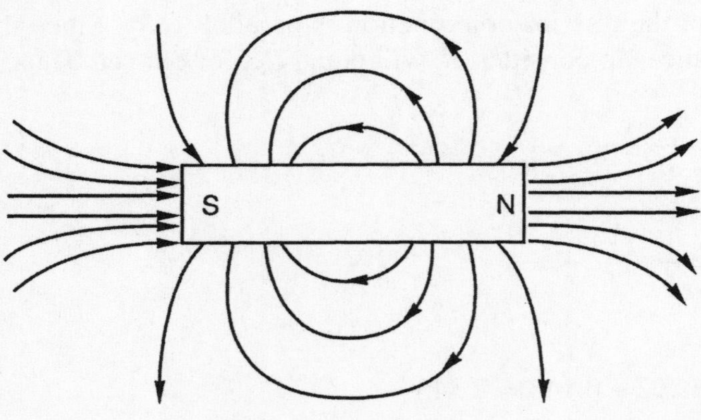

Figure 33

Similar to electric charges, opposite magnetic poles attract one another and like poles repel each other. The lines shown are called **magnetic lines of flux**. A line of flux is drawn so that the tangent to the line at any point shows the direction of the magnetic field. Keep in mind that both magnetic and electric fields surround the source in three dimensions, not just in a single plane, as shown on paper.

MAGNETOSTATICS

A **magnetic field** is defined as a field that exerts a force perpendicular to a moving charge's velocity. This force is proportional to the strength of the field, the magnitude of the charge, and the velocity of the charge; it is expressed mathematically as:

$$\mathbf{F_B} = q\mathbf{v} \times \mathbf{B} \text{ (or } F_B = qvB\sin\,\theta\text{)},$$

with the direction of $\mathbf{F_B}$ given by the right-hand rule.

In the figure shown below, a uniform magnetic field points upwards. The force and velocity of the particle are drawn in various stages of its movement.

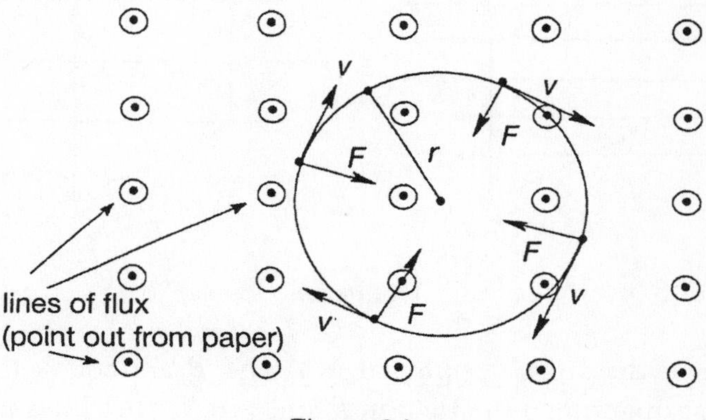

Figure 34

The particle acted upon by a magnetic field follows a circular path of radius

$$r = mv/QB,$$

where m, v, and Q are the mass, speed, and electric charge of the particle, respectively, and B is the strength of the magnetic field. The unit measure for a magnetic field is tesla (T).

Note, however, that any component of particle velocity parallel to the magnetic field is unaffected. So, in general, the actual particle trajectory is helical in nature.

The magnetic force (known as **Lorentz force**), $\mathbf{F_B} = q\mathbf{v} \times \mathbf{B}$, affects charges moving as currents in wires, thus exerting force on such wires.

The force on a length (ℓ) of a straight current-carrying wire in a uniform magnetic field (B) is given by

$F_B = BI\ell \sin\theta$,

where ℓ points in the direction of the current. Such force is known as the **Ampere force**.

The strength of a magnetic field is related to the flux density. **Flux density** is a measure of the number of flux lines per unit area perpendicular to the lines. This idea is illustrated by Figure 35.

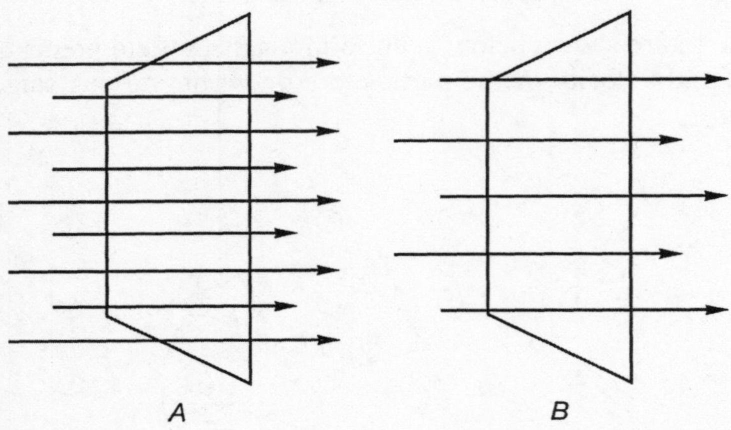

Figure 35

Given that the areas designated in A and B are equal, the magnetic field in A is stronger than the field in B since more flux lines pass through the area. Thus, the field in A is more dense than the field in B.

Flux density can be calculated by

$B = \phi_m/A$,

where B is the field, ϕ is the flux, and A is the area of flux. Since flux is measured in **webers** (Wb), B can be measured in Wb/m2 (1 T = 1 Wb/1 m^2).

Current-carrying wires are themselves sources of magnetic fields. For instance, the magnetic field around a long straight current-carrying wire is

$$B = \frac{\mu_0 I}{2\pi r},$$

where I is the current and r is the distance from the wire. Here, μ_0 is a magnetic constant; $\mu_0 = 4\pi \times 10^{-7}$ SI units.

Figure 36 shows how the direction of the magnetic field lines can be found. If a straight conductor is grasped in the right hand with the thumb pointing in the direction of current, then the fingers wrap the wire in the direction of magnetic field lines.

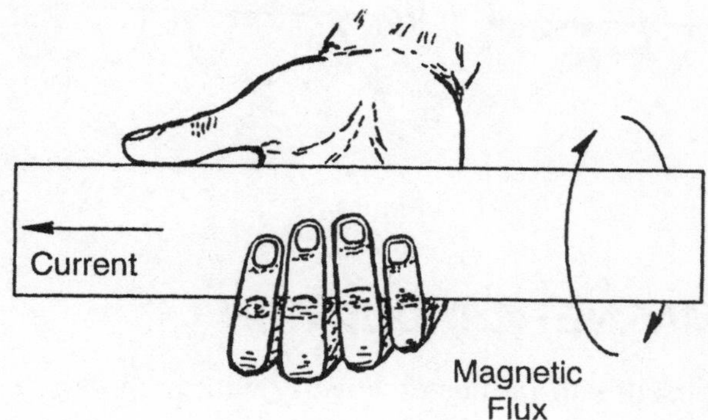

Figure 36

If a conducting wire is looped into a coil, a new situation occurs. Current traveling around a cylindrical core generates a magnetic field through the core, as illustrated by Figure 37.

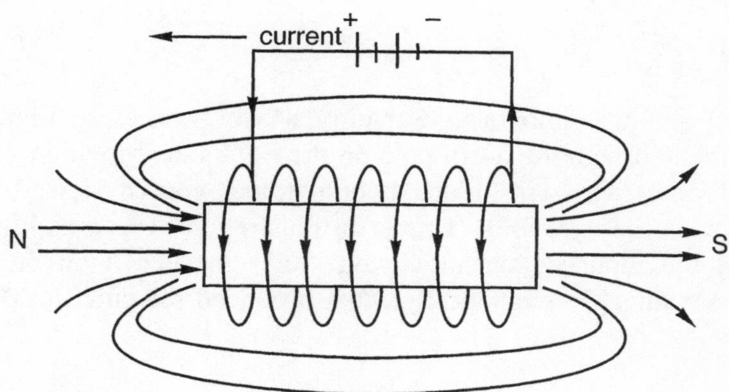

Figure 37

To find the direction of the magnetic field lines, the following technique is used. Figure 38 shows that if the coil is grasped with the right hand so that the fingers wrap in the direction of the current, then the thumb will point in the direction of magnetic flux.

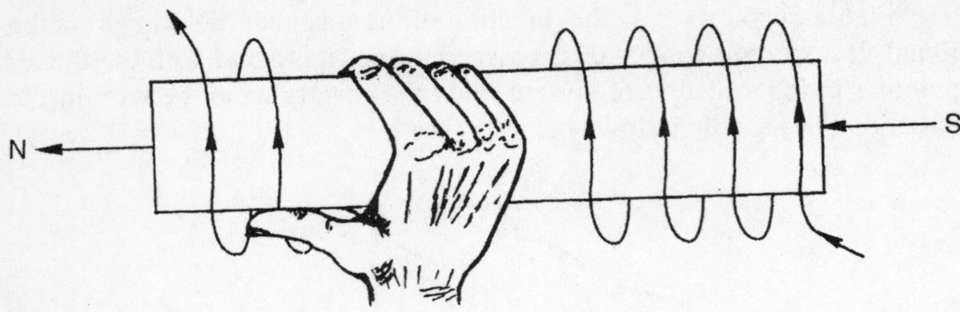

Figure 38

ELECTROMAGNETIC INDUCTION

It is also possible to induce electricity with magnetism. This phenomenon is called **electromagnetic induction**. More specifically, if the magnetic flux through a conducting loop changes, an electromagnetic force (emf) is induced, which is called the emf of induction (ε_i). This emf may, in turn, induce current. The formula used to calculate the emf of induction is

$$\varepsilon_i = -(\text{change in magnetic flux})/\text{time, or}$$

$$\varepsilon_i = -\frac{\Delta\phi}{\Delta t}.$$

This formula is known as **Faraday's law**. As seen in Figure 39, a magnet, oriented with the north pole on the right side, moving to the right toward a loop of wire will induce a counterclockwise (if viewed from the left) current in the wire loop. This is an illustration of **Lenz's law**, which states that the induced current always flows in such a direction as to oppose the change in magnetic flux that produced the current. The coun-

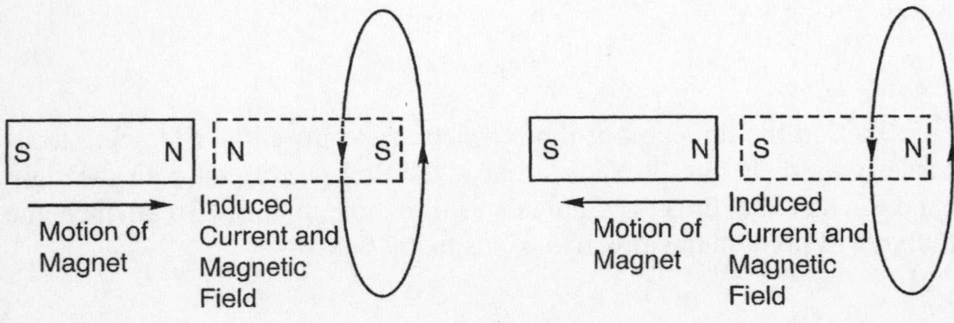

Figure 39

terclockwise induced current produces a magnetic field (as found from the right-hand rule) that has its north pole oriented to the left, which opposes, and thus diminishes, the effect of the flux increase caused by the magnet moving toward the loop. If the magnet were pulled away from the loop, the induced current would be clockwise (if viewed from the left) and the induced magnetic field would attract the magnet, thus opposing its motion away from the coil.

AP PHYSICS B

Chapter 4
Waves & Optics

Chapter 4

WAVES AND OPTICS

GENERAL WAVE PROPERTIES

A **wave** is a disturbance that propagates through some material medium or space. There are two types of waves. Waves that travel through a material medium are called **mechanical waves**. Waves that carry various forms of electromagnetic energy are **electromagnetic waves**, and travel at the speed of light through a vacuum.

An important thing to understand about any kind of mechanical wave (circles on the water, sound, shock wave, etc.) is that only energy is carried through large distances—particles of the medium are not. Rather, these particles vibrate around their local equilibrium positions, transferring energy from one particle to another. The direction of vibration relative to the direction in which the energy travels determines whether a wave is **longitudinal** or **transverse**. Mechanical waves can be either longitudinal or transverse; electromagnetic waves are always transverse.

Transverse waves cause matter to move in a direction perpendicular to the direction of wave propagation. Figure 40 shows 4 points along a wave medium. As the wave travels to the right, the matter within the medium moves up, then down as the wave passes. Thus, the wave is transverse.

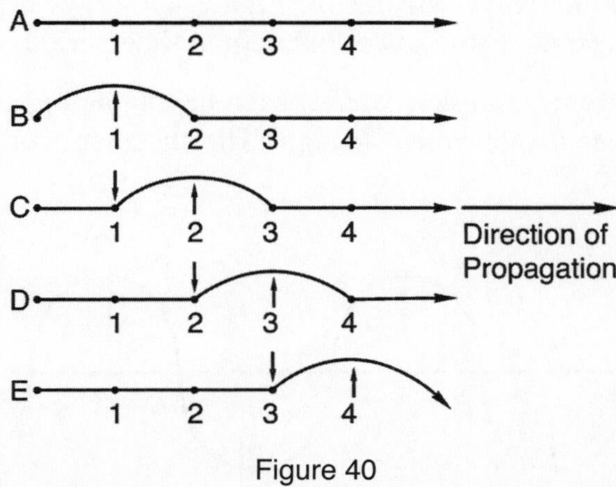

Figure 40

A second type of mechanical wave is the longitudinal wave. Longitudinal waves cause material in the medium to vibrate *parallel* to the direction of wave propagation. Figure 41 shows a longitudinal wave pulse moving through a coil spring. When released, the compressed area attempts to spread out, which will compress the coils to their right. This process continues throughout the length of the spring.

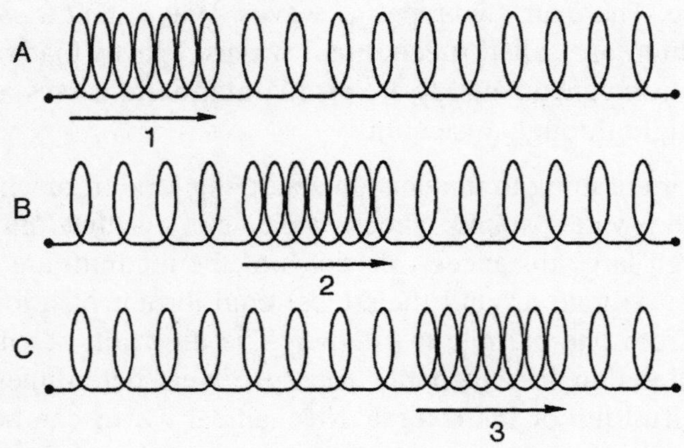

Figure 41

Sound waves are a good example of compression waves. The shock from a sound source compresses the air near the source, which sends a compression wave through the air in all directions. You hear the sound when the compression shock hits your eardrum.

If a source that creates a wave does so repeatedly at equal time intervals, a periodic wave will result. Figure 42 shows a periodic transverse wave with equal disturbances over equal time periods.

Shown are three complete waves, each having an upper displacement crest and a lower displacement trough. The distance from a point on a

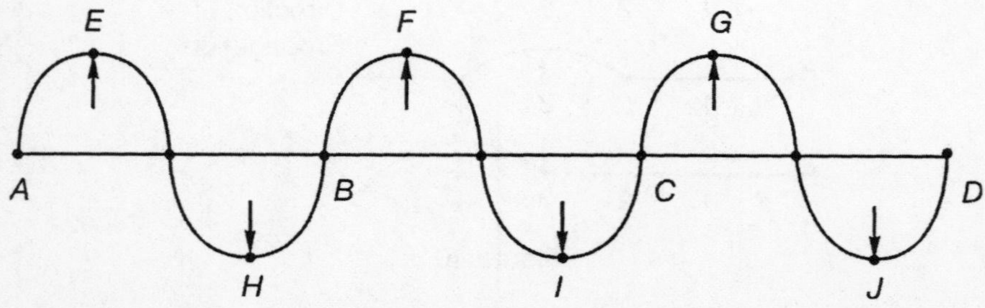

Figure 42

wave to the same point on the next is called one wavelength. For our wave, the wavelength (λ, lambda) could be measured from *A* to *B*, one crest and one trough; from *E* to *F*, crest to crest, or from *H* to *I*, trough to trough.

A wave that travels through one crest and one trough completes one cycle. The number of cycles completed per second is known as **wave frequency** (*f*). Frequency is measured in cycles per second (Hz). The **period** (*T*) for a wave is the time for one complete wave to pass a reference point. Finally, a wave that moves in a given direction must have velocity in that direction. Wavelength, frequency, period, and velocity all relate to each other. Figure 43 shows two waves traveling one meter from *x* to *y*. Each wave can travel from *x* to *y* in one second.

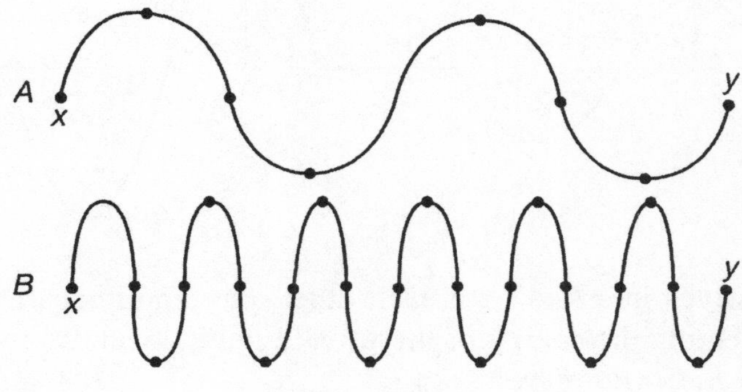

Figure 43

Looking at wave *A*, we find that in one second, two complete waves will pass point *y*, which gives a frequency equal to 2 Hz. For wave *B*, six waves pass *y* in one second, which gives a frequency of 6 Hz. Since the waves are traveling 2 per second in *A*, the period for wave *A* is $\frac{1}{2}$ second. In *B*, waves pass 6 per second, and the period is $\frac{1}{6}$ second. Note that

$f = 1/T$ and $T = 1/f$.

Since each wave travels a distance (λ) in time *T*,

$v = \lambda/T$.

Substituting for $1/T$ results in

$v = \lambda/T = (1/T)(\lambda) = f\lambda$:

$v = f\lambda$

This final equation is true for all periodic waves, transverse or longitudinal, regardless of medium material.

INTERFERENCE OF WAVES

The behavior of waves can be affected by other waves or by instruments designed to produce a desired effect. The **principle of superposition** states that, if several disturbances exist in the same region of space, the resulting wave is the net result of all individual disturbances. Superposition is especially interesting if waves have the same frequency and wavelength. When two or more such waves meet, the resulting phenomenon is known as **interference**. Figure 44 shows two transverse waves. The maximum displacement of a crest or a trough from the center is the amplitude of the wave. Here, amplitude a_1 is half that of a_2.

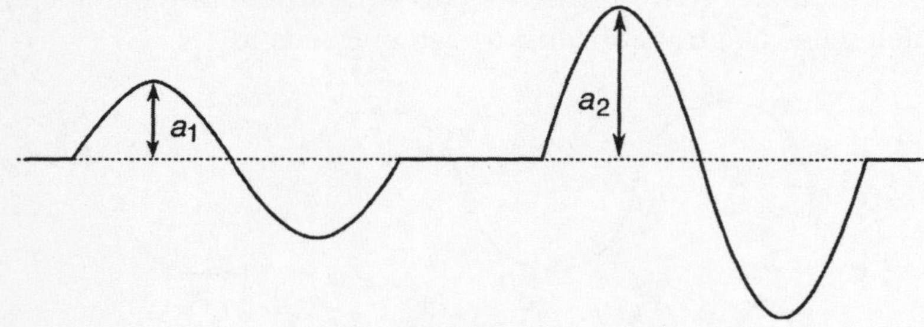

Figure 44

When waves interfere with each other, the amplitudes are affected, indirectly affecting the energy of the wave. Figure 45 shows two identical waves, *A* and *B*, traveling from *x* to *y*.

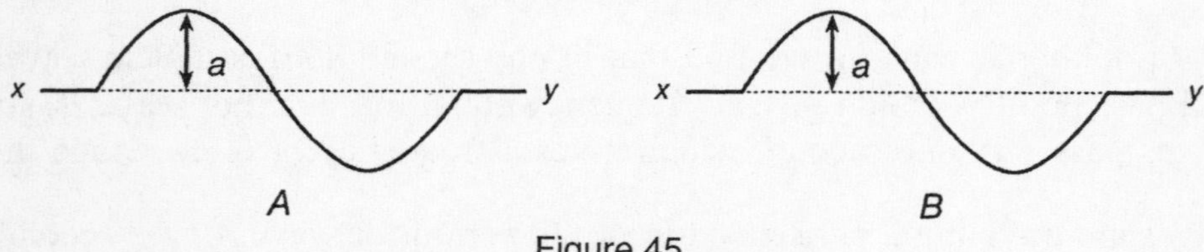

Figure 45

If these waves are added together, **constructive interference** occurs. The crests of *A* and *B* will combine as well as their troughs. This would create a new wave (*C*), shown in Figure 46.

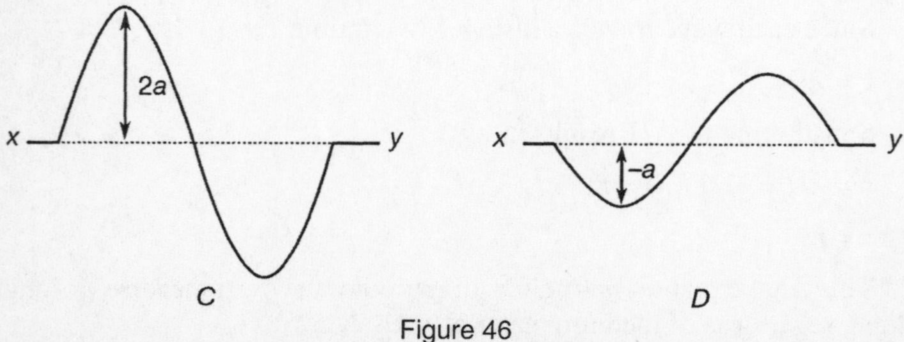

Figure 46

If wave *A* were to combine with wave *D*, each crest would combine with a trough, effectively canceling out both waves. This effect is **destructive interference**.

Interference creates definite patterns within a wave system. Figure 47 shows an interference pattern resulting from two point sources of light waves. The solid lines represent crests and the dotted lines represent troughs. The dark regions appear at points of destructive interference and the bright regions appear where constructive interference occurs.

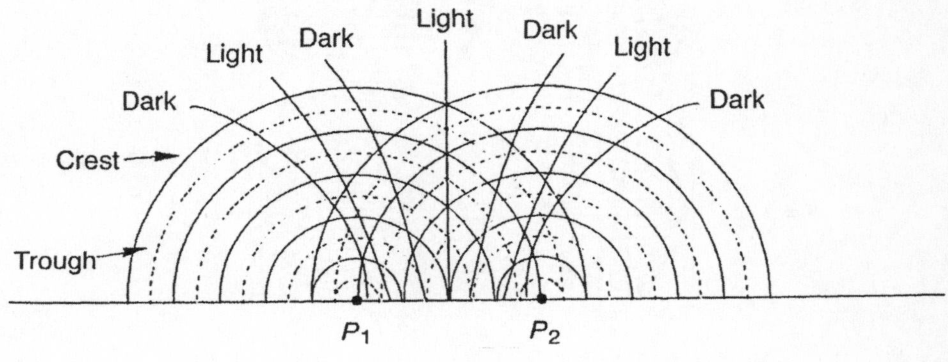

Figure 47

PROPERTIES OF STANDING WAVES

When two waves of the same wavelength and the same amplitude travel at the same speed but in opposite directions, a **standing wave** occurs. At certain locations in the medium, the two waves interfere destructively. These locations are called **nodes**. At other points, constructive interference occurs; such locations are called **antinodes**. Adjacent nodes are $(^1/_2)\lambda$ apart, as are adjacent antinodes. The geometry of the medium and the medium itself determine which wavelengths may result in standing waves; not every wavelength (or, in other words, not every frequency) would produce a standing wave in a given medium.

For instance, standing waves can occur on a string of a length (L) fixed at both ends, so that each end is a node. In such a situation, possible wavelengths are given by

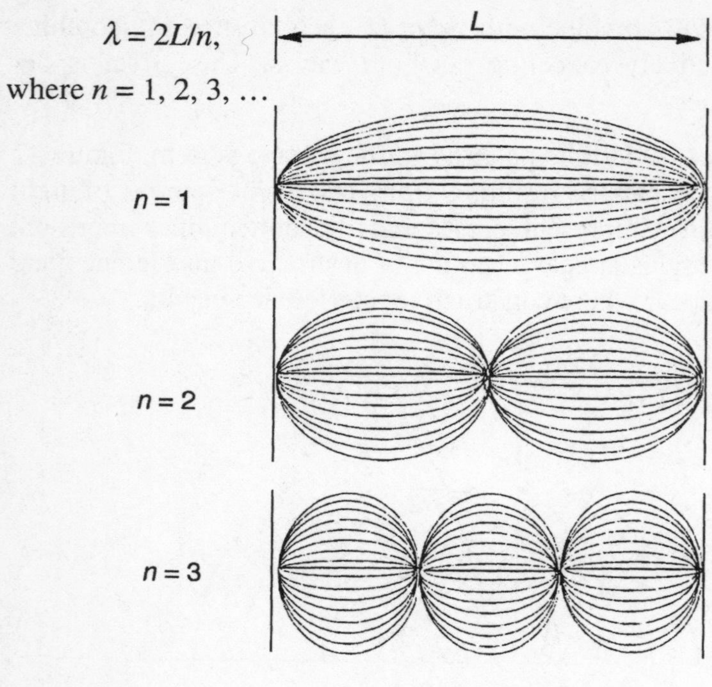

Figure 48

One interesting wave phenomenon is the **Doppler effect**. This effect refers to a wave that originates from a source which is traveling with some velocity. The Doppler effect is best illustrated by examining sound waves. In essence, the source frequency depends on the relative motion of the source and the observer of sound. If the source and the observer approach each other, the observer hears a sound that has a frequency higher than that emitted by the source; if the source and the observer are moving away from each other, the observed frequency is lower than the one emitted by the source. The Doppler effect can be observed for any type of wave, including electromagnetic waves.

GEOMETRIC OPTICS

Optics is the study of light, which can be considered an electromagnetic wave. However, for many purposes, the actual wave nature of light is not important. **Geometric optics** focuses on the study of **light rays**, which can be thought of as very thin beams of light. Such a model allows us to examine the laws of image formation by lenses, mirrors, and other optical systems. Also, this model allows for the exploration of natural laws that apply to *all* waves, not just light waves.

Reflection and Mirrors

Waves can be **reflected**. This means that waves can bounce off certain surfaces, such as a mirror. The reflection of waves follows geometric principles. In Figure 49, the line *xy* represents the surface of a plane mirror. Line *AB* is an incident light ray that strikes the surface at *B*. Dotted line *NB* is the normal reference line perpendicular to the surface. Line *BC* is the reflected light ray. The **first law of reflection** states that the angle of incidence, measured from the normal to the incident ray, is equal to the angle of reflection (*r*) measured from the normal to the reflected ray. The **second law of reflection** simply states that the incident ray, the reflected ray, and the normal all lie in the same plane.

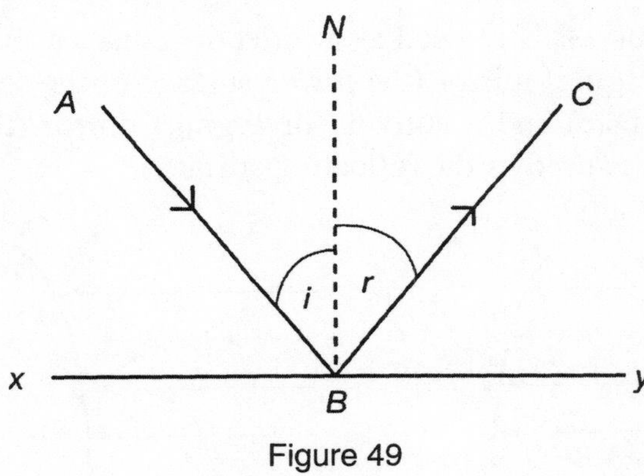

Figure 49

Reflection of light can cause the formation of images. **Real images** are formed by converging light passing through an image point, and **virtual images** are formed by light that appears to have diverged from an image point, but no light actually passes through this point. Two rays of light are needed to locate an image point from an object point.

Figure 50 shows the location of the image of object line *AB*. Rays 1 and 2 begin at point *A* and are reflected according to the first law. The point at which reflected rays intersect is the **image point**. Since the reflected rays for 1 and 2 are diverging, they appear to have intersected behind the mirror. Tracing these reflected rays back, we find the intersection at *A′*. *B′* is found by tracing rays 3 and 4 in a similar manner. Line *A′B′* is the virtual image for line *AB* since there is no light behind the mirror. Note that for plane mirrors, the images are always virtual, erect (oriented the same way as the object itself), and equal in size to the object; they appear to be the same distance behind the mirror as the object is in front of it.

Curved spherical mirrors present a greater challenge. Spherical mir-

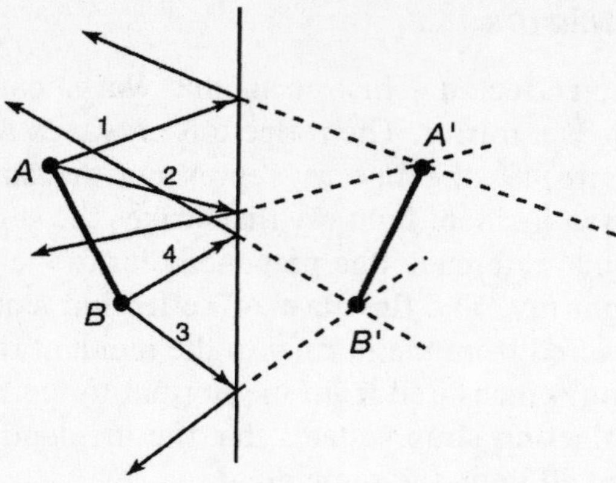

Figure 50

rors are sections of a sphere used as a reflecting surface. Figure 51 shows a **concave** (converging) mirror (the *inside* surface of the sphere is used as the reflecting surface) and a **convex** (diverging) mirror (the *outside* surface of the sphere is used as the reflecting surface).

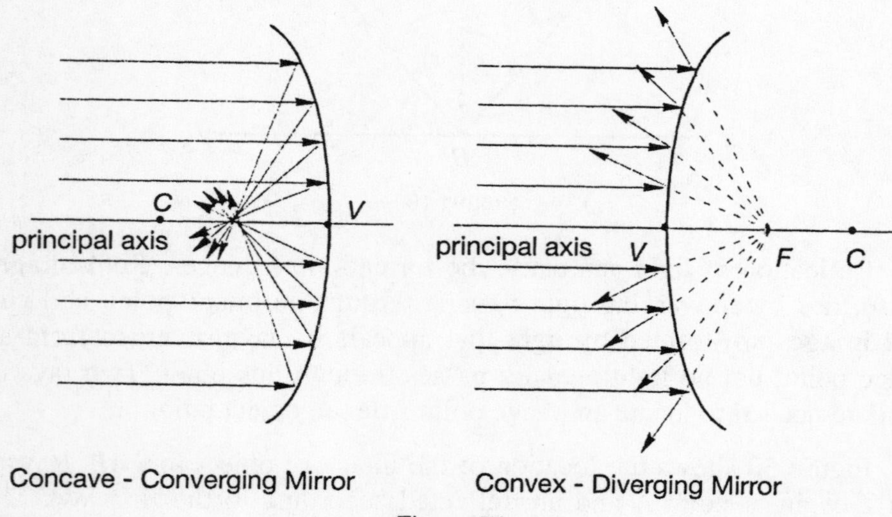

Figure 51

The exact center of the spherical surface of the mirror is called the **vertex** (*V*). The imaginary line that passes through the vertex perpendicular to the face of the mirror is the **principal axis**. Along the axis lies point *C*, the **center point of curvature** for the mirror. It represents the center of the sphere from which the mirror was taken. Any line from *C* to the mirror is normal to the mirror and is a secondary axis. Point *F* is the **focal point** of the mirror. It is located exactly half the distance from *V* to *C*. Any light ray that is parallel to the principal axis converges to, or appears to diverge from, the focal point. The distance from *V* to *F* is called the **focal length**.

These mirrors form images, the characteristics of which can be determined graphically or mathematically.

When locating images formed by spherical mirrors, the following rules are useful:

1. If the incident ray is coming from an object parallel to the principal axis, the reflected ray (or its extension) passes through the focal point.
2. If the incident ray is passing through or is going towards the focal point, the reflected ray is parallel to the principal axis.
3. If the incident ray is passing through the center of curvature, the reflected ray (or its extension) passes through the center of curvature.

Figures 52(a)-(f) show the six general curved mirror situations.

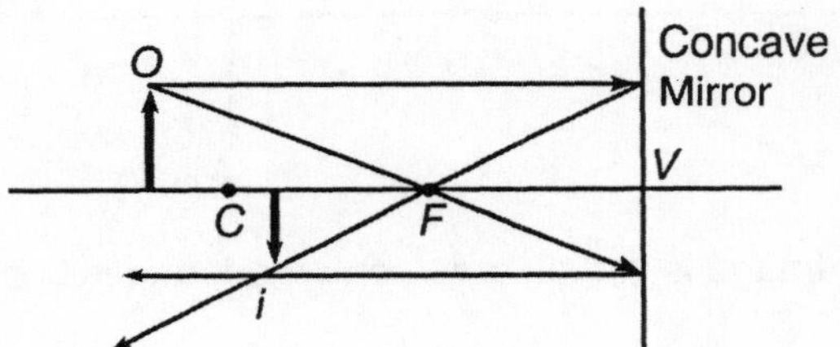

Figure 52(a) — Image is real, inverted, reduced, and is between *C* and *F*.

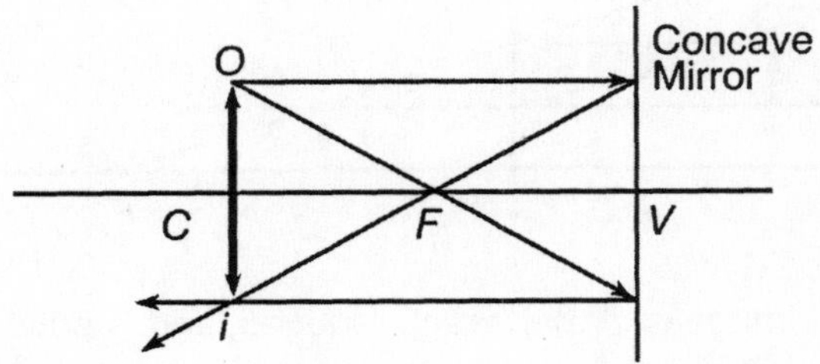

Figure 52(b)— Image is real, inverted, equal in size, and is at *C*.

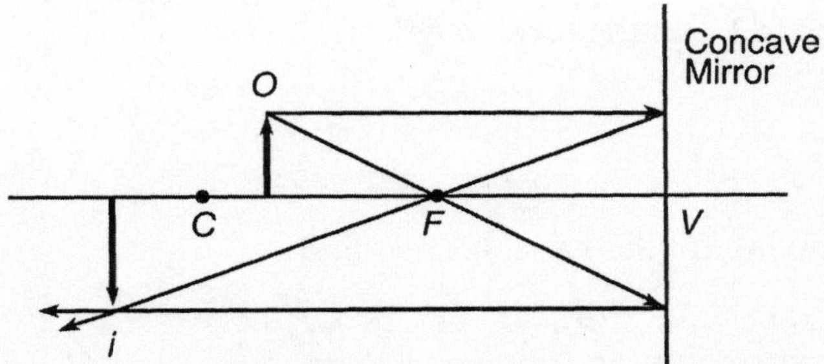

Figure 52(c) — Image is real, inverted, enlarged, and is beyond *C*.

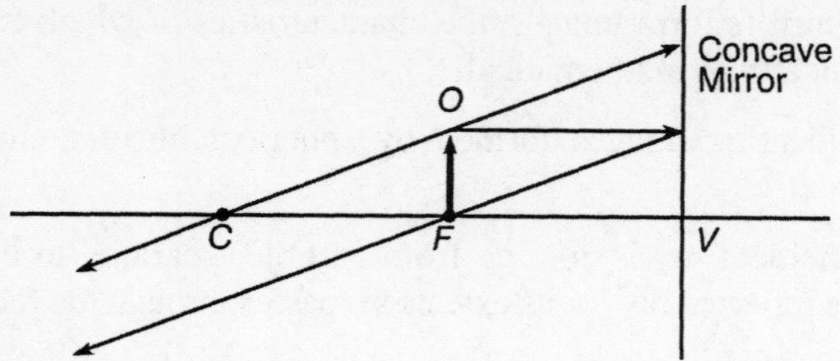

Figure 52(d) — The reflected rays are parallel; no image is formed.

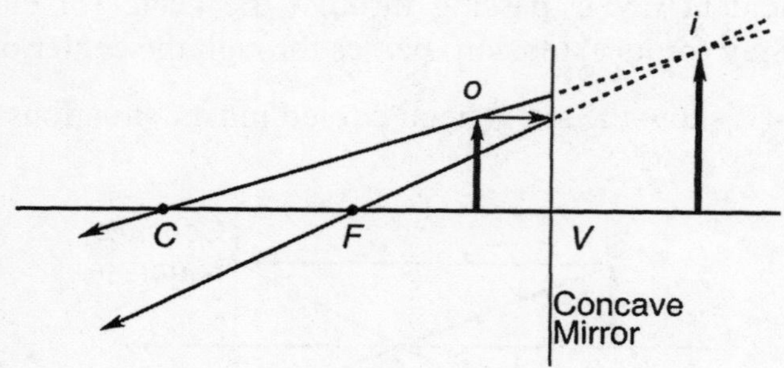

Figure 52(e) — Image is virtual, erect, enlarged, and is behind the mirror.

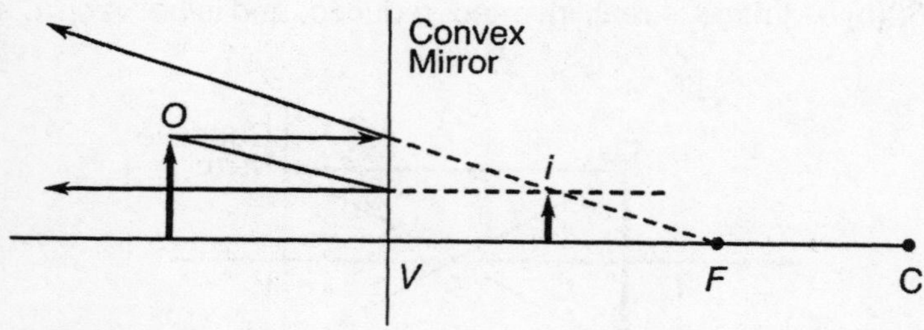

Figure 52(f) — Image is virtual, erect, reduced, and is between *V* and *F*.

The mathematical equation for mirrors (often called the **mirror equation**) relates the distance from *V* to the object (d_o), the distance from *V* to the image (d_i), and the focal length (f):

$$\frac{1}{f} = \frac{1}{d_o} + \frac{1}{d_i}.$$

When solving for the variables, we find

$$f = \frac{d_o d_i}{d_o + d_i};\ d_o = \frac{d_i f}{d_i - f};\ d_i = \frac{d_o f}{d_o - f}.$$

According to the applicable rules, d_i is assumed to be negative for virtual images and f is assumed to be negative for convex mirrors. All other quantities are considered positive. The size of an image is given by

$$\frac{h_i}{h_o} = \frac{d_i}{d_o},$$

where h_i is the height of the image and h_o is the height of the object. This shows that the size ratio is equal to the distance ratio for each situation. Since height cannot be negative, h_i is always positive and any negative sign on a d_i value is ignored.

The examples below illustrate the use of the mirror equation.

PROBLEM

A 4-cm tall object is placed 12 cm from a concave mirror with a focal length of 8 cm. Where is the image? What is the height of the image? What is its type?

SOLUTION

Solve the mirror equation for d_i,

$$d_i = d_o f/(d_o - f) = (12)(8)/(12 - 8) = 96/4 = 24 \text{ cm},$$

and then solve for h_i,

$$h_i = d_i h_o / d_o = (24)(4)/12 = 8 \text{ cm}.$$

Since d_i is positive, the image is real; it is also inverted, as are all real images.

PROBLEM

A 10-cm tall object is 6 cm from a convex mirror with a focal length of 5 cm. Where is the image? What is its height? What is its type?

SOLUTION

Solve for d_i, remembering that d_i is negative for convex mirrors:

$$d_i = d_o f/(d_o - f) = (6)(-5)/[6 - (-5)] = -30/11 = -2.7 \text{ cm}.$$

Solve for h_i, remembering that h_i is positive:

$$h_i = d_i h_o / d_o = (2.7)(10)/6 = 4.5 \text{ cm}.$$

Since d_i is negative, the image is virtual.

Refraction and Lenses

Another characteristic of waves is that they can be refracted. **Refraction** is the phenomenon that takes place when light travels from one medium to another. The light ray usually bends at the boundary between the two media. This change of direction is related to the speed of light in each medium. Figure 53 shows how light may be refracted.

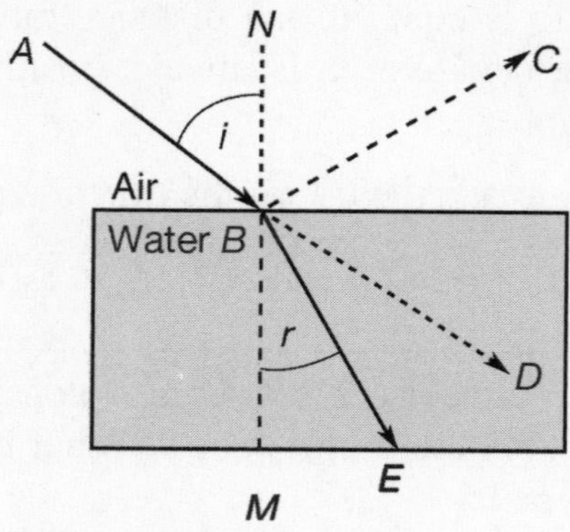

Figure 53

Line *AB* is the incident ray. Line *NM* is the perpendicular normal at the point of refraction. Line *BC* represents a small amount of light reflected by the surface. Here, *i* is the **angle of incidence** and *r* is the **angle of refraction**. Line *BD* is the original path of the incident ray, and *BE* is the refracted light ray. The respective directions of the incident ray and the refracted ray are related by **Snell's law**:

$$n = \sin i / \sin r,$$

where *n*, known as the **index of refraction**, is a property of an optical medium. The index of refraction can also be expressed in terms of the speed of light:

$$n = c / v_m,$$

where *c* is the velocity of light in a vacuum and v_m is the velocity of light in the medium.

The refraction of light can be summarized by two laws. First, the incident ray, the refracted ray, and the normal are in the same plane. Second, the index of refraction for any medium is constant for any incident angle. The effects of refraction are shown in Figure 54.

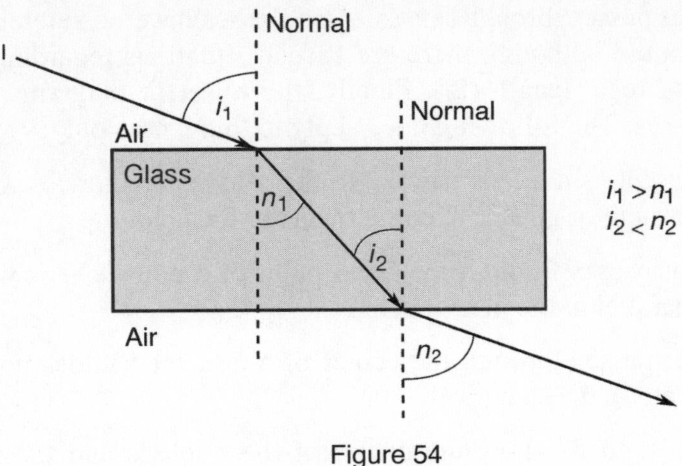

Figure 54

According to Snell's law, it would be possible to reach an angle of refraction equal to 90° when light is moving from a medium with lower speed to one with higher speed. Such an effect, called **total internal reflection**, is illustrated in Figure 55.

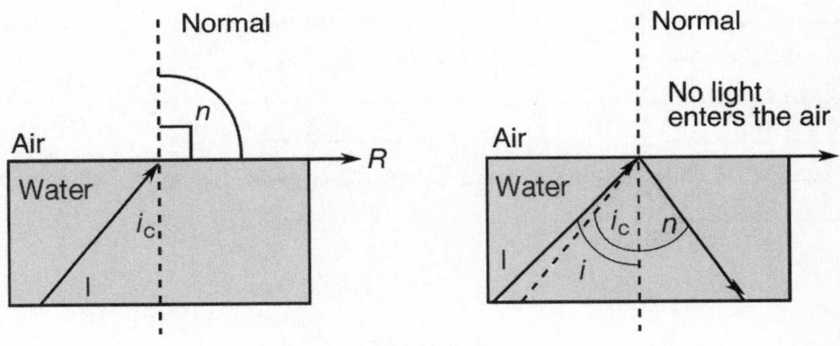

Figure 55

The angle of incidence that produces the 90° refraction is called the **critical angle** (i_c). If the angle of incidence is larger than i_c, all light is reflected by the surface. Since i_c is a characteristic of the medium, it is related to the index of refraction by $\sin i_c = 1/n$; thus, $i_c = \arcsin 1/n$.

The most useful type of refraction is the bending of light with **lenses**. A lens is a piece of transparent material bound by two fragments of spherical surfaces. There are **convex** (converging) and **concave** (diverging) lenses. Lenses are used to produce eyeglasses, microscopes, telescopes, cameras, and many other commonly used devices. Much of the terminology is the same as for curved mirrors, but there are differences to recognize.

First, light passes through lenses. Also, lenses have no reference to a center of curvature, although there are special situations regarding a distance twice the focal length (2*f*). Finally, the rules for diagrams change slightly for lenses. The following laws apply to thin lenses only:

1. A ray that enters the lens parallel to the principal axis will exit so as to pass through or appear to come from the focal point.
2. A ray that passes through the focal point of a convex lens will exit the lens parallel to the principal axis.
3. A ray that passes through the center of a lens (at *V*) does not bend, and exits along the same path.

Figures 56 and 57 show the nature of these lenses and the general image formations.

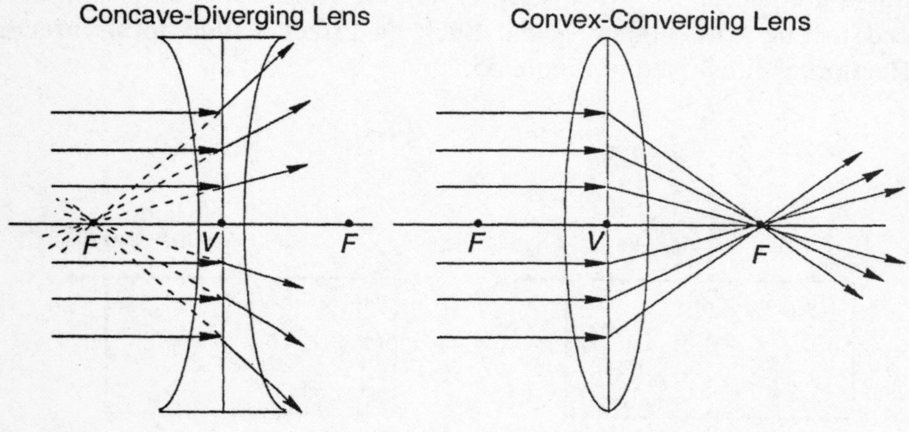

Figure 56

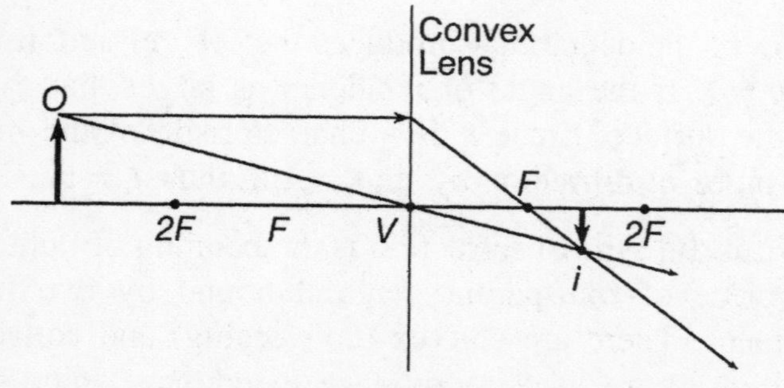

Figure 57(a) — Image is real, inverted, reduced, and is located between *F* and 2*F*.

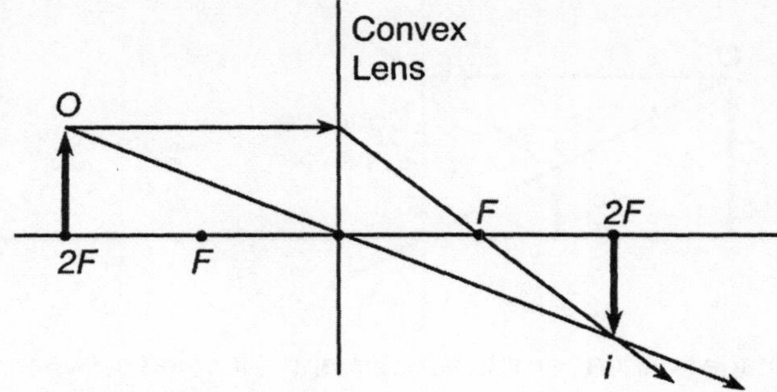

Figure 57(b) — Image is real, inverted, equal in size, and is located at 2*F*.

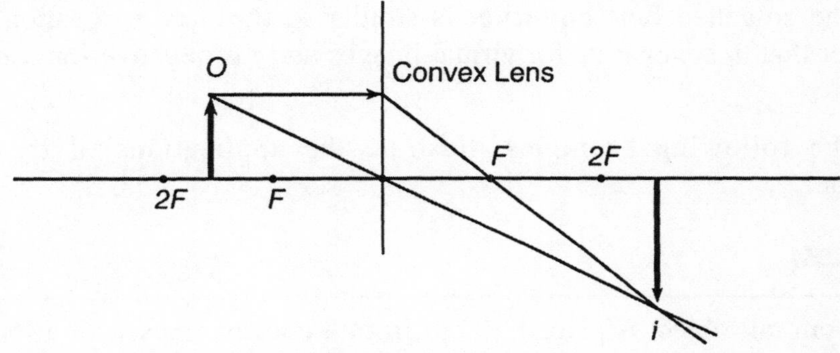

Figure 57(c) — Image is real, inverted, enlarged, and is located beyond 2*F*.

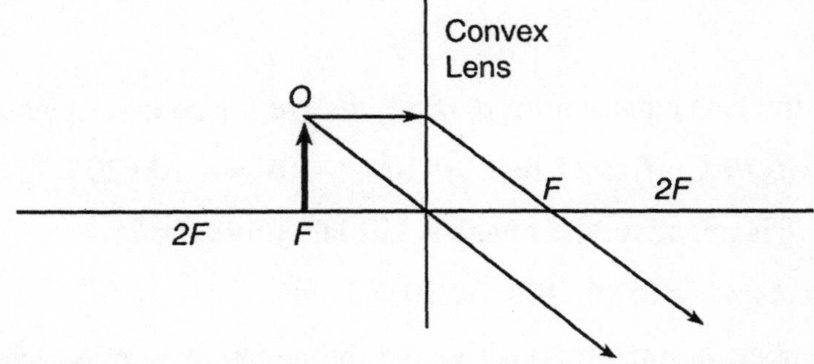

Figure 57(d) — The reflected rays are parallel, no image is formed.

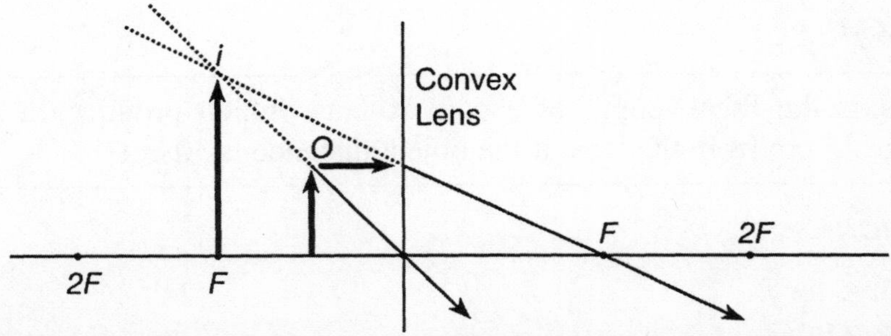

Figure 57(e) — Image is virtual, erect, enlarged, and is located behind the object.

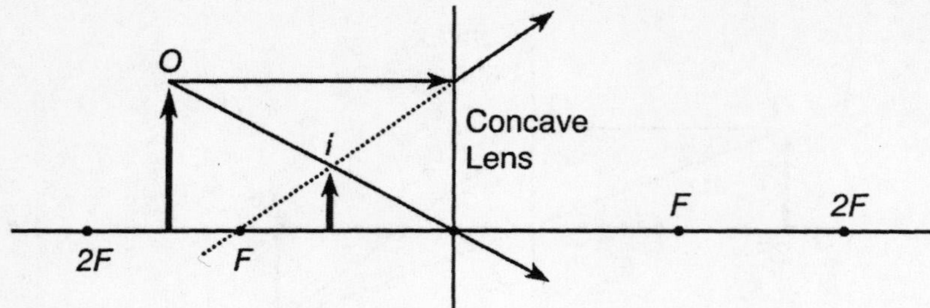

Figure 57(f)—Image is virtual, erect, reduced, and is located between the object and the lens.

The so-called **lens equation** is similar to the mirror equation. Remember that d_i is negative for virtual images and f is negative for concave lenses.

The following examples illustrate the applications of the lens equation.

PROBLEM

A 6-cm tall object is placed 10 cm from a concave lens with a focal length of 10 cm. Where is the image? What is its type? What is its height?

SOLUTION

Solve the lens equation for d_i (f is negative for concave lenses):

$$d_i = d_o f/(d_o - f) = (10)(-10)/[10 - (-10)] = -100/20 = -5 \text{ cm.}$$

Since d_i is negative, the image is virtual. Solve for h_i:

$$h_i = d_i h_o/d_o = (5)(6)/10 = 30/10 = 3 \text{ cm.}$$

Remember, h_i must be positive, so the negative sign associated with d_i is ignored.

PROBLEM

What is the focal length of a convex lens, which produces a real image 15 cm from the lens, if the object distance is 30 cm?

SOLUTION

Solve for f:

$$f = d_o d_i/(d_o + d_i) = (30)(15)/(30 + 15) = 450/45 = 10 \text{ cm.}$$

PHYSICAL OPTICS

Light waves are not just abstract rays of light; they are electromagnetic waves that interact with each other and with the medium in which they propagate. The nature and the effects of such interactions are studied by **physical optics**. In AP Physics B, the following phenomena are considered: interference (discussed earlier), diffraction, dispersion, and polarization.

Through a process known as diffraction, waves can be bent. **Diffraction** is the process of a light wave interacting with a small obstruction (whose size is comparable with the wavelength). As is the case with many wave phenomena, diffraction can be explained by the **Huygens' principle**, which states that every point in a medium that has been brought to vibration can be considered a source of secondary waves (wavelets); the wave picture at any moment can be explained as the result of interference of all the wavelets produced by secondary sources.

Items such as slit openings, pin holes, or sharp edges can produce a diffraction pattern. In general, diffraction occurs when the obstacles have dimensions comparable to the wavelength of light. Due to diffraction, white light may be split into spectral colors; also, light and dark regions may be observed.

One instrument used to observe diffraction is called a **diffraction grating**. A grating is a transparent slide with etched lines that cause diffraction. Each grating could have hundreds or thousands of lines per centimeter of surface area. Diffraction gratings can measure the wavelength of unknown light using the interference pattern produced on a screen.

Waves can also be physically affected by a process known as **polarization**. In principle, all transverse waves can be polarized; however, only polarization of electromagnetic waves has common applications in everyday life; the AP curriculum only considers polarization of light.

Usually, when transverse electromagnetic waves travel through a medium, both electric and magnetic fields vibrate in all directions perpendicular to the direction of the wave. When these waves encounter a special material called **polarizer**, only the waves that vibrate in a predetermined plane may pass through. Figure 58 shows the effect of a polarizer.

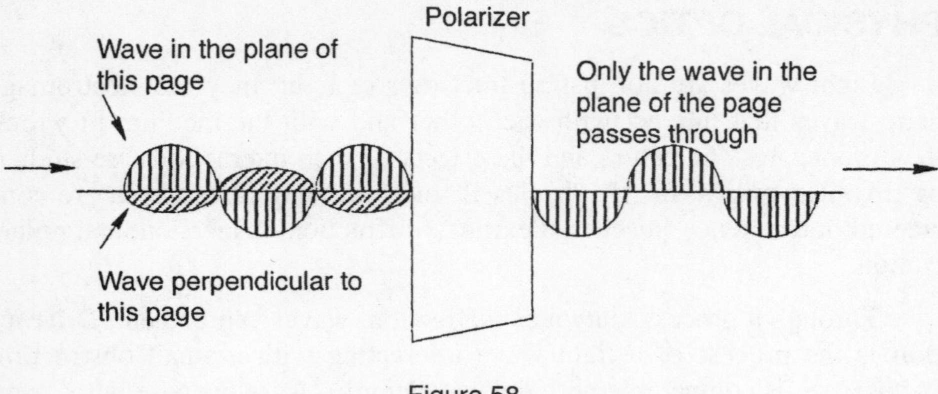

Figure 58

Dispersion and Electromagnetic Spectrum

In vacuum, all electromagnetic waves travel at the same speed, known as the speed of light ($c = 3.00 \times 10^8$ m/s). However, in any other medium, waves of differing frequency travel at slightly different speeds, which means that they refract through different angles. For instance, when a beam of white light travels through a prism, it is separated into different colors. This phenomenon is called **dispersion**. Dispersion can be useful, especially for research purposes—or it can be harmful. For instance, because of dispersion, all high-quality telescopes use mirrors rather than lenses, so that the images are not distorted.

Of course, dispersion pertains to electromagnetic waves of all frequencies, not just visible light. While all electromagnetic waves have the same nature and similar properties, they do differ. The frequency of a wave determines how it can be classified, what type of properties it has, and what its practical applications are. The table below describes electromagnetic waves of different kinds. The entire array of electromagnetic waves is called the **electromagnetic spectrum**. Note that the boundaries between different types of waves are rather fuzzy; sometimes, they overlap.

Type of wave	Wavelength (m)	Applications
Radio waves	> 0.3	radio, television
Microwaves	0.3 to 10^{-3}	radar, navigation, research of atoms, cooking
Infrared	10^{-3} to 750×10^{-9}	physical therapy, heating, infrared imaging
Visible light	750×10^{-9} to 400×10^{-9}	vision and all that is related: photography, microscopy, etc.
Ultraviolet	400×10^{-9} to 60×10^{-9}	sterilization of medical equipment, medical treatment, research
X-rays	60×10^{-9} to 10^{-13}	cancer treatment, medical imaging of bones and internal organs
Gamma rays	10^{-10} to 10^{-15}	material quality control, food irradiation, cancer treatment

All electromagnetic waves, except for gamma rays, are produced by electron transitions within atoms and molecules; gamma rays are produced during transformations taking place in atomic nuclei.

AP PHYSICS B

Chapter 5
Heat, Kinetic Theory & Thermodynamics

Chapter 5

HEAT, KINETIC THEORY, AND THERMODYNAMICS

In this chapter, the central concept is **temperature**. Conceptually, temperature can be understood as the measure of "hotness"; the hotter the object, the higher the temperature. However, there are specific ways of measuring temperature and relating it to some fundamental properties of matter, especially energy.

THERMAL PROPERTIES

Much of the energy we deal with day to day is **thermal**, or **heat energy**. This is the energy associated with the temperature of an object. Objects exchange this type of energy regularly; for instance, hot objects cool over time and some substances burn and release heat. When a substance is hot, it has more thermal energy than when it is cold. The thermal energy of matter is the total potential and kinetic energy associated with the internal motion of the constituent particles. The term heat is actually a reference to the amount of thermal energy that is released, absorbed, or transferred from one body to the next.

Although heat and temperature are related, they are different quantities. A temperature is a quantity proportional to the **average kinetic energy** of the internal particles. These two quantities are related as

$$K_{avg} = (3/2)k_B T,$$

where K_{avg} is the average kinetic energy of the internal particles, k_B is Boltzmann's constant ($k_B = 1.38 \times 10^{-23}$ J/K), and T is the absolute temperature (see below).

For scientific purposes, temperature is usually measured on the Celsius or Kelvin scales. The Kelvin scale is an absolute scale containing no negative temperatures; its unit is one **kelvin** (K). 0 K is called the absolute zero of temperature. At this temperature, molecular motion is at a minimum, thus it is the lowest possible temperature. Celsius is another scale often used; its unit is degree Celsius (°C). The magnitude of 1 °C is equal to that of 1 K. The difference is that the temperature of 0 °C is assigned to the freezing point of water at normal atmospheric pressure. 0 K is approximately 273° below this point. Therefore,

$$K = {}^\circ C + 273.$$

For instance, the temperature of 273 K is the same as 0 °C; 100 °C = 373 K; 200 K = –73 °C, etc.

When a body absorbs heat, its temperature increases. The amount of heat needed to change the temperature of a body by 1 °C (or by 1 K) is called the **heat capacity**:

$$\text{heat capacity} = \Delta Q/\Delta T,$$

where ΔQ is the heat needed to cause the temperature change of ΔT. Since heat capacity is affected by the mass of material, it is not considered a descriptive property of matter. If, however, we consider different substances with equal masses, we can define a property unique to each substance, known as **specific heat**. Specific heat is the heat capacity per unit mass of substance. Specific heat (c) is given by

$$c = \Delta Q/m\Delta T.$$

From this we can see that $\Delta Q = mc\Delta T$, which allows the change in heat to be calculated since m and T are measurable, and c can be found from a reference table of specific heat values. Examine the following problems:

PROBLEM

What is the specific heat of copper if a 150 g sample absorbs 6930 calories as the temperature increases from 20 °C to 520 °C?

SOLUTION

Solving for c,

$$c = \Delta Q/m\Delta T = 6930/(150)(500) = 6930/75{,}000 = 0.0924 \text{ cal/g°C}.$$

NOTE: In the international system of units (SI), the unit of specific heat is J/(kg × K). Since 1 cal = 4.186 J, and 1 kg = 10^3 g, the specific heat of copper can be calculated as

$$c = 387 \text{ J/(kg} \times \text{K)}.$$

PROBLEM

How many calories of heat are required to raise the temperature of 875 g of copper by 200 °C?

SOLUTION

Solving for ΔQ,

$$\Delta Q = mc\Delta T = (875)(0.0924)(200) = 16{,}200 \text{ cal} = 6.77 \times 10^5 \text{ J.}$$

Another interesting property of substances is **thermal expansion.** With few exceptions (water is a notable one), materials expand when heated and contract when cooled. When we consider the expansion of solids in one dimension, we are referring to **linear expansion** (α). The change in length per unit length of a solid for a 1° change is called the **coefficient of linear expansion.** From this we conclude that the longer an object is, the greater the expansion for a given change in temperature. This is illustrated in Figure 59.

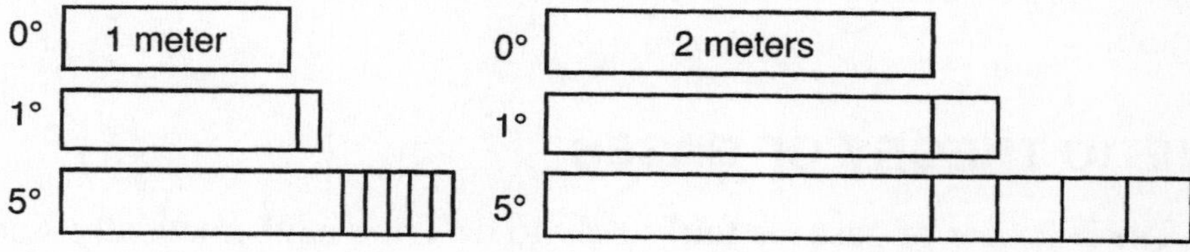

Figure 59

Note that the expansion shown here is greatly exaggerated for the purposes of the diagram. The rods' lengths are first measured at 0 °C. At 1 °C, the rods expand according to their coefficients of thermal expansion. Since the 2 m rod is twice as long, its expansion is twice as much for any given change in temperature. The diagram illustrates that effect for 1 °C and for 5 °C. This means that the change in length ($\Delta \ell$) is equal to the product of the original length (ℓ), its temperature change (ΔT), and the coefficient of linear expansion (a), such that

$$\Delta \ell = \alpha \ell_0 \Delta T.$$

PROBLEM

> The coefficient of thermal expansion for aluminum is 2.3×10^{-5}/°C. If a 12.000 m aluminum rod is heated from 20° to 100°, what is the length of the rod at 100°?

SOLUTION

$$\Delta \ell = \alpha \ell_0 \Delta T = (2.3 \times 10^{-5})(12.000)(80) = 0.022 \text{ m}$$

The new length of the rod is

$$12.000 \text{ m} + 0.022 \text{ m} = 12.022 \text{ m}.$$

We must remember that solids expand in three dimensions. It can be shown mathematically that the **thermal coefficient of volume expansion** for any substance is approximately 3 times the linear coefficient for that same substance.

Most liquids also tend to expand when heated. Since liquids have no definite shape, we consider their volume expansion (ΔV) as

$$\Delta V = \beta V \Delta T.$$

Here, β is the coefficient of volume expansion.

Water is an exception to the expansion rule. Water has its maximum density at 4 °C, at which point heating or cooling causes expansion. Also, ice has a lower density than water does, due to its specific molecular structure.

KINETIC THEORY OF GASES

The behavior of gases is fairly easy to describe mathematically since the interactions between the particles are weak. We will only consider gases under low pressures, when the interaction between particles is negligible. Such gases are called **ideal gases**.

There are several laws that help explain the behavior of the ideal gases. **Charles' law** states that at constant pressure, the volume of any dry gas is directly proportional to its absolute (Kelvin) temperature. Figure 60 illustrates Charles' law.

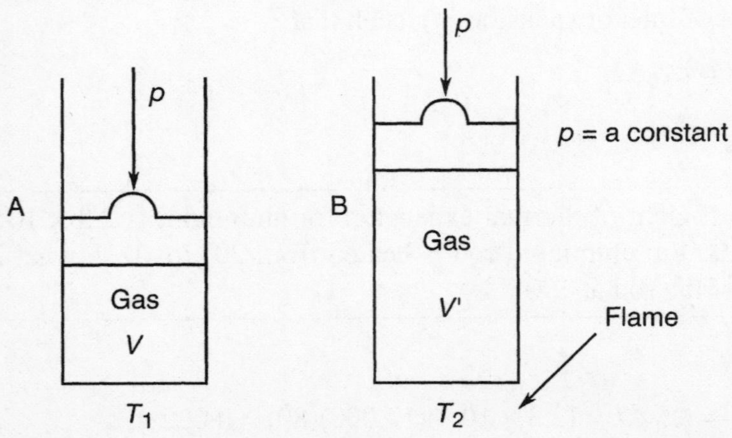

Figure 60

The gas has a larger volume at a higher temperature. The mathematical expression of Charles' law is

$$V'T = VT',$$

where V is the original volume, T is the original temperature, V' is the new volume, and T' is the new temperature. For calculations, the temperatures must be expressed in kelvins (K). Charles' law can be applied to the following problem.

PROBLEM

When a 3.0 liter quantity of oxygen is heated from 20 °C to 50 °C under constant pressure, what is the resulting volume of oxygen?

SOLUTION

First, we must convert °C to K,

$$K = °C + 273$$

$$20 + 273 = 293 \text{ and } 50 + 273 = 323.$$

Solving for V',

$$V' = VT'/T = (3)(323)/293 = 3.3 \text{ liters.}$$

Boyle's law states that, at constant temperature, the volume of any dry gas is inversely proportional to the pressure exerted on it. Figure 61 illustrates Boyle's law. The increase in pressure from p_1 to p_2 decreases the volume of gas.

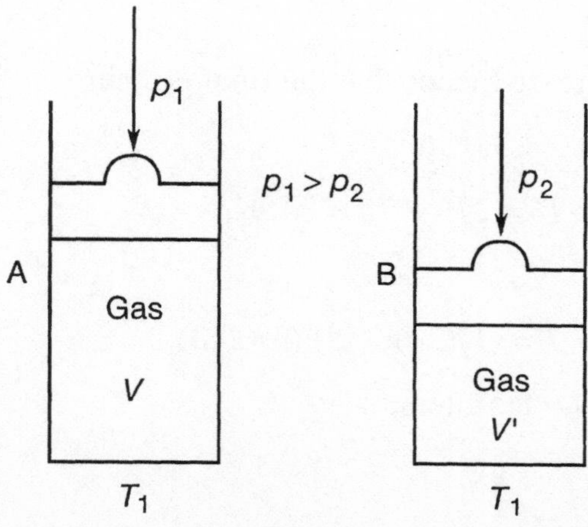

Figure 61

Since pressure and volume are inversely proportional, their product is a constant. This means that the equation for Boyle's law is

$$pV = p'V'.$$

The pressure of a gas is measured in pascals (Pa) or atmospheres (atm). One atmosphere is the normal pressure of the earth's atmosphere at sea level, and is often called standard pressure. 1 atm is approximately equal to 1.01×10^5 Pa. Standard temperature is 0 °C, or 273 K. These values are often referred to as STP (standard temperature and pressure). Boyle's law can be applied to the following problem.

PROBLEM

What pressure is needed to reduce 10 liters of a gas at STP to a volume of 2.0 liters?

SOLUTION

Solving for p',

$$p' = Vp/V' = (10)(1)/2 = 5 \text{ atm}.$$

The combination of the two laws (Charles' and Boyle's) gives:

$$pV/T = p'V'/T'.$$

PROBLEM

What is the volume of 20 liters of gas, initially at STP, after a pressure increase of 2.0 atm and a temperature increase of 75°?

SOLUTION

A 2.0-atm increase means that the final pressure is

$$p' = 1.0 + 2.0 = 3.0 \text{ atm};$$

$$T = 273 \text{ and } T' = 273 + 75 = 348\text{K}.$$

Solving for V',

$$V' = pVT'/p'T = (1)(20)(348)/(3)(273)$$

$$= 6960/819 = 8.5 \text{ liters}.$$

Mole and the Ideal Gas Law

Amedeo Avogadro found that at the same temperature and pressure, different gases had densities proportional to their **molecular masses**. The molecular mass is the total mass of all atoms that form the molecule. He also suggested a unit called a **mole**, containing 6.02×10^{23} particles of a substance. This number, 6.02×10^{23}, called **Avogadro's number**, equals the ratio of one gram to one atomic mass unit (amu). For example, helium has an atomic mass of about 4 amu. Therefore, 4 grams of helium contain about 6.02×10^{23} atoms of helium. The mass of one mole of a substance is called its **molar mass**; for instance, helium has a molar mass of 4 grams.

As is evident from Charles' law and Boyle's law, the quantity pV/T is the same for one mole of any gas, and can be expressed as a constant (R). Quantity R is called the **Universal Gas Constant**:

$$R = 8.31 \text{ J/(kg} \times {}^\circ\text{C)} = 8.31 \text{ J/(mol} \times \text{K)};$$

$$R = pV/T \text{ for one mole of an ideal gas.}$$

For any given number of moles of the ideal gas, n, one can write

$$nR = pV/T.$$

This equation is most commonly written as

$$pV = nRT,$$

which is known as the **Ideal Gas Law**.

PROBLEM

15g of carbon dioxide (CO_2) occupy a volume of 0.013 m^3 under 1.5×10^5 Pa of pressure. What is the temperature of the CO_2?

SOLUTION

Determine the number of moles of CO_2.

The molar mass of CO_2 is:

$$CO_2 = C + O + O = 12 + 16 + 16 = 44 \text{ g/mol};$$

$$15 \text{ grams} \times 1 \text{ mol/44 g} = 0.34 \text{ mol of } CO_2.$$

Solving for T,

$$T = pV/nR = (1.5 \times 10^5)(.013)/(0.34)(8.31) = 690\text{K}.$$

THERMODYNAMICS

Thermal, or **internal energy**, can be changed into other types of energy. This is one of the central concepts of **thermodynamics. Internal energy** is the total potential and kinetic energy of particles within a substance.

Many problems deal with converting heat into mechanical energy. The transformation of heat into mechanical energy is governed by the First and Second Laws of Thermodynamics. The **First Law of Thermodynamics** states that the energy supplied to a system in the form of heat is equal to the work done by the system plus the change in internal energy of the system; this is just another way to state the law of conservation of energy. To state the law mathematically, consider ΔQ, the quantity of heat added to a substance with internal energy U. This addition causes an increase in internal energy to U_f and also helps the gas do a quantity of work (W). Thus, according to the First Law of Thermodynamics,

$$\Delta Q = (U_f - U) + W.$$

The First Law of Thermodynamics can be written as

$$\Delta Q = \Delta U + W,$$

where ΔQ is the total heat input, ΔU is the change in the internal energy of the gas, and W is the work done *by* (not *on*) the system.

For instance, if the internal energy increased by 200 J, and 60 J of work is done by the system, a heat input of (200 + 60) = 260 J is required.

Often, it is important to calculate the internal energy of the ideal gas:

$U = (3/2)nRT = (3/2)pV$ for a monoatomic gas (such as He, Ar, Ne, etc.) and

$U = (5/2)nRT = (5/2)pV$ for a diatomic gas (such as H_2, N_2, O_2, etc.).

The diagrams showing the gas pressure as a function of its volume (so-called p-V diagrams), are useful in examining the amount of work done by the gas. This amount of work is numerically equal to the area under the graph. Let us consider two examples, showing the processes undergone by helium (a monoatomic gas):

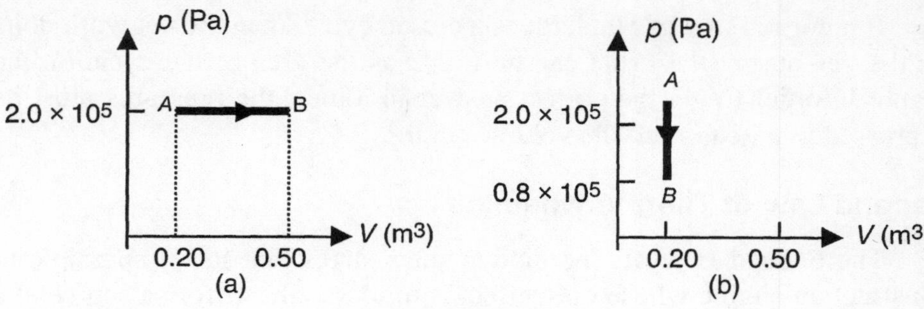

Figure 62

In diagram (a), gas expands and, therefore, so does work. The pressure remains constant (such a process is called **isobaric**). For an isobaric process,

$$W = p(V_f - V_i),$$

where W is work done by the gas, p is its pressure, V_f is the final volume of the gas, and V_i is its initial volume. In our case,

$$W = 2.0 \times 10^5(0.50 - 0.20) = 6.0 \times 10^4 \text{ J}.$$

If we want to know how much heat the gas absorbs during this process, we need to find the change in the internal energy:

$$\Delta U = U_f - U_i = 1.5p(V_f - V_i);$$

$$\Delta U = 1.5 \times 2.0 \times 10^5(0.50 - 0.20) = 9.0 \times 10^4 \text{ J}.$$

Therefore, in this process, the gas increases its internal energy by 9.0×10^4 J and does 6.0×10^4 J of work. The total heat input, according to the First Law, is: $\Delta Q = 9.0 \times 10^4 \text{ J} + 9.0 \times 10^4 \text{ J} = 1.5 \times 10^5 \text{ J}$.

As a reminder, we discussed case (a). In diagram (b), the volume of the gas does not change (the process is **isovolumetric**) and, therefore, no work is being done. However, the internal energy changes from

$$U_i = 1.5 \times 2.0 \times 10^5 \times 0.2 = 6.0 \times 10^4 \text{ J}$$

to

$$U_f = 1.5 \times 0.8 \times 10^5 \times 0.2 = 2.4 \times 10^4 \text{ J}.$$

$\Delta U = U_f - U_i = -3.6 \times 10^4$ J—note the negative sign indicating that internal energy decreases.

Since $W = 0$, the heat input is also negative:

$$\Delta Q = \Delta U + W = \Delta U = -3.6 \times 10^4 \text{ J}.$$

If a portion of a gas undergoes a closed cycle, then the net work done by the gas during the cycle can be found as the area of the cycle on the graph. In order to get the correct answer in joules, the pressures must be expressed in pascals, and the volumes in m^3.

Second Law of Thermodynamics

The Second Law of Thermodynamics states that it is impossible to construct an engine whose only effect is to extract heat from a source at a constant temperature and convert all the heat into work. The examination of a basic heat engine can help clarify the second law.

In an engine, the working substance goes through a cycle. The heat taken in during the cycle is partially converted into work. However, any heat that is not converted must be delivered to a low temperature reservoir or "heat sink." The heat sink absorbs the exhaust from the cycle. Figure 63 illustrates the basic process for heat engines.

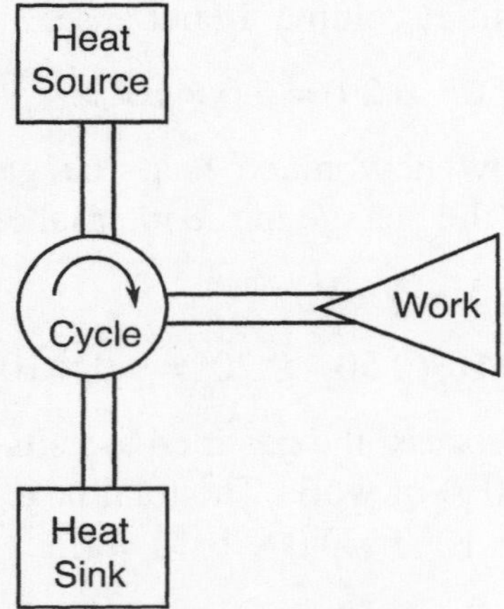

Figure 63

In essence, the second law says that heat flows from objects with high temperatures to objects with low temperatures. In a single temperature system, no heat flows.

The efficiency (e) of a heat engine is equal to the work done during one cycle divided by the heat input during the cycle:

$$e = W/Q_H.$$

From the First Law, we find that the work is the difference between the heat taken in (Q_i) and the heat exhaust (Q_o),

$$W = \Delta Q_i - \Delta Q_o.$$

Therefore,

$$e = (\Delta Q_i - \Delta Q_o)/Q_i,$$

$$e = 1 - (\Delta Q_o/\Delta Q_i).$$

The French scientist Sadi Carnot showed that an engine working between the input temperature (T_i) and the exhaust temperature (T_o) cannot have an efficiency greater than

$$e = 1 - (T_o/T_i) \times 100\%.$$

From this, we conclude that the efficiency can be increased by raising the temperature of the source, lowering the temperature of the sink, or both. Maximum efficiency is achieved by keeping the source temperature as high as possible while keeping the sink temperature as low as possible. Also, maximum efficiency can only be reached if the engine uses a special cycle, called the Carnot cycle. This cycle includes **isothermal** processes (meaning T is a constant), which tend to be extremely slow; therefore, the Carnot cycle is not practical (its power would approach zero). However, the problems related to the Carnot cycle are often posed on the AP Exam.

Examine the following problems:

What is the maximum efficiency of a heat engine that has an input temperature of 300 °C and a sink temperature of 150 °C?

SOLUTION

First, we must convert the temperatures to the Kelvin scale:

300 °C = 573 K and

150 °C = 423 K.

Solving for e,

$$e = 1 - (T_o/T_i) = 1 - (423/573) = 0.26$$

$$e = 0.26 \times 100\% = 26\%$$

Some problems involve "real" engines that do not involve the Carnot cycle.

PROBLEM

During each cycle, an engine takes in 20.0×10^3 J of energy and releases 14.0×10^3 J in the heat sink. What is the efficiency of such a heat engine?

SOLUTION

The amount of work (W) done during each cycle can be found from the First Law:

$$W = 20.0 \times 10^3 \text{ J} - 14.0 \times 10^3 \text{ J} = 6.0 \times 10^3 \text{ J};$$

$$e = W/\Delta Q_i = 6.0 \times 10^3 \text{ J}/20.0 \times 10^3 \text{ J} = 0.30;$$

$$e = 0.3 \times 100\% = 30\%.$$

AP PHYSICS B

Chapter 6
Modern Physics

Chapter 6

MODERN PHYSICS

NUCLEAR STRUCTURE AND TRANSFORMATION

Early atomic scientists believed that atoms were composed of an equal number of positive and negative electrical charges but the actual internal structure of these charges was undetermined. Ernest Rutherford performed an experiment that led to a new theory of atomic structure.

Rutherford shot a beam of positively charged alpha particles through a thin layer of gold foil. An alpha particle is a heavy subatomic particle, with a positive charge twice that of a proton, and a mass about four times that of a proton. In the experiment, the alpha particles had a velocity of about 1.6×10^7 m/s. The thickness of the foil was 1×10^{-7} m. Rutherford found that most of the particles passed through the foil as if it had not been there, as expected. But, to his surprise, he found that approximately one of 8,000 alphas was deflected backward by the foil. From this, Rutherford concluded that the positive charge in an atom must be concentrated in a very small region within the atom. This would be the only possible structure that could repel an alpha particle as observed. Therefore, Rutherford proposed a **nuclear theory** of atoms. According to the theory, every atom contains a **nucleus** in which 99.95% of its mass is concentrated. The nucleus holds all the positive charge within the atom, and is surrounded by negatively charged electrons. The nucleus itself is made of positively charged and neutral particles of about equal mass. The positive nuclear particles are called **protons**. Protons have a mass of 1.00728 amu, which is approximately equivalent to 1.67×10^{-27} kg. The number of protons in the atom nucleus is called the **atomic number**. The neutral particles, **neutrons**, have a slightly larger mass. They were first isolated by James Chadwick. From his experiments it was evident that neutrons were regular components of atomic nuclei with a size comparable to a proton and a slightly higher mass of 1.00867 amu. Note that both protons and neutrons are often called **nucleons** since they both are found in atomic nuclei.

The electron's mass is only 1/1836 that of the proton, 9.1×10^{-31} kg, or about 0.00055 amu. Electrons do not, therefore, significantly contribute to the total mass of the atom.

It may seem strange that many protons may be compacted into the nucleus of an atom without repelling each other electrically. Protons and neutrons in a nucleus are held together by the **nuclear binding force,** otherwise known as **strong force**. Nuclear binding is a unique attraction force that acts between nucleons which are closer than 2.0×10^{-15} m. The magnitude of the binding energy can be found by considering the nuclear **mass defect**. Measurements show that the mass of a nucleus is always less than the sum of the masses of its individual particles. This is true because when particles combine to form a nucleus, a small amount of mass is converted to energy. The energy released is the nuclear binding energy, which can be calculated from Einstein's equation,

$$E = mc^2.$$

PROBLEM

Find the binding energy of a helium nucleus.

SOLUTION

To find the binding energy of a helium nucleus, let us examine the following information:

a helium nucleus is made of 2 protons and 2 neutrons;

the mass of 2 protons = $2 \times 1.007276 = 2.014552$ amu;

the mass of 2 neutrons = $2 \times 1.008665 = 2.017330$ amu;

the total mass of 4 nucleons = 4.031882 amu;

the mass of a helium nucleus = 4.001509 amu;

the nuclear mass defect = 0.030373 amu.

This result can be converted into energy units; however, joules are rarely used in nuclear physics. Instead, nuclear energies are measured in electron-volts. One electron-volt (eV) is the energy needed to move an electron through a potential difference of 1 volt. Since electron-volts is a small unit (1 eV = 1.6×10^{-19} J), energies are more commonly measured in Megaelectron-volts (MeV). 1 MeV = 10^6 V. The conversion of one amu to energy yields 931 MeV. To find the binding energy of helium,

$$0.030373 \text{ amu} \times 931 \text{ MeV/amu} = 28.3 \text{ MeV or } 7.1 \text{ MeV/nucleon}.$$

One important characteristic of many nuclei is **radioactivity**. This is the process of spontaneous breakdown of unstable nuclei that emit particles and/or rays. This process is most commonly referred to as **radioactive decay**. A heavy nucleus can decay by emitting two kinds of particles, alpha or beta, or by emitting gamma rays. The alpha particle is a helium nucleus. Alpha particles formed as a result of decay travel fast; they reach speeds of up to one-tenth the speed of light. They are positively charged and do not have a very large penetrating power; they can be stopped by a sheet of paper. Beta particles are actually electrons that travel near the speed of light, have a negative charge, and have more penetrating power than alpha particles. Of course, there are no electrons inside a stable nucleus; however, they can be formed in the process of decay. For example, a single neutron can decay, forming a proton and an electron (remember that the mass of a neutron exceeds that of a proton). Gamma rays are electromagnetic waves that carry no mass and no charge, travel at the speed of light, and have high energies and very high penetration power.

The emission of these radiation particles causes conversion of the atom into a new **isotope** of the same element, or into a new element. Isotopes have nuclei with the same charge (same atomic number, or number of protons) but different mass, due to a different number of neutrons.

For example, uranium-238 is radioactive and decays by a series of reactions. We can examine nuclear transformations by looking at some of these uranium decay reactions. Uranium-238 decays by the emission of an alpha particle. The reaction is

$$^{238}_{92}\text{U} \rightarrow {}^{234}_{90}\text{Th} + {}^{4}_{2}\text{He}\cdot$$

The letters shown are the element symbols. The number written as the superscript is the atomic mass of the isotope, and the number written as the subscript is the number of protons in the nucleus (the atomic number). Uranium-238 emits an alpha particle, which carries away 2 protons and 2 neutrons. Thus the mass is reduced by 4 nucleons, 238 – 4 = 234. Losing 2 protons changes the atomic number from 92 to 90. This means that the element now present is element 90, thorium. This thorium isotope has a mass of 234 amu. In nuclear equations, the laws of conservation of charge and mass apply, of course. Therefore, the sums of the masses must be equal on either side (same for the number of protons). Reactions in which gamma rays are emitted do not change the atom, since gamma rays carry no mass and no protons. Thorium-234 is also radioactive, and decays by the emission of a beta particle. By looking at the following equation, we can predict the resulting element and its mass:

$$^{234}_{90}\text{Th} \rightarrow {}^{0}_{-1}\text{e} + {}^{?}_{?}?$$

The symbol for beta shows that it carries no mass and a – 1 proton number. These numbers are significant in that betas must come from a transformation which results in the loss of a neutron and the gain of a proton. Thus, the mass is the same but the element will change. Since,

$$234 = 0 + ? \text{ and } 90 = -1 + ?$$

then

$$^{234}_{90}\text{Th} \rightarrow {}^{0}_{-1}\text{e} + {}^{234}_{91}\text{Pa}.$$

Thus, the element produced is protactinium-234. After 14 such reactions, all of which produce radioactive products, uranium-238 is eventually reduced to a very stable lead-206 atom.

As a sample of radioactive atoms decays, the decay activity decreases over time since there are fewer atoms of the original element left. The time period associated with a decay rate is called **half-life**. The half-life is the time necessary for exactly one-half of a radioactive sample to decay. The following chart and graph show an example of half-life analysis for iodine-131. Given that the half-life for iodine-131 is 8 days:

Time in days	Number of I-131 atoms	Number of half lives
0	100%	0
8	50%	1
16	25%	2
24	12.5%	3
32	6.25%	4
40	3.125%	5

Shown graphically, we see how the decay activity decreases over time.

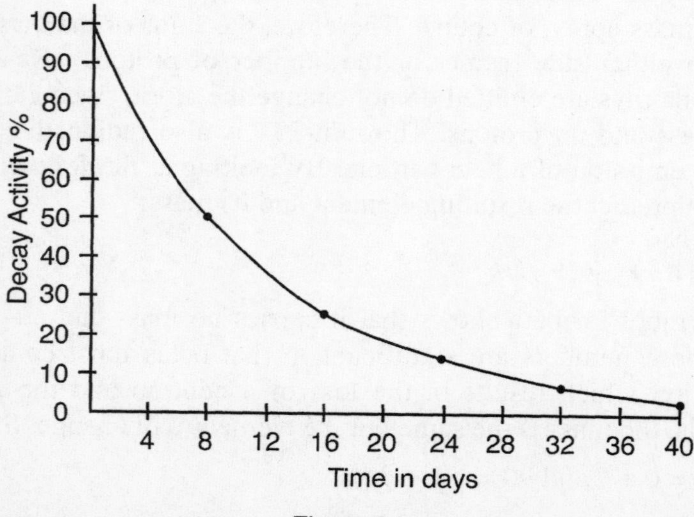

Figure 64

Radioactive decay is not the only nuclear process. Other reactions may occur by the bombardment of one nucleus with another. One example is the bombardment of beryllium with alpha particles:

$$^{9}_{4}\text{Be} + ^{4}_{2}\text{He} \rightarrow ^{12}_{6}\text{C} + ^{1}_{0}\text{n} + \text{energy},$$

which produces carbon-12 and a free neutron, as well as the release of the binding energy.

Nuclear **fission** is another reaction that releases a great amount of energy. Fission occurs in some isotopes of atoms with large nuclei. Fission is the splitting of the nucleus into smaller nuclei. For instance, uranium-235 is a common fission fuel for power plants. When a uranium-235 nucleus absorbs a neutron, the uranium nucleus divides to produce any number of different element combinations. In any case, the energy released is very large and can be used for the production of electricity. The products produced most often by uranium-235 fission are barium, krypton, and free neutrons. Many other materials, notably, plutonium-239, can also undergo fission.

Since the number of neutrons produced in such reaction exceeds the number of neutrons bombarding the nucleus, the reaction, under certain conditions, may self-accelerate. Such a process, in which energy is released very rapidly, is called **chain reaction**. Chain reactions are used in nuclear weapons.

QUANTUM THEORY AND ATOMIC STRUCTURE

Around 1900, physicists were examining a phenomenon they called the Photoelectric Effect. The **photoelectric effect** is the emission of electrons by a substance when illuminated by electromagnetic radiation. If an electron on the surface of the substance absorbs enough energy, it would escape the surface. Such electrons are called **photoelectrons**. Experiments showed that the photoelectrons are ejected only when they can instantly absorb the energy required to do so. This fact contradicted the assumptions of the classic wave theory that suggested that the electron should be able to absorb energy over a period of time until it has enough for ejection. The evidence presented by the photoelectric effect lead to the conception of the **quantum theory of radiation**.

Max Planck showed that the experimental results could be explained if the energy provided by radiation was an integral multiple of a quantity he called hf, where h is Planck's constant ($h = 6.63 \times 10^{-34}$ J $\times$ s) and f is the frequency of the radiation wave. Thus, light energy is radiated or absorbed in particles containing energy equal to some multiple of hf. Today, these particles are called **photons**. The fact that light can be considered and described as either a particle or a wave is called **wave-particle duality**.

Eventually, Einstein used the photon theory to explain the photoelectric effect. According to Einstein, an electron can absorb the entire energy of an incident photon. If that energy exceeds the work function, the electron is ejected. The maximum kinetic energy (K_{max}) possessed by a photoelectron is, according to **Einstein's equation**:

$$K_{max} = hf - \phi = (1/2)mv^2,$$

where m and v are the mass and velocity of the ejected photoelectron, h is Planck's constant, f is the photon frequency, and ϕ is called the **work function**: the minimum energy needed (or the work done) for an electron to escape the surface of a material. The value of the work function depends on the material and the condition of its surface; for well-polished metals, the work function's values are on the order of several electron-volts.

If the photon's energy is just enough to free it with a zero velocity, then $hf = \phi$, and f is called the **cut-off frequency**. This means that any photons with a frequency below the cut-off frequency cannot cause a photoelectric effect regardless of exposure time and the intensity of light.

The quantum theory led to new theories regarding atomic structure. Neils Bohr theorized that the electron around the nucleus of an atom must exist only in certain distinct, or **quantized**, orbitals since they do not radiate energy. Also, the closer the orbital is to the nucleus, the lower the energy for that orbital.

If an electron in an atomic orbital absorbs a photon with the exact amount of energy so as to land in a higher level, it may do so and become **excited**. Similarly, if an excited electron emits a photon, it falls to a lower orbital, and the energy of the photon will be equal to the energy difference between the orbitals. This is shown by Figure 65.

Before absorption, we have an electron in level 1. The photon absorbs a 5-eV photon. Since the difference between level 1 and level 3 is 5 eV, the electron jumps to level 3. Once in level 3, there are two possible outcomes. The first is that the electron could emit a 5 eV photon and return to level 1. The second possibility is that the electron would emit a 3 eV photon and fall to level 2, then emit a second photon with 2 eV energy as it falls to level 1.

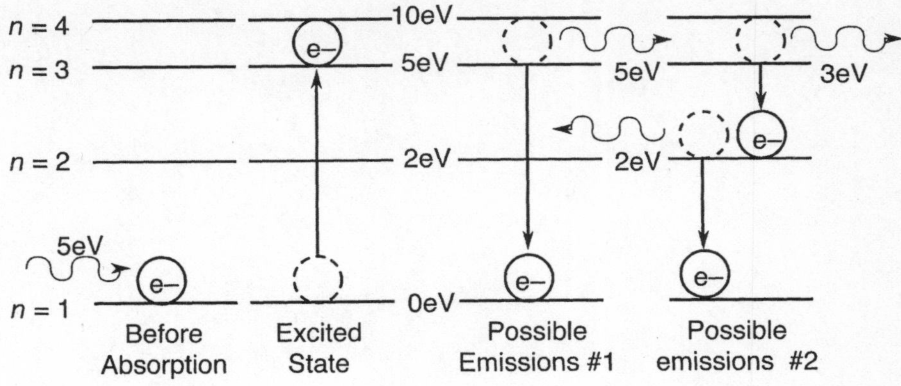

Figure 65

Bohr's idea has since been modified to incorporate such ideas as electron spin, magnetic effects, and angular momentum—factors that he did not include in his original atomic explanations.

* * *

This concludes the theoretical material that should be helpful in your studies for the AP Physics B exam. However, only *practice* can help you acquire and refine the problem-solving skills necessary for success on the exam. Please refer to our Practice Tests for further training.

	Dimension	**Units**
	Length	Meter
	Time	Second
	Mass	Kilogram
Derived Dimensions	Acceleration	m/s^2
	Velocity	m/s
	Force	$kg \times m/s^2$
	Momentum	$kg \times m/s$
	Torque	$kg \times m^2/s^2$
	Angular Momentum	$kg \times m^2/s^2$
	Electrostatic Charge	coulomb (C)
	Energy/Work	joule ($kg \times m^2/s^2$)
	Power	watt ($kg \times m^2/s^3$)
	Potential Difference	volt ($kg \times m^2/C \times s^2$)
	Current	ampere (C/s)

AP PHYSICS C

Chapter 7
Classical Mechanics

Chapter 7

CLASSICAL MECHANICS*

VECTORS

A vector is a quantity that can be assigned both direction and magnitude. Vector variables are usually indicated in **boldface**, or with an arrow, such as $\vec{v}$.

The Components of a Vector

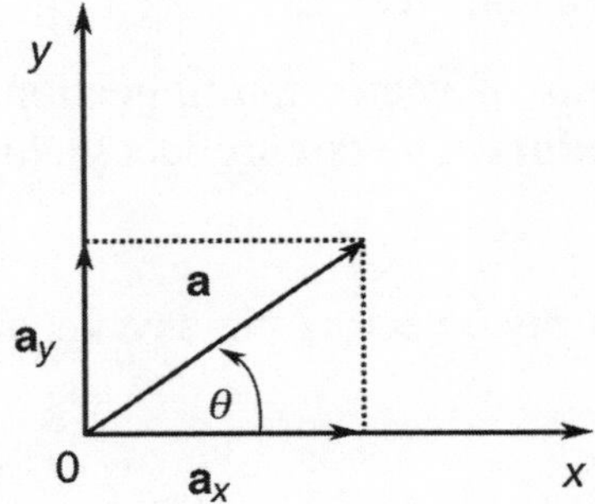

Figure 1 — The Formation of Vector Components on the x–y axes

The components of a vector are given by:

$A_x = A\cos\theta$, and

$A_y = A\sin\theta$.

A component is equal to the product of the magnitude of vector **A** and the cosine of the angle between the positive direction of the corresponding axis and the vector.

The magnitude of a vector can be expressed in terms of its components:

$$a = \sqrt{a_x^2 + a_y^2}\,.$$

* Note: AP Physics C examines Classical Mechanics and Electricity & Magnetism in greater depth than AP Physics B does. Also, AP Physics C uses calculus, whereas AP Physics B is algebra- and trigonometry-based. However, most concepts discussed in the C course are also covered in the B course. Therefore, the discussion of such concepts in the following two chapters is rather brief. We will only repeat enough to make the reading process smooth; the main focus of AP Physics C review is on the concepts and principles not covered in AP Physics B. For basic terminology and principles, you are encouraged to refer to Chapters 1-6.

Finally, the angle θ, in terms of the vector components, is given by:

$$\tan \theta = \frac{a_y}{a_x}.$$

Like scalars, vectors can be added, subtracted, and multiplied.

To add or subtract vectors, one can add or subtract the corresponding x and y coordinates. For example, to find **A** – **B**:

First, find $A_x - B_x = C_x$;

then, find $A_y - B_y = C_y$;

therefore, **C** is the sum vector.

There are two forms of vector multiplication: the **dot product** and the **vector**, or **cross product**. The dot product yields a scalar value:

$$\mathbf{a} \cdot \mathbf{b} = ab\cos \theta.$$

The cross product of two vectors yields a vector:

$$\mathbf{a} \times \mathbf{b} = \mathbf{c}$$

and

$$|\mathbf{c}| = ab\sin \theta.$$

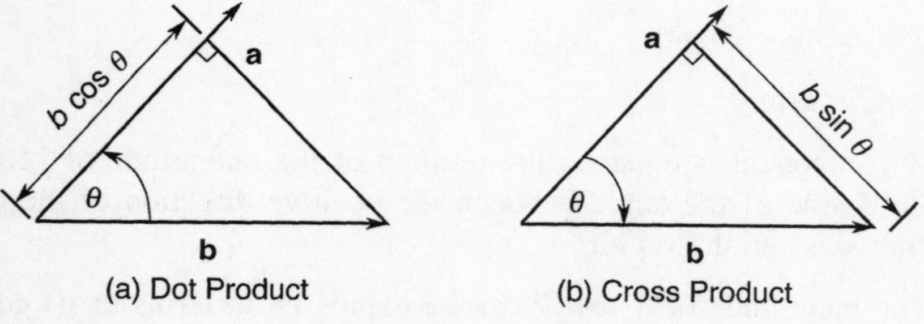

(a) Dot Product

(b) Cross Product

Figure 2 — Vector Multiplication

The direction of the vector product $\mathbf{a} \times \mathbf{b} = \mathbf{c}$ is given by the "Right-Hand Rule":

1) With **a** and **b** tail-to-tail, draw the angle θ from **a** to **b**.

2) With your right hand, curl your fingers in the direction of the angle drawn. The extended thumb points in the direction of **c**.

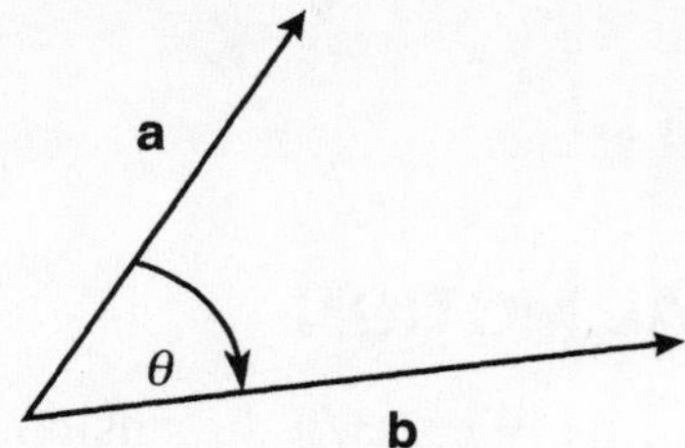

Figure 3 — The direction of the vector product, **c** = **a** × **b**, (|**c**| = $ab\sin\theta$), is into the page.

Properties of the cross product:

$$\mathbf{A} \times \mathbf{B} = -\mathbf{B} \times \mathbf{A}$$

$$\mathbf{A} \times (\mathbf{B} + \mathbf{C}) = (\mathbf{A} \times \mathbf{B}) + (\mathbf{A} \times \mathbf{C})$$

$c(\mathbf{A} \times \mathbf{B}) = (c\mathbf{A}) \times \mathbf{B} = \mathbf{A} \times (c\mathbf{B})$, where c is a scalar.

$$|\mathbf{A} \times \mathbf{B}|^2 = A^2B^2 - (\mathbf{A} \cdot \mathbf{B})^2$$

LINEAR MOTION

For any object in motion, it makes sense to discuss both **average** and **instantaneous velocity**:

Average Velocity

$$v = \frac{\Delta x}{\Delta t} = \frac{x_2 - x_1}{t_2 - t_1} \rightarrow \text{units: m/s.}$$

Instantaneous Velocity

$$v = \lim_{\Delta t \to 0} \frac{\Delta x}{\Delta t} = \frac{dx}{dt} = v(t) \rightarrow \text{units: m/s.}$$

Just as the average and instantaneous velocities are the rate of change of position with respect to time, acceleration is the rate of change of velocity with respect to time. In many cases, the acceleration of a moving object is a constant. With this assumption ($\Delta v/\Delta t$ = constant = a), the following basic kinematic equations of motion can be derived:

1. $v = v_0 + at$
2. $v^2 = v_0^2 + 2a(x - x_0)$
3. $x = x_0 + v_0t + 1/2\, at^2$

4. $x = x_0 + 1/2\,(v_0 + v)t$,

where v_0 and x_0 are initial values.

TWO-DIMENSIONAL MOTION

To solve problems involving two-dimensional (or planar) motion, one can break the velocity and acceleration vectors down into their x and y components. Once this is done, the preceding one-dimensional equations can apply.

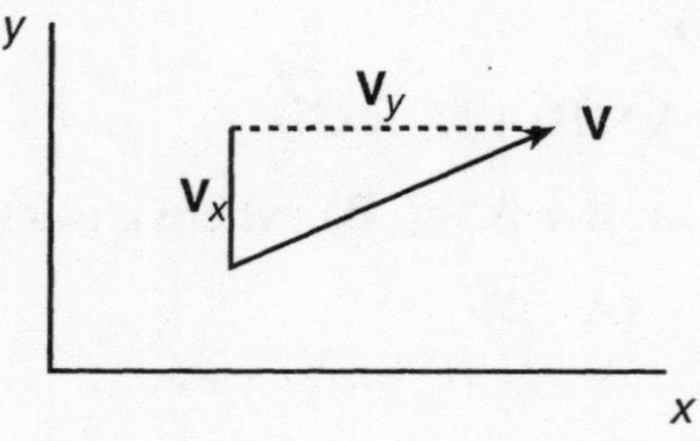

Figure 4

A special case of two-dimensional motion is **Uniform Circular Motion**. For a particle following a circular path, the acceleration is directed radially inward. This acceleration is called **centripetal acceleration**.

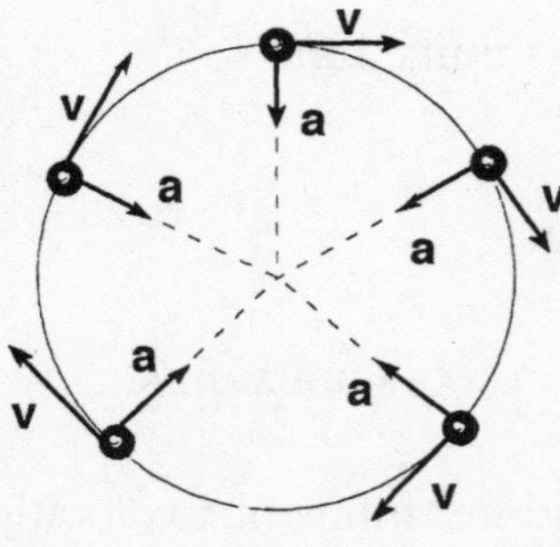

Figure 5

Centripetal Acceleration

$$a = \frac{v^2}{r},$$

where a represents acceleration, v represents the tangential component of velocity, and r represents the radius of the path.

For uniform circular motion, a can also be written as:

$$a = \frac{4\pi^2 r}{T^2},$$

where T, the period or time for one revolution, is given by:

$$T = \frac{2\pi r}{v}.$$

The tangential component of the acceleration is the rate at which the particle speed changes:

$$a_T = \lim_{\Delta t \to 0} \frac{\Delta v}{\Delta t} = \frac{dv}{dt}.$$

In describing circular motion, the angular quantities are often useful:

1. ω represents angular velocity,

$$\omega = \frac{d\theta}{dt};$$

2. α represents angular acceleration,

$$\alpha = \frac{d\omega}{dt}.$$

If angular acceleration (α) is constant, then equations correlating to those previously stated for linear motion can be shown to apply.

Similarity Table

Rotational Motion	Linear Motion Equivalent
$\alpha = \text{constant}$	$a = \text{constant}$
$\omega = \omega_0 + \alpha t$	$v = v_0 + at$
$\theta = \frac{\omega_0 + \omega}{2} t$	$x = \frac{v_0 + v}{2} t$
$\theta = \omega_0 t + (1/2)\alpha t^2$	$x = v_0 t + (1/2)at^2$
$\omega 2 = \omega_0^2 + 2\alpha\theta$	$v^2 = v_0^2 + 2ax$
θ_0, θ = initial and final angular displacements	
ω_0, ω = initial and final angular velocities	

NEWTON'S LAWS

First Law

In an inertial frame of reference, every body remains in a state of rest or uniform linear motion, unless a non-zero external force is applied.

Second Law

If the net force, or the vector sum of the forces (**F**), acting on a particle of mass (m) is different from zero, then the particle has an acceleration (**a**) directly proportional to, and in the same direction as, **F**, but inversely proportional to mass m. Symbolically,

$$\mathbf{F} = m\mathbf{a},$$

(if mass is constant).

Third Law

For every force, there exists a corresponding equal and opposing force of the same nature; in other words, the mutual actions of two bodies in contact are always equal in magnitude and opposite in direction. Sometimes, it is said that "for every action, there is an equal and opposite reaction."

Newton's laws all refer to the effects of forces on particles or bodies. These forces can be represented in vector form.

Force

1. Force is a cause of acceleration; it can be thought of as a push or pull that bodies exert on each other.
2. Force can be represented by a vector.

MOMENTUM

Linear Momentum

Linear momentum is defined as

$$\mathbf{p} = m\mathbf{v} \rightarrow \text{units: (kg} \times \text{m)/s},$$

where p represents the linear momentum of a particle, m represents the mass of the particle, and v represents the velocity of the particle.

Newton's Second Law in its Momentum Form

$$\mathbf{F} = d\mathbf{p}/dt = d(m\mathbf{v})/dt,$$

where $\mathbf{F}$ is the net force acting on the particle.

LINEAR MOMENTUM OF A SYSTEM OF PARTICLES

Total Linear Momentum

$$\mathbf{p}_{total} = \sum_{i=1}^{n} \mathbf{p}_i = \mathbf{p}_1 + \mathbf{p}_2 + \ldots + \mathbf{p}_n$$

$$= m_1\mathbf{v}_1 + m_2\mathbf{v}_2 + \ldots + m_n\mathbf{v}_n,$$

where $\mathbf{p}_{total}$ represents the total linear momentum of a system and $\mathbf{p}_i$, m_i, $\mathbf{v}_i$, represent the linear momentum, mass, and velocity of the ith particle, respectively.

Newton's Second Law for a System of Particles (Momentum Form)

$$\mathbf{F}_{ext} = d\mathbf{p}_{total}/dt,$$

where $\mathbf{F}_{ext}$ = the sum of all external forces.

Momentum is conserved. The total linear momentum of the system remains unchanged if the sum of all forces acting on the system is zero or if there are no external forces at all (in other words, if the system is closed).

According to Newton's Second Law,

$$d\mathbf{p}_{total}/dt = \sum \mathbf{F}_{ext} = 0.$$

Impulse and Momentum

The **Impulse-Momentum Method** is an alternate method to solving problems in which forces are expressed as a function of time.

Linear Impulse-Momentum Equation

$$\sum \mathbf{F}\Delta t = M\mathbf{v}_2 - M\mathbf{v}_1$$

COLLISIONS

When kinetic energy is conserved, a collision is called **elastic**; otherwise, a collision is said to be **inelastic**.

1. For an elastic collision,

$$\frac{1}{2}m_1v_{1_i}^2 + \frac{1}{2}m_2v_{2_i}^2 = \frac{1}{2}m_1v_{1_f}^2 + \frac{1}{2}m_2v_{2_f}^2.$$

2. For an inelastic collision, some kinetic energy is transformed into internal energy. However, linear momentum is still conserved. If the two bodies stick and travel together with a common final velocity after collision, it is said to be completely inelastic. From conservation of momentum, we have

$$m_1v_{1_i} + m_2v_{2_i} = (m_1 + m_2)v_f.$$

Collisions in Two Dimensions

Since momentum is linearly conserved, the resultant components must be found and then the conservation laws applied in each direction.

1. The x-component

$$m_1v_{1_i} = m_1v_{1_f}\cos\theta_1 + m_2v_{2_f}\cos\theta_2$$

2. The y-component

$$m_2v_{2_i} = m_1v_{1_f}\sin\theta_1 + m_2v_{2_f}\sin\theta_2$$

In the equations above, θ_1 represents the angle of deflection (after the collision) of mass m_1 and θ_2 represents the angle of deflection (after the collision) of mass m_2.

Note that for the above cases, i denotes initial value; f denotes final value.

ANGULAR MOMENTUM

Angular Momentum (**L**) is a conserved quantity, pertaining to rotational motion, corresponding to linear momentum.

Angular momentum can be calculated with respect to a given axis of rotation. The vector equation for the angular momentum of a particle is

$$\mathbf{L} = \mathbf{r} \times \mathbf{p};$$

and the scalar equation for the angular momentum of a particle is

$$L = rp(\sin\theta),$$

Where L represents angular momentum, r is the radius-vector from the axis toward the particle, p represents linear momentum, and θ is the angle formed by r and p.

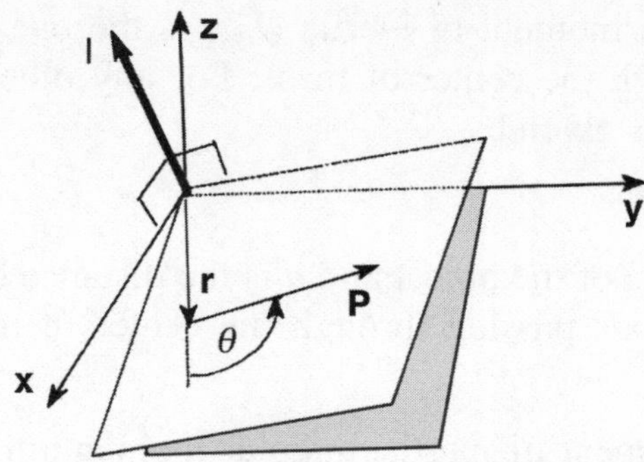

Figure 6 — Angular Momentum

The rotational correlation to force is **torque** ($\boldsymbol{\tau}$), which relates to angular momentum by the equation:

$$\boldsymbol{\tau} = d\mathbf{L}/dt.$$

Torque is given by:

$$\boldsymbol{\tau} = \mathbf{r} \times \mathbf{F}_{\text{tangential}}$$

When the net torque is zero, a state of **rotational equilibrium** is achieved; in other words, ω is a constant (not necessarily zero).

Another way to calculate angular momentum is through the use of **moment of inertia**. The moment of inertia corresponds to mass in rotational motion. It depends on the mass of the object, its geometry (shape and mass distribution), and the axis of rotation.

Calculating the Moment of Inertia of Various Objects

$$I = \int r^2 \, dm$$

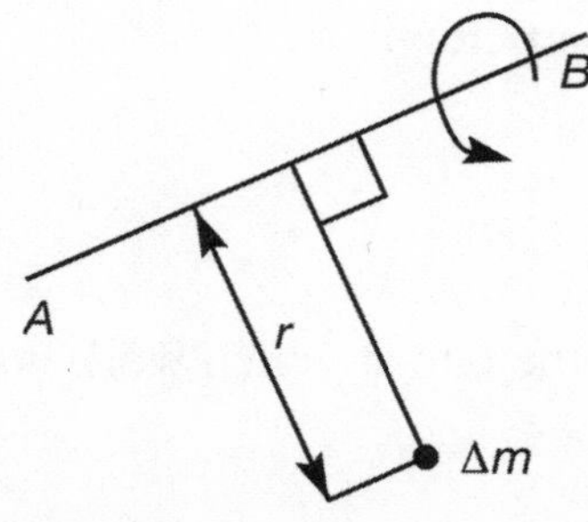

Figure 7

The minimum moment of inertia (I_{cm}) is the one with respect to an axis passing through the center of mass. For any other parallel axis, the moment of inertia is given by

$$I = I_{cm} + md^2,$$

where m is the mass of the object and d is the distance between the axis in question and the axis passing through the center of mass (**the parallel-axis theorem**).

Using the moment of inertia, angular momentum of a rotating rigid body can be calculated as:

$$\mathbf{L} = I\boldsymbol{\omega}.$$

ENERGY AND WORK

The work done by a force (**F**) through a displacement (d**r**) is defined as:

$$W = \int \mathbf{F} \cdot d\mathbf{r}, \text{ in Joules (SI units).}$$

Over a finite distance from point 1 to point 2:

$$W_{1\text{-}2} = \int_1^2 \mathbf{F} \cdot d\mathbf{r}.$$

Work-Energy Principle

Kinetic energy is the energy possessed by a particle by virtue of its motion. Kinetic energy for a particle of mass m and velocity v is defined as

$$K = (1/2)mv^2.$$

The **Work-Energy Principle**—if a particle undergoes displacement under the influence of a net force **F**, the work done by **F** equals the change in kinetic energy of the particle:

$$W_{1\text{-}2} = K_2 - K_1.$$

Power and Efficiency

Power is defined as the rate at which work is done:

$$P = dW/dt$$

Often, when an object is moving at constant velocity v, and force F has the same direction as v, power can be found as

$P = \mathbf{F} \cdot \mathbf{v}.$

Mechanical Efficiency

Mechanical efficiency is defined as the percentage of useful work obtained when a certain amount of total work is done (or, in other words, the work output corresponding to a given amount of energy spent):

$$\eta = W_{useful}/K_{spent}$$

Note: η is always < 1.

Potential Energy

Potential Energy (U) is defined as the stored energy of a system associated with the mutual position of the particles and the interaction existing between them.

The potential energy of a particle in the gravitational field of Earth is given by the following equation:

$$\Delta U_g = mgh.$$

Other types of potential energy include:

1) Gravitational Potential Energy of a system of two particles with masses m_1 and m_2 at a distance r from each other:

$$U_G = -G\frac{m_1 m_2}{r}.$$

2) Spring Potential Energy:

$$U_s = (1/2)kx^2.$$

Conservation of Energy

Conservative Forces are forces whose work on an object do not depend on the object's trajectory, and are defined only by the initial and the final positions of the object. Most forces we deal with are, in fact, conservative, with friction being an exception: friction is a non-conservative force.

For a particle under the action of *only* conservative forces:

$(K)_1 + (U)_1 = (K)_2 + (U)_2 = E,$ where E is the total energy of the system. (1)

The sum of kinetic and potential energy at a given point is constant.

Equation (1) can be written as

$$E = (1/2)mv^2 + U.$$

The potential energy must be less than or equal to the total energy.

In a conservative system, if $U = E$, then $V = 0$.

In a non-conservative system, relating potential and kinetic energy with the non-conservative force $\mathbf{F}'$ can be done as follows:

$$\Delta(U + K) = \int \mathbf{F}' \cdot d\mathbf{r}.$$

HARMONIC MOTION

Simple Harmonic Motion—linear motion of a body where the acceleration is proportional to the displacement from a fixed origin and is always directed towards the origin. The direction of acceleration is always opposite to that of the displacement.

Equation of motion:

$$mx'' + kx = 0 \qquad (1)$$

$$x'' + \omega^2 x = 0 \qquad (2)$$

where $\omega^2 = k/m$.

General solution of Equation (2):

$$x = c_1 \sin \omega t + c_2 \cos \omega t, \qquad (3)$$

where c_1 and c_2 may be obtained from initial conditions.

An alternate form of Equation (3):

$$x = x_m \sin(\omega t + \theta),$$

where x_m represents the amplitude (maximum displacement from equilibrium), ω is the angular speed of the oscillations, and θ is the phase angle.

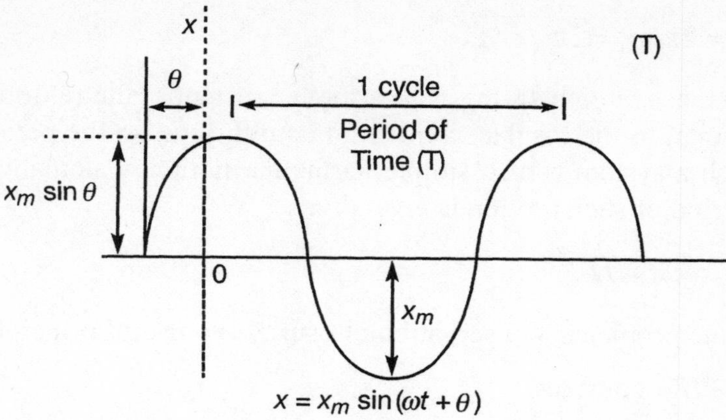

Figure 8 — Period — $T = 2\pi/\omega$
Frequency — $f = 1/T = \omega/2\pi$

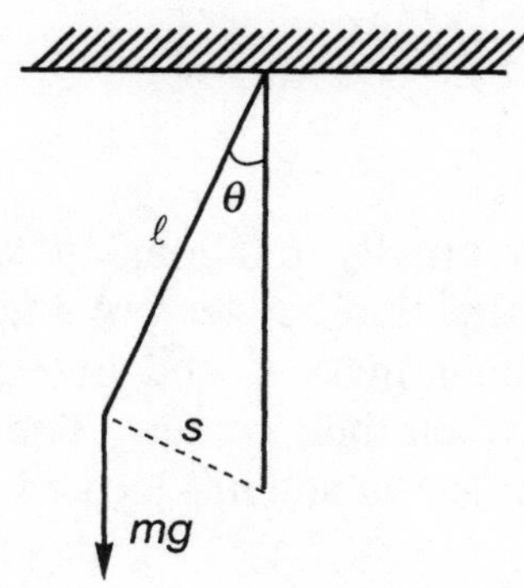

Figure 9

For small angles of vibration, the motion of a simple pendulum can be approximated by simple harmonic motion:

$$\theta = s/\ell.$$

Equation of Motion:

$$\theta'' + (g/\ell)\theta = 0.$$

The solution is:

$$\theta = \theta_0 \cos(\omega_0 t + \alpha_0),$$

where ω_0 equals $\sqrt{g/\ell}$, θ_0 is the max amplitude of oscillation, and α_0 represents the phase angle.

The period of oscillation of a simple pendulum is

$$T_0 = 2\pi/\omega_0 = 2\pi\sqrt{\ell / g}.$$

For a mass m on a spring with a force constant k, the returning force is proportional to the displacement from equilibrium, so the periodic motion of such a system is also simple harmonic motion. Calculations show that the period of such motion is given by:

$$T = 2\pi\sqrt{m / k}.$$

In some problems, conservation of energy is a useful principle to use:

$$K + U = \text{constant}.$$

Since $K = 0$ at the maximum displacement, and $U = 0$ at equilibrium (when speed is at a maximum), one can also write that at any given moment,

$$K + U = K_{max} = (1/2)mv_m^2, \text{ and}$$

$$K + U = U_{max} = (1/2)kx_m^2.$$

Universal Gravity

Newton developed a gravity relationship known as the Universal Law of Gravitation. The attraction between two masses is directly proportional to the product of their masses, and inversely proportional to the square of the distance between their centers. The equation describing the attraction between two masses (m and m') located a distance (d) from each other is

$$\mathbf{F} = \frac{Gmm'}{d^2},$$

where G is the universal gravitational constant. The value of G is 6.67×10^{-11} Nm^2/kg^2.

The motion of planets and satellites can be approximated by considering their orbits as circular. The gravitational force between the masses is the centripetal force that maintains circular motion. From the Law of Gravitation,

$$\mathbf{F} = Gmm'/d^2$$

and the centripetal force is given by

$$\mathbf{F}_c = m\omega^2 r.$$

Since $\mathbf{F} = \mathbf{F}_c$ and d can be considered the radius of the orbit,

$Gmm'/r^2 = m\omega^2 r$, and

$\omega^2 = Gm'/r^3$.

This equation is the determination of the angular velocity for planetary or satellite orbits, where m' is the larger mass that holds the planet or satellite. This equation also shows that the mass of the orbiting satellite (m) does not affect its velocity.

In most problems, planets and satellites are assumed to have circular orbits. In reality, the orbits are always **elliptical**. Figure 10 shows the orbit of the Earth around the Sun. The Earth is shown at the closest point of the orbit (called the **perigee**). The point farthest from the Sun is called the **apogee**. Note that, in reality, the Earth's orbit is nearly circular: the separation from the Sun varies from 149,000,000 km to 151,000,000 km.

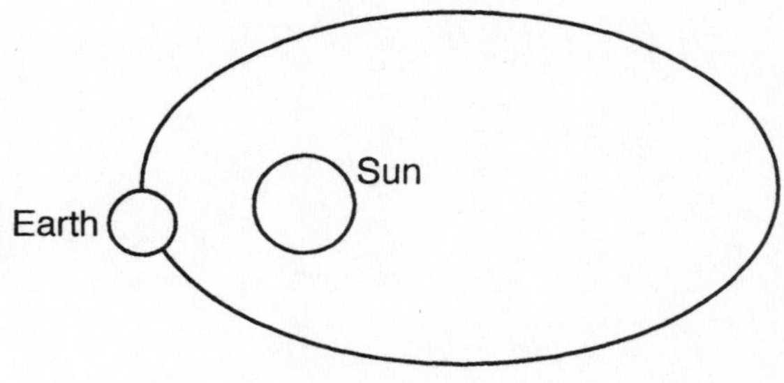

Figure 10

For satellites in elliptical orbits, the potential energy is at a maximum in the apogee and at a minimum in the perigee. The kinetic energy, correspondingly, is at a maximum in the perigee and at a minimum in the apogee. Thus, the total energy of the satellite remains constant.

The elliptical orbits are governed by **Kepler's laws**:

1. **The law of orbits**: each planet moves around the Sun in an elliptical orbit. The Sun is located at one focus of the ellipse.

2. **The law of areas**: a radius-vector connecting a planet to the Sun sweeps out equal areas in equal periods of time.

3. **The law of periods**: the square of the orbital period of a planet is proportional to the cube of the semi-major axis of the orbit. (A semi-major axis is one-half of the "longest measurement" of the ellipse).

Kepler's laws are useful in calculating the various parameters of the orbits. For instance, a useful formula for the period of a satellite (or a planet) orbiting an object of mass m is $T^2 = (4\pi^2/Gm)r^3$.

AP PHYSICS C

Chapter 8
Electricity & Magnetism

Chapter 8

ELECTRICITY AND MAGNETISM

ELECTRIC FIELDS

Definition of an Electric Field

$$\mathbf{E} = \mathbf{F}/q,$$

where **E** is the electric field and **F** is an electric force acting on the positive test charge q.

COULOMB'S LAW

By definition, the force between two point charges in vacuum is given by Coulomb's law:

$$F = \frac{q_1 q_2}{4\pi\epsilon_0 r^2},$$

where q_1 and q_2 are the values of the charges (positive or negative), r is the distance separating the two point charges, and ϵ_0 is the permittivity in free space (8.854×10^{-12} F/m).

The force F can be expressed in vector form to indicate its direction as follows:

$$\mathbf{F} = \frac{q_1 q_2}{4\pi\epsilon_0 r^2}\mathbf{a}_d.$$

The unit vector **a**d is in the direction of d:

$$\mathbf{a}_d = \mathbf{d}/|\mathbf{d}| = \mathbf{d}/d.$$

Since q_1 and q_2 can each be either positive or negative, the resultant force can also be either positive (repulsive) or negative (attractive).

GAUSS'S LAW

By definition, the electric flux of electric field E through a small element of a surface dA equals

$$d\phi = \mathbf{E} \cdot d\mathbf{A} = E\cos\,\theta dA.$$

To find the total flux through the surface, one must integrate:

$$\phi = \oint_A \mathbf{E} \cdot d\mathbf{A} = \oint_A E\,dA\cos\,\theta.$$

Gauss's law states that the net electric flux ϕ passing through a closed surface is equal to the total charge Q within that surface divided by ϵ_0:

$$f = \oint \mathbf{E} \cdot d\mathbf{A} = \mathrm{Q}/\epsilon_0.$$

Applications of Gauss's Law

Gauss's law helps in calculating the electric fields of highly symmetrical charge distributions, namely, spherical, cylindrical and planar. It is easier to solve a problem if we can choose a special, convenient Gaussian surface.

Some hints for choosing a convenient Gaussian surface:

1. The surface must be closed.
2. The electric field must remain constant through, and normal to, the surface.

PROBLEM

Find the electric field (E) of a point charge (q) at a given distance (r) from the charge.

SOLUTION

First, choose the Gaussian surface. In this case, it is convenient to choose a sphere with the center at q and with a radius of r. Here, E is a constant at any point of the surface; moreover, vector E is at all times perpendicular to the surface. Therefore,

$$\phi = EA = E(4\pi r^2)$$

We also know that

$$\phi = q/\epsilon_0.$$

Using both equations, we arrive at the answer, a familiar formula from Coulomb's law:

$$E = q/4\pi\epsilon_0 r^2.$$

ELECTRIC POTENTIAL, ENERGY, AND WORK

Electric Potential Difference:

$$V_B - V_A = \frac{W_{AB}}{q_0} \rightarrow \text{units: volts (V)},$$

where V_B is the electric potential at Point B, V_A is the electric potential at Point A, W_{AB} is the work done by an external force, and q_0 is the electrical test charge.

In more general terms, the potential difference between two points (1 and 2), symbolized as $V_{1\text{-}2}$, is defined as the work done in moving a unit positive charge by an external force from the initial point (1) to the final point (2).

The potential difference between points 1 and 2, located along direction x sin a non-uniform electric field E, can be found as

$$V_{1\text{-}2} = -\int_{x_1}^{x_2} \mathbf{E} \cdot d\mathbf{x}.$$

The unit for potential difference is the volt (V): 1 V = 1 J/1 C.

It is useful to know the formulas for electric field and potential due to typical charge distributions:

1. Point charge.

   $E = q/4\pi\epsilon_0 r^2$; $V = q/4\pi\epsilon_0 r$

2. Uniformly charged conducting, thin spherical shell of radius R.

   $E = q/4\pi\epsilon_0 r^2$ and $V = q/4\pi\epsilon_0 r$, if $r > R$; $E = 0$ and $V = q/4\pi\epsilon_0 R$, if $r < R$

3. Uniformly charged conducting, thin long cylindrical shell of radius R and linear density (charge/length) λ.

   $E = \lambda/2\pi\epsilon_0 r$, if $r > R$; $E = 0$, if $r < R$

4. Uniformly charged conducting plane with surface charge density (charge/surface area) σ.

   $E = \sigma/2\epsilon_0$

Reminder: potential difference for any charge distribution can be found through

$$V_{1\text{-}2} = -\int_{x_1}^{x_2} \mathbf{E} \cdot d\mathbf{x}.$$

CAPACITORS

The capacitance of two oppositely charged conductors in a uniform dielectric medium is

$$C = \frac{Q}{V_0},$$

where Q is the total charge in either conductor and V_0 is the potential difference between the two conductors.

The unit for capacitance is the Farad (F); 1 F = 1 C/1 V.

PROBLEM

> Find the capacitance of the parallel-plate capacitor with the charge Q, plate area A, and plate separation d (the plate separation is assumed to be much smaller than the size of the plates).

SOLUTION

$$C = Q/V,$$

where V is the voltage (potential difference between the plates). Since the field is uniform, $V = Ed$, where E is the electric field inside the capacitor.

$$E = 2E_0,$$

where E_0 is the electric field due to each plate (since charges are opposite, the fields add up inside)—see Figure 11.

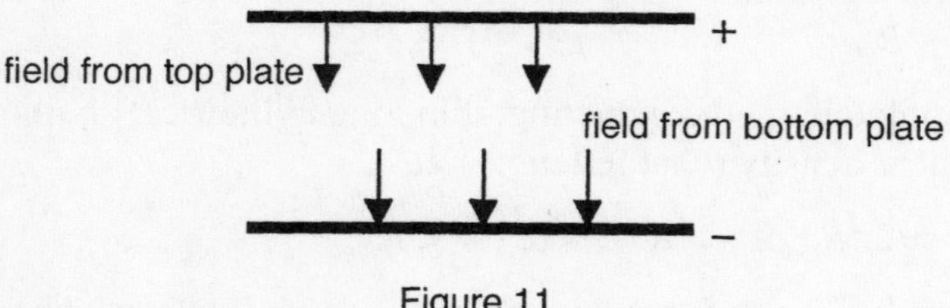

Figure 11

To find E_0, consider a box-like Gaussian surface surrounding a plate. Only the sides of the box parallel to the plate will experience electric flux. Since the area of each side is A, the flux equals:

$$\phi = 2AQ.$$

From Gauss's law,

$\phi = Q/\epsilon_0$.

Therefore,

$E_0 = Q/2A\epsilon_0$,

$E = Q/A\epsilon_0$,

$V = Ed = Qd/A\epsilon_0$, and

$C = Q/V = A\epsilon_0/d$.

The total energy stored in the capacitor is:

$U = (1/2)QV = (1/2)(Q^2/C) = (1/2)CV^2$.

It is also useful to know the formulas for capacitance of a **spherical** capacitor (two concentric spheres with radii r and R):

$C = 2\pi\epsilon_0(rR/(R - r))$,

and the **cylindrical** capacitor (two coaxial cylinders of length ℓ, with radii r and R):

$C = 2\pi\epsilon_0\ell/(\ln R/r)$.

Capacitors with Dielectric

A dielectric weakens the electric field by a factor of k (dielectric constant, which depends on the nature of the dielectric material). Therefore, for a capacitor with dielectric,

$C = Q/V = \epsilon_0 kA/d$.

COMBINATIONS OF CAPACITORS

The capacitance value for combinations of capacitors depends upon the connections within the circuit. Sometimes, capacitors are connected **in parallel** (they have the same voltage across them). In such cases, the total capacitance (C_{total}) is given by

$C_{total} = C_1 + C_2 + C_3 \ldots + C_n$.

For capacitors **in series** (same charge on each capacitor), C_{total} can be found:

$1/C_{total} = 1/C_1 + 1/C_2 + 1/C_3 \ldots + 1/C_n$.

CURRENT AND RESISTANCE

Definitions

Current

$$I = dQ/dt,$$

where I is the electric current, Q is the net charge, d is distance, and t is the time. Current is measured in amperes (A); 1 A = 1 C/1 s.

Current Density and Current

$$j = I/A,$$

where j is the current density, I is current, and A is the cross-sectional area. Current density is measured in A/m^2.

Resistance

$$R = V/I,$$

where R is resistance, V is potential difference, and I is current. The unit of resistance is the ohm (Ω).

Resistivity

$$\rho = E/j,$$

where ρ is resistivity, E is the electric field, and j is the current density. Resistivity is measured in ohm-meters (Ω-m).

Power

$$P = VI = I^2R = V^2/R,$$

where P is power, I is current, V is potential difference, and R is resistance.

Circuits

The strength of the energy source (a battery, for instance) within a circuit can be described by the source's **Electromotive Force (emf**, or simply $\boldsymbol{\varepsilon}$):

$$\varepsilon = dw/dq,$$

$$\varepsilon = -(d\phi_m/dt), \text{ and}$$

$$\varepsilon = -L(dI/dt),$$

where ε is the emf, w is the work done on a charge by the source (as the charge completes a loop around a circuit), q is the electric charge, ϕ_m is the magnetic flux, d is distance, t is time, I is current, and L is inductance.

Current in a Simple Circuit

$$I = \varepsilon/R,$$

where I is the current, ε is the emf, and R is the total resistance, including the internal resistance of the battery.

Resistances

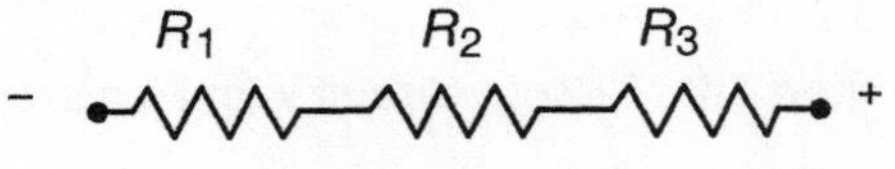

Figure 12

$$R_{total} = (R_1 + R_2 + R_3), \text{ (in series).}$$

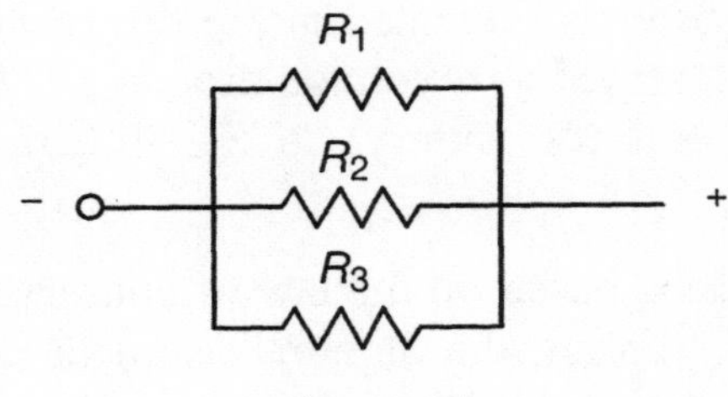

Figure 13

$$1/R_{total} = (1/R_1 + 1/R_2 + 1/R_3), \text{ (in parallel).}$$

Kirchhoff's rules

Two simple rules allow the calculation of currents in complex, multi-loop circuits.

1. The **Loop Rule** is based on the law of conservation of energy. For a closed loop within a circuit, the algebraic sum of all voltages equals zero:

   $$\Delta V_1 + \Delta V_2 + \Delta V_3 \ldots = 0.$$

EXAMPLE

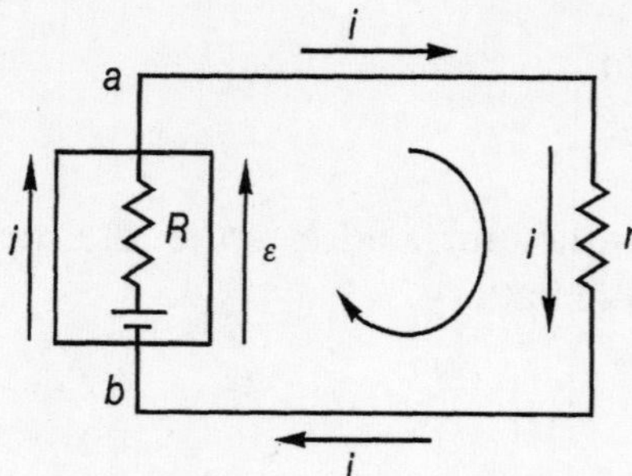

Figure 14—Simple Circuit with Resistor

$V_{ab} = \varepsilon - IR = + Ir.$

Then, $\varepsilon - IR - Ir = 0.$

Note that if a resistor is traversed in the direction of the current, the voltage change is represented as a voltage drop, $- IR$. A change in voltage while traversing the emf (or battery) in the direction of the emf is a voltage rise, $+ \varepsilon$.

2. The **junction rule** is based on the law of conservation of charge. For any junction in a circuit, the algebraic sum of all currents entering and exiting the junction equals zero.

EXAMPLE

$I_1 + I_2 + I_3 = 0.$

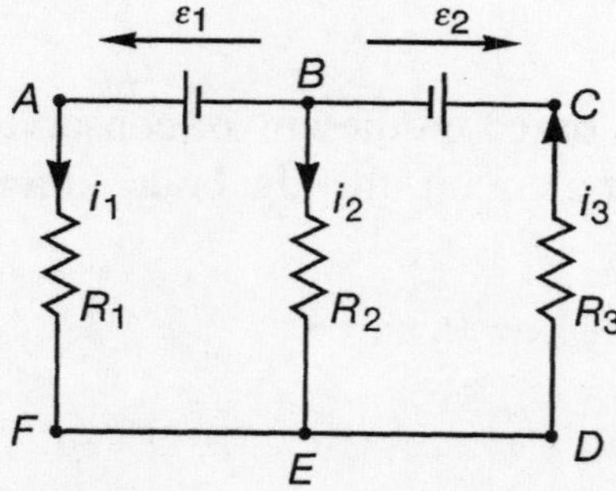

Figure 15—Multiloop Circuit

RC CIRCUITS (RESISTORS AND CAPACITORS)

Sometimes, circuits include both capacitors and resistors. In such circuits, the current may flow when the conditions are changed. Under steady conditions, there is no current through any capacitor; the circuit, in effect, is broken at every point where a capacitor is inserted.

Formulas below describe the behavior of the RC circuits when a source of *e* is connected (capacitor is charging) or disconnected (capacitor is discharging).

Differential Equations

$\varepsilon = R(dq)/(dt) + q/C$ (charging) and

$O = R(dq)/(dt) + q/C$ (discharging).

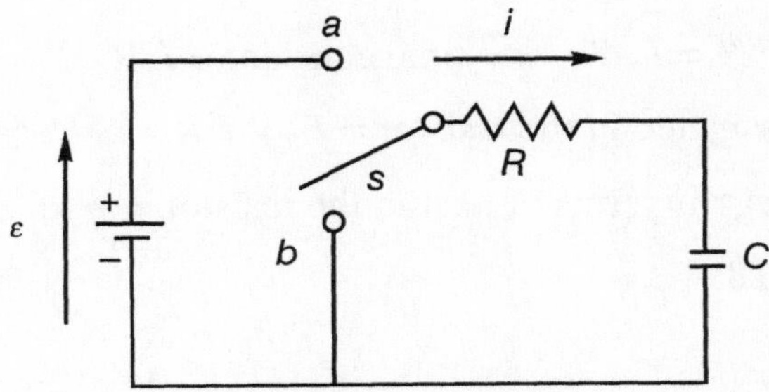

Figure 16—An RC Circuit

Charge on the Capacitor

$q = (C\varepsilon)(1 - e^{\frac{-t}{RC}})$ (charging), and

$q = (C\varepsilon)\ e^{\frac{-t}{RC}}$ (discharging).

Current in the Resistor

$I = (\varepsilon/R)\ e^{\frac{-t}{RC}}$ (charging), and

$I = -\ (\varepsilon/R)\ e^{\frac{-t}{RC}}$ (discharging),

where *e* is equal to 2.71828. . . (exponential constant).

Source Free RC Circuit

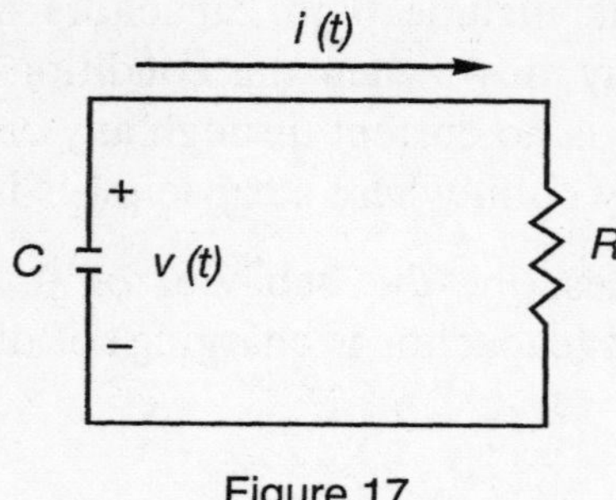

Figure 17

Properties: Initially, assume that $v(0) = V_0$.

1. $v_R + v_L = RI + L(dI/dt) = 0$
2. $I(t) = I_0 e^{-Rt/L} = I_0 e^{-t/\tau}$, τ = time constant = L/R
3. Power dissipated in the resistor = $P_R = I^2R = I_0^2 R e^{-2Rt/L}$
4. Total energy in terms of heat in the resistor = $W_R = (1/2)LI_0^2$

   $e = 2.71828$

MAGNETISM

The Magnetic Field

The force on a charged particle moving in a magnetic field can be calculated using the following equation:

$$\mathbf{F}_\mathrm{B} = q\mathbf{v} \times \mathbf{B},$$

where $\mathbf{F}_\mathrm{B}$ is the force on a particle due to the field, q is the charge on the particle, $\mathbf{v}$ is the velocity of the particle, and $\mathbf{B}$ is the strength of the magnetic field. The unit of magnetic field is the tesla (T).

Similarly, the magnetic force on a current-carrying wire is given by:

$$\mathbf{F}_\mathrm{B} = I\boldsymbol{\ell} \times \mathbf{B},$$

where $\mathbf{F}_\mathrm{B}$ is the force on a particle due to the field, I is the current through the wire, $\boldsymbol{\ell}$ is the length of the wire, and $\mathbf{B}$ is the strength of the magnetic field.

Magnetic Fields and Currents

Biot-Savart Law

This law describes the magnetic field due to a short piece of wire carrying a current:

$$d\mathbf{B} = \frac{\mu_0 I}{4\pi}\frac{\sin\theta d\ell}{r^2},$$

where **B** is the magnetic field, μ_0 is the permeability constant, I is the current through a wire, ℓ is the length of the wire, r is the distance from the wire to a point in the magnetic field, and θ is the angle between r and the direction of the current.

Note: $\mu_0 = 4p \times 10^{-7}$ (T · m)/A.

Integral form:

$$\mathbf{B} = \frac{\mu_0 I}{4\pi}\oint_c \frac{d\ell' \times \mathbf{a}_R}{r^2},$$

where primed terms refer to points along the source of the magnetic field (usually, a current carrying a wire).

Ampere's Law

The line integral of the tangential component of **B** along a closed path is equal to the total current enclosed by that path multiplied by the magnetic constant (μ_0):

$$\oint \mathbf{B} \cdot d\ell = \mu_0 I_{total}.$$

Many magnetic fields, due to highly symmetrical current distributions, can be calculated using either the Biot-Savart law or Ampere's law. For instance, the magnetic field due to a long straight wire carrying current I, at a distance r from the wire, is given by:

$$B = \mu_0 I/2\pi r.$$

ELECTROMAGNETIC INDUCTION

As demonstrated, electric currents can create magnetic fields—or, in more general terms, electric fields can create magnetic fields. Specifically, if the magnetic flux through a conducting loop changes, the emf (ε) is induced in that loop. If the loop is also closed, electric current is generated. The magnitude of the induced emf is given by **Faraday's law**:

$$\varepsilon = \oint \mathbf{E} \cdot d\ell = -d\phi_m/dt.$$

The negative sign is necessary here according to Lenz's law, which indicates that the induced emf is always acting against the changing magnetic fields that produce that emf.

Note that the unit of magnetic flux (ϕ_m) is weber (Wb). 1 Wb = 1 T-m^2.

Inductance (*L*)

Inductance is defined as the coefficient of proportionality between the flux through a loop of current and the magnitude of the current:

$L = \phi/I$, or

$\phi = LI.$

Inductance depends on the geometry of the loop and the possible presence of special materials that may change the flux. Inductance does not depend on the current. The unit of inductance is the henry (H), which is equivalent to Wb/A.

EXAMPLES

1. Inductance per meter length of a coaxial cable of inner radius a and outer radius b:

$$L = \frac{\mu_0}{2\pi} \ln \frac{b}{a} \text{ H/m.}$$

2. Inductance of a long solenoid:

$L = \mu_0 n^2 A,$

where n is the number of turns per unit length and A is the cross-sectional area of the solenoid.

3. Energy stored in a solenoid (L carrying current I):

$U_L = (1/2)LI^2.$

4. Self-induction is the situation in which the induced emf affects the current in the very coil that generates the emf, due to the current change (dI/dt). For the self-induced emf,

$\varepsilon = -L dI/dt.$

SIMPLE RL CIRCUITS

Source Free RL Circuit

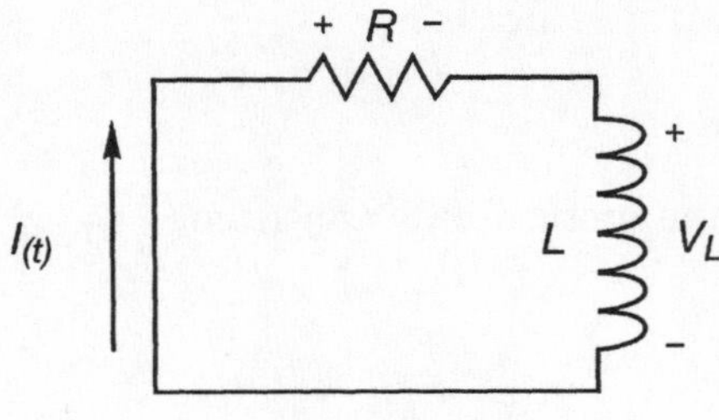

Figure 18

Properties **(Assume, initially, $I(0) = I_0$):**

1. $v_R + v_L = RI + L(dI/dt) = 0$
2. $I(t) = I_0 e^{-Rt/L} = I_0 e^{-t/\tau}$, $\quad \tau$ = time constant = L/R
3. Power dissipated in the resistor = $P_R = I^2R = I_0^2 Re^{-2Rt/L}$
4. Total energy in terms of heat in the resistor = $W_R = (1/2)LI_0^2$

OSCILLATIONS IN ELECTRIC LC CIRCUITS

These oscillations are analogous, and described mathematically similar, to mechanical harmonic motion in its various forms.

When a circuit that only includes a solenoid (L) and a charged capacitor (C), initially having a charge (Q), is closed, the oscillation process begins. Its parameters can be calculated using the energy considerations (the total energy (U) in the circuit is constant):

$$U = (1/2)LI^2 + (1/2)(q^2/2C).$$

Since $dU/dt = 0$ (U is a constant due to the conservation of energy), calculations give:

$L(d^2q/dt^2) = -\, q/C$. This is the basic differential equation describing the electromagnetic oscillations. Its solution is

$$q(t) = Q\cos(\omega t),$$

where $\omega = 1/\sqrt{LC}$.

Correspondingly, the current is given by

$$I(t) = dq/dt = -\,\omega Q\sin(\omega t).$$

MAXWELL'S EQUATIONS

Listed below are Maxwell's "famous four" equations, the most fundamental laws describing electromagnetic phenomena.

1. Gauss's law for electric fields

$$\oint \mathbf{E} \cdot d\mathbf{A} = Q/\epsilon_0$$

2. Gauss's law for magnetic fields (postulates the absence of "magnetic charges")

$$\oint \mathbf{B} \cdot d\mathbf{A} = 0$$

3. Faraday's law of induction

$$\oint \mathbf{E} \cdot d\ell = -\frac{d\phi_B}{dt}$$

4. Ampere-Maxwell law (including the "displacement current" introduced by Maxwell to account for a changing electric field)

$$\oint Bds = \mu_0\epsilon_0\frac{d\phi_E}{dt} + \mu_0 I$$

AP PHYSICS B

Test 1

AP PHYSICS B
Test I

Section I

TIME: 90 Minutes
70 Questions

DIRECTIONS: Each of the questions or incomplete statements below is followed by five answer choices or completions. Select the one that is best in each case.

Questions 1–3

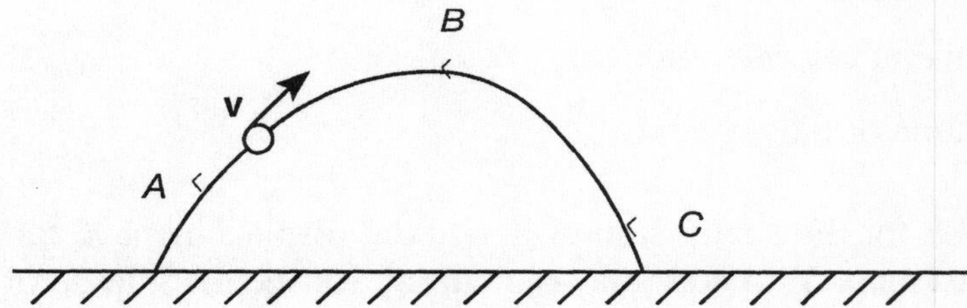

A ball is thrown into the air as shown above and follows a parabolic path. Air friction is negligible. *B* is highest point. Point *A* is higher above the ground than point *C*.

1. At which point(s) is/are the ball's speed highest?

   (A) *A*

   (B) *B*

   (C) *C*

   (D) Cannot be determined with given information

   (E) *A*, *B*, and *C*, as the ball speed is constant

2. At which point(s) will the vertical component of velocity be zero?

   (A) *A*

   (B) *B*

   (C) *C*

   (D) None of the three points

   (E) All of the three points

3. The horizontal component of velocity at point *B* is

   (A) equal to the horizontal component of velocity at point *A*.

   (B) zero.

   (C) equal to the vertical component of velocity at point *C*.

   (D) equal to the initial velocity.

   (E) equal to the vertical component of velocity at point *B*.

4. The change in velocity divided by the corresponding change in time represents

   (A) net displacement.

   (B) average velocity.

   (C) instantaneous velocity.

   (D) average acceleration.

   (E) none of the above.

5. In order for the vector sum of horizontal displacement **X** and vertical displacement **Y** to add to a resultant of 10, the magnitude of **X** must be

   (A) 8.

   (B) 3.

   (C) 6.

   (D) 12.

   (E) 2.

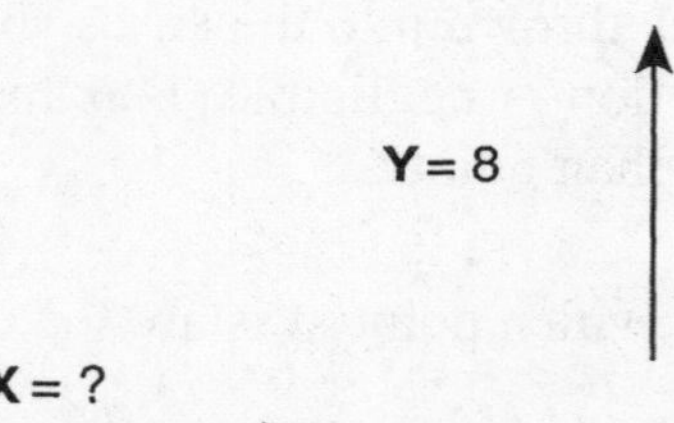

6. Three 5-N forces are applied at fixed point *P* as shown. The magnitude of the resultant of combining these three forces is

   (A) $15\sqrt{2}$ N.

   (B) 5 N.

   (C) $(5\sqrt{2} - 5)$ N.

   (D) $(5\sqrt{2} + 5)$ N.

   (E) 0 N.

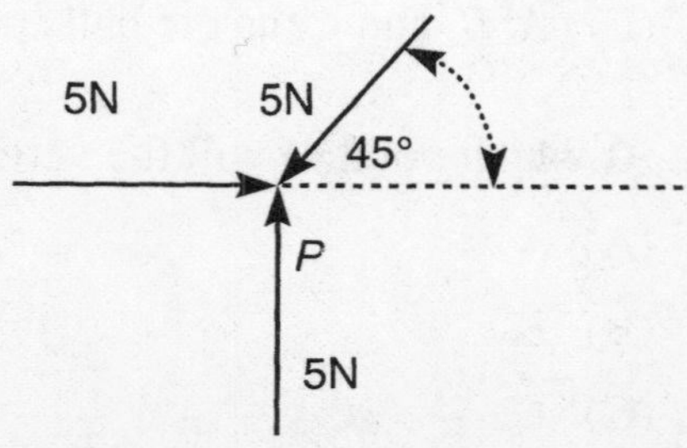

7. A weight of mass m hangs from a string of length l and is whirled in a circle contained in the vertical plane. The angular velocity ω is constant. The maximum tension on the string is

(A) $m(g + l\omega^2)$.

(B) mg.

(C) $m(g - l\omega^2)$.

(D) $ml\omega^2$.

(E) zero.

8. Two blocks are in contact and accelerated by a horizontal force **F** = 8 N over a frictionless surface as shown. The contact forces between the blocks are

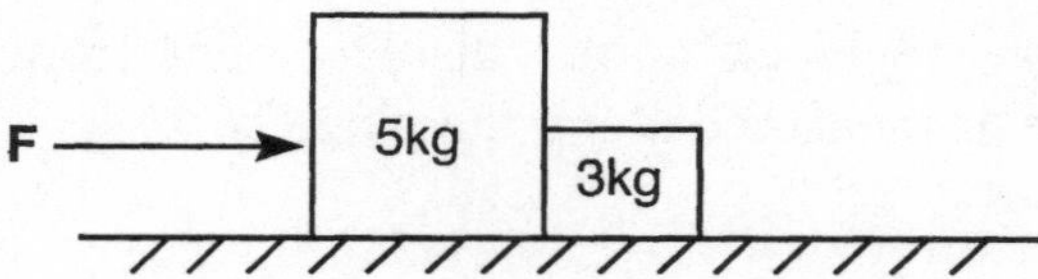

(A) 3 N, both to the left.

(B) 0 N.

(C) 2 N, both to the right.

(D) 5 N, equal and oppositely directed.

(E) 3 N, equal and oppositely directed.

9. An object of mass 10 kg is traveling in a straight line and is accelerated from 10 m/s to 25 m/s in one second. The average acceleration during this interval of time is

(A) 25 m/s^2.

(B) 15 m/s^2.

(C) 150 m/s^2.

(D) 30 m/s^2.

(E) 9.8 m/s^2.

10. A satellite is orbiting a planet in a circular path at radial distance r. If the radial distance is increased to $3r$, the new orbital speed required for circular orbit is

(A) the same as at distance r.

(B) 3 times that at distance r.

(C) 9 times that at distance r.

(D) 1/3 that at distance r.

(E) $\frac{1}{\sqrt{3}}$ that at distance r.

11. A mass-spring system with negligible friction is vibrating at a frequency of 5 Hz. If the mass is doubled, the new vibration frequency is

(A) 20 Hz.

(B) 25 Hz.

(C) 10 Hz.

(D) $(5/\sqrt{2})$ Hz.

(E) $5\sqrt{2}$ Hz.

12. A block of mass m is attached to a spring with spring constant k (as shown) atop an inclined plane. l is the length of the unstretched spring. There is negligible friction between the block and plane. The expression for the block's total displacement from the top of the inclined plane as measured along the plane is

(A) $l + mg/k$.

(B) $mg \cos \theta$.

(C) $l + (mg/k) \sin \theta$.

(D) $l + (mg/k) \cos \theta$.

(E) $l - mg/k$.

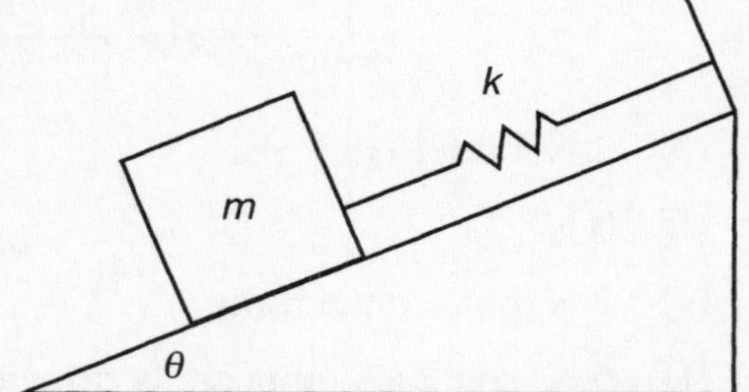

Questions 13-15 relate to the following diagram, which shows a 5-kg block given an initial velocity of 2 m/s at the base of a frictionless plane.

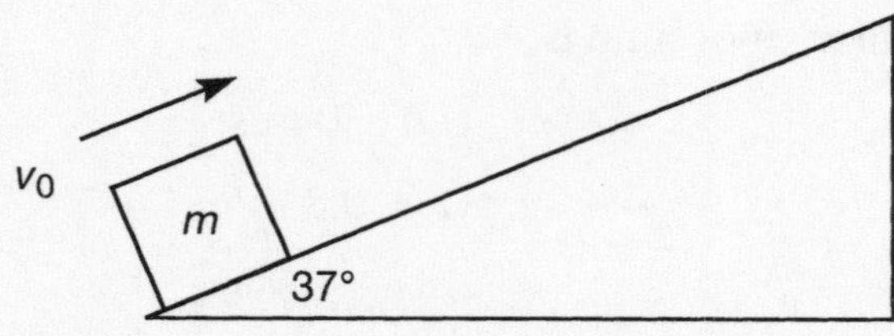

13. The maximum vertical displacement of the block is most nearly

(A) 0.1 m.

(B) 0.2 m.

(C) 0.4 m.

(D) 0.5 m.

(E) 0.6 m.

14. If the mass of the block were halved, the vertical displacement of the block would be

    (A) unchanged.

    (B) doubled.

    (C) halved.

    (D) four times as much as before.

    (E) one-fourth as much as before.

15. If the kinetic energy of the 5-kg block were completely converted to work, it would total

    (A) 4 J.

    (B) 1 J.

    (C) 5 J.

    (D) 20 J.

    (E) 10 J.

16. A stationary ball of mass 0.1 kg is struck, causing it to acquire a speed of 200 m/s. If the applied force is 10,000 N, the contact time for the strike is most nearly

    (A) 2 ms.

    (B) 10 ms.

    (C) 100 ms.

    (D) 0.2 ms.

    (E) 0.02 ms.

17. A sphere with mass m moving with velocity v_1 strikes head-on another sphere of mass $3m$ moving at velocity v_2 in the opposite direction. Both are stopped dead. (Assume the collision is perfectly elastic.) The ratio of v_2 to v_1 is

    (A) 3.

    (B) 1/3.

    (C) 1/9.

    (D) 9.

    (E) 3.

18. The equation $\mathbf{F}\Delta t = \Delta \mathbf{p}$ relates impulse to momentum change. ($\mathbf{F}$ is force, t is time and $\mathbf{p}$ is momentum.) Which of the following statements apply?

I – The equation relates two vector quantities.

II – Impulse has the same direction as change in momentum, but a different magnitude.

III – Decreasing $\mathbf{F}$, with Δt held constant, decreases $\Delta \mathbf{p}$.

(A) I and II
(B) II only
(C) I only
(D) II and III
(E) I and III

19. A train is rounding a circular curve traveling at a speed of 40 m/s. The radius of the curve is 400 m. The train's angular velocity is most nearly

(A) 0.2 rad/s.
(B) 5.0 rad/s.
(C) 1600 rad/s.
(D) 0.1 rad/s.
(E) 10 rad/s.

20. Given the torque equation $\tau = Fr\sin\theta$ (where τ is the torque, F is applied force, r is distance, and θ is the angle between the applied force vector and the distance vector from the axis of rotation to the point of application of F), which of the following statements is correct?

I – Torque is a scalar quantity.

II – Torque magnitude depends on the direction of F relative to r.

III – When F and r are parallel, torque magnitude is maximum.

(A) I and II
(B) II and III
(C) I and III
(D) II only
(E) III only

21. A wheel is rotating at a constant speed of 6 rev/sec. Its moment of inertia about the axis of rotation is 10 kgm^2. The wheel's kinetic energy is nearest to

(A) 7100 J.
(B) 380 J.
(C) 190 J.
(D) 5000 J.
(E) 2500 J.

Questions 22-23 refer to a particle that undergoes simple harmonic motion according to the equation $X = 10 \sin (8t)$.

22. A maximum value of X occurs when t is most nearly

(A) $\pi/8$.
(B) $\pi/4$.
(C) $\pi/16$.
(D) $3\pi/4$.
(E) $\pi/6$.

23. The magnitude of both the minimum and maximum value for X is

(A) zero.
(B) 5.
(C) infinite.
(D) 20.
(E) 10.

24. A pendulum has length l and mass m. At a distance far removed from the surface of Earth, it has a period $T/6$. On the surface of Earth, the pendulum period is T. The acceleration of gravity at the far distance is

(A) $g/\sqrt{6}$.
(B) $6g$.
(C) $g/6$.
(D) $g/36$.
(E) $36g$.

25. Identify which is/are NOT a factor(s) when calculating the gravitational attraction between two spheres of differing mass that are separated by a distance that is large in comparison to their radii.

    I – Mass of each sphere

    II – Separation distance

    III – Radius of each sphere

    (A) III only
    (B) III and I
    (C) II and I
    (D) I only
    (E) II only

26. A plastic rod has a net negative charge. A possible explanation for its charged condition is that

    (A) electrons were transferred from the rod.
    (B) positive charges are flowing on the rod surface.
    (C) there is spontaneous polarization of the rod.
    (D) positive charges were transferred to the rod.
    (E) electrons were transferred to the rod.

27. An E-field region in a vacuum is shown. An electron placed and released at point P will

    (A) move to the left and accelerate.
    (B) move to the right and accelerate.
    (C) move to the right at a constant speed.
    (D) move to the left at a constant speed.
    (E) not move at all.

• P E

28. Two stationary point charges are both positively charged and separated by distance r. If they are moved closer together and then held in place, the resulting force acting on either charge is

    (A) increased and repulsive.
    (B) increased and attractive.
    (C) decreased and attractive.

(D) decreased and repulsive.

(E) unchanged and attractive.

29. A positive charge is brought near a large metal plate. Which of the following statements is/are true?

I – The surface of the plate becomes negatively charged.

II – The surface of the plate becomes positively charged.

III – Electric field lines originate at the positive charge and terminate on the plate.

(A) I only

(B) II only

(C) I and III

(D) II and III

(E) III only

30. A capacitor has a charge of 1 nC, when 10 V is applied. The capacitance is

(A) 100 pF.

(B) 10 μF.

(C) 1 μF.

(D) 1 pF.

(E) 10 pF.

31. A parallel plate capacitor in air has a capacitance of 1 μF. If the area of both plates is tripled and the distance between the plates is halved, then the new value for capacitance is

(A) 6 μF.

(B) 3 μF.

(C) 1/6 μF.

(D) 1/3 μF.

(E) 18 μF.

32. The equivalent resistor R_{eq} for the resistive network shown is nearest

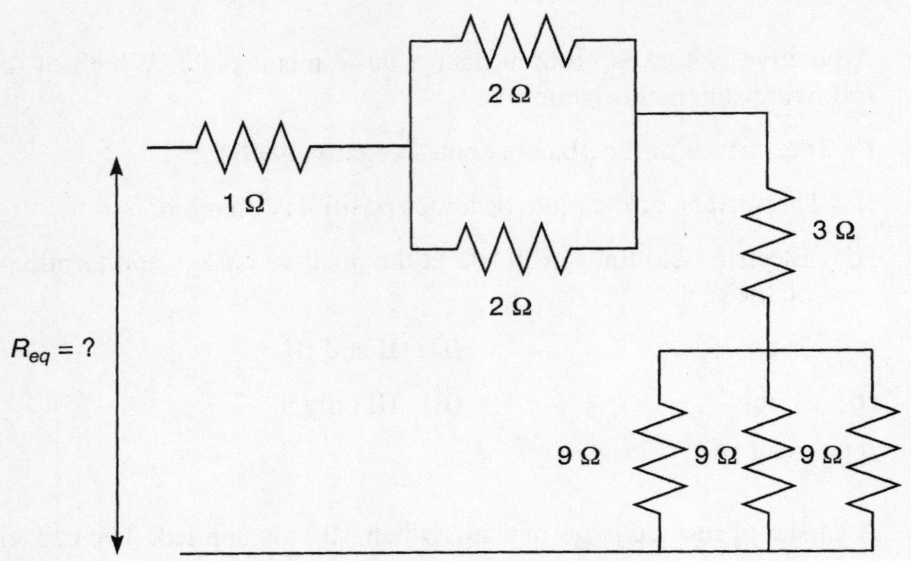

(A) 5 Ω.
(B) 8 Ω.
(C) 6 Ω.
(D) 3 Ω.
(E) 1 Ω.

33. A 5000-Ω resistor has 1 mA of current flowing through it. The power dissipated by the resistor is

(A) 5 mW.
(B) 5 W.
(C) 50 mW.
(D) 0.5 W.
(E) 0.2 W.

34. The ammeter A shown in the circuit would most nearly read

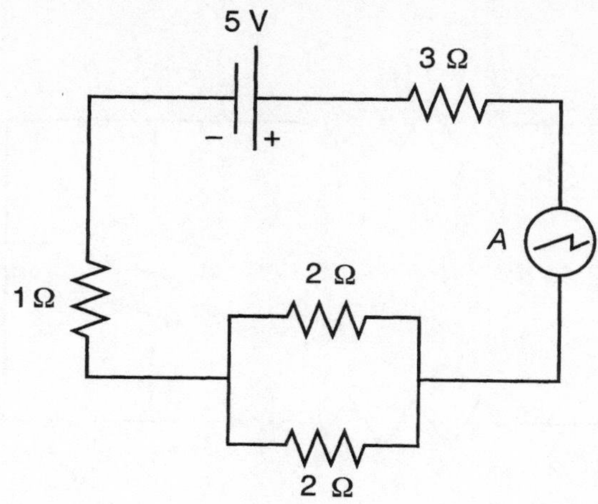

(A) 5/8 A.

(B) 1/2 A.

(C) 7/8 A.

(D) 1 A.

(E) 2 A.

35. A single capacitor C equivalent to the capacitor network shown is most nearly

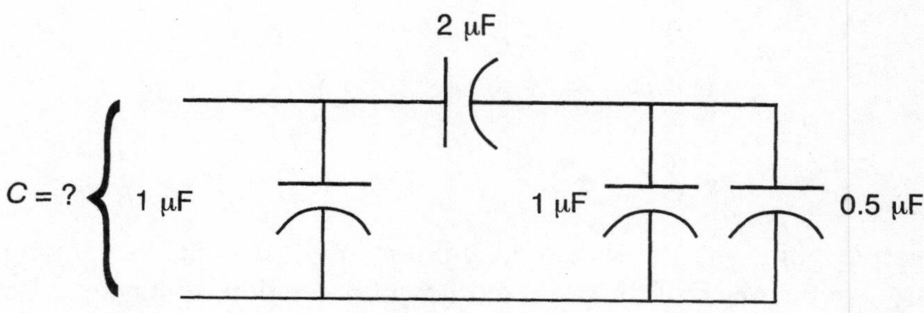

(A) 0.6 μF.

(B) 0.7 μF.

(C) 1.0 μF.

(D) 1.9 μF.

(E) 1.5 μF.

36. After a long time, the potential difference across the capacitor for the circuit shown is

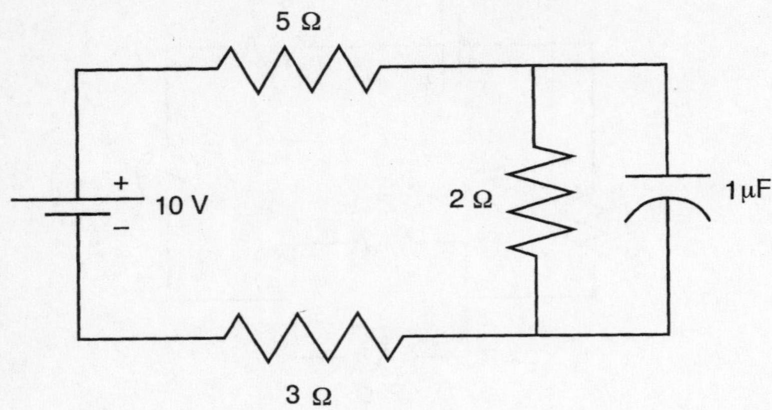

(A) 1 V.

(B) 2 V.

(C) 10 V.

(D) 0 V.

(E) 5 V.

Questions 37-38

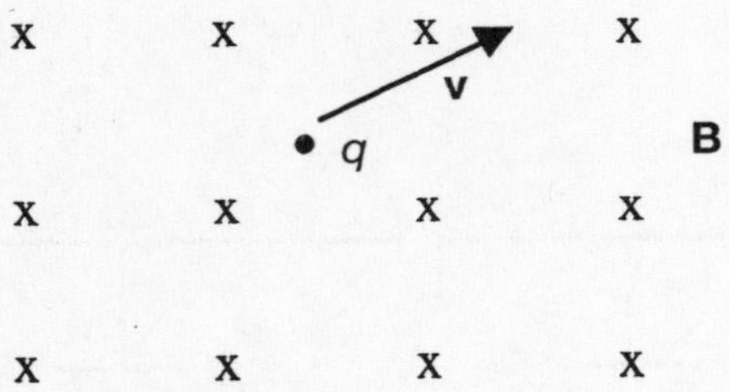

A negative point-charge with a magnitude of $q = 4$ nC is moving at velocity v in the plane of the paper as shown in a region of magnetic field.

37. The magnitude of the force acting on q is

(A) different than for a negative charge of the same magnitude moving at the same speed in the opposite direction.

(B) different than for a positive charge of the same magnitude moving at the same speed in the same direction.

(C) zero.

(D) the same as a negative charge of the same magnitude moving at velocity v parallel to the magnetic field.

(E) the same as for a positive charge of the same magnitude moving at velocity v in the opposite direction.

38. The direction of the force acting on q is

(A) perpendicular to and out of the plane of the paper.

(B) perpendicular to and into the plane of the paper.

(C) perpendicular to the plane formed by vectors **v** and **B**.

(D) parallel to **v**.

(E) parallel to **B**.

39. A compass is placed near a long current-carrying wire. The north end of the compass needle is observed to rotate 180° once every 10 seconds. The cause of this behavior is most likely

(A) a varying current in the wire with no change in polarity.

(B) variations in Earth's magnetic field.

(C) heating of the wire by the current.

(D) a varying current in the wire with alternating polarity.

(E) electric field variations due to current flowing in the wire.

Questions 40-42 relate to the magnetic field through a one-turn loop of wire of radius $r = 1$ cm, as shown in the figure.

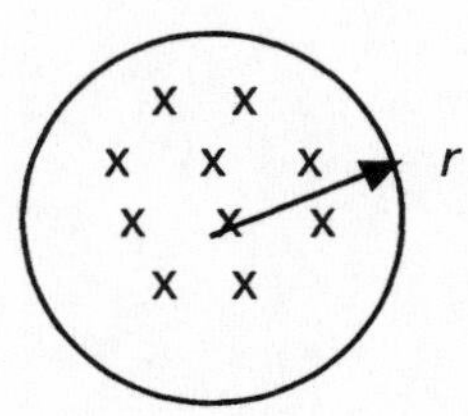

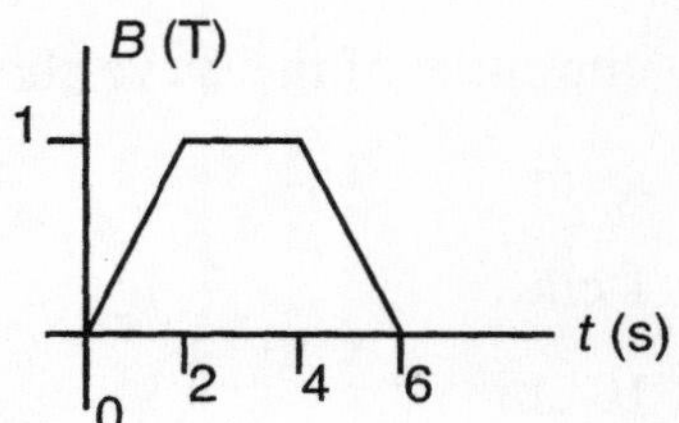

40. The magnitude of the induced emf (ε) during the interval from 0 to 2 seconds is nearest

(A) 0.8×10^{-4} V.

(B) 3.2×10^{-4} V.

(C) 0 V.

(D) 1.6 V.

(E) 1.6×10^{-4} V.

41. The magnitude of the induced ε in the interval from 2 to 4 seconds is nearest

(A) 1.6×10^{-4} V.
(B) 3.2×10^{-4} V.
(C) 0 V.
(D) 1.6 V.
(E) 0.8×10^{-4} V.

42. The polarity of the conventional induced current in the interval from 4 to 6 sec is

(A) clockwise.
(B) parallel to *B*.
(C) not defined.
(D) antiparallel to *B*.
(E) counterclockwise.

Questions 43-45

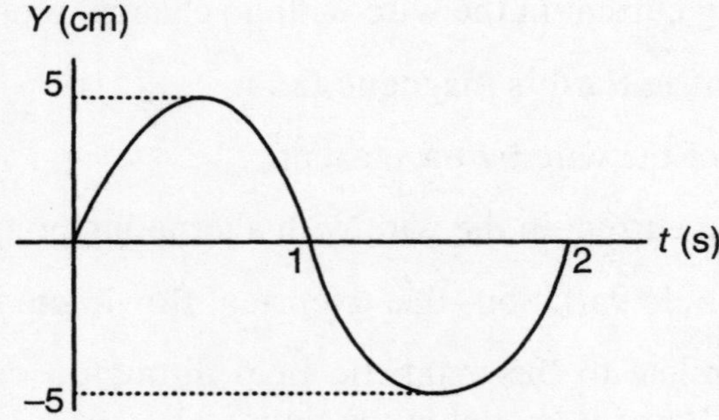

43. The amplitude of the wave shown is

(A) 2 cm.
(B) 1 cm.
(C) 10 cm.
(D) 5 cm.
(E) 0.5 cm.

44. The period of the wave is

(A) 2 s.
(B) 1 s.
(C) 10 s.
(D) 5 s.
(E) 20 s.

45. The wave has a wavelength of 10 m. Its speed is equal to

(A) 1 m/s.
(B) 0.1 m/s.
(C) 0.025 m/s.
(D) 2.5 m/s.
(E) 5.0 m/s.

46. A lightning flash is observed, and 5 seconds later a thunderclap is heard. (The speed of sound is about 330 m/s.) The distance from observer to flash location is nearest

(A) 3300 m.
(B) 825 m.
(C) 1650 m.
(D) 1000 m.
(E) 500 m.

47. The Doppler effect causes the frequency of sound heard by an observer to

(A) increase with speed for a moving source separating from the observer.

(B) remain constant with speed for a moving source separating from the observer.

(C) remain constant with speed for a moving source nearing the observer.

(D) increase with speed for a moving source nearing the observer.

(E) decrease with speed for a moving source nearing the observer.

48. A standing wave is established on a string fixed at both ends as shown. The wavelength is

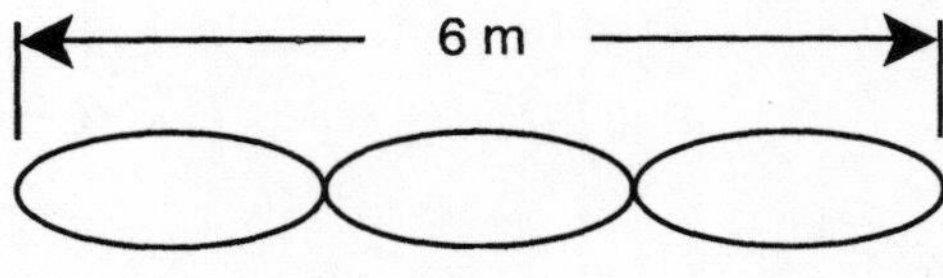

(A) 4 m.
(B) 2 m.
(C) 1 m.
(D) 6 m.
(E) 3 m.

49. Shown is a plane wave in medium 1 moving at speed v approaching a slit (the width of which is small compared to the wavelength). Upon passing through the slit into medium 2, the wave is

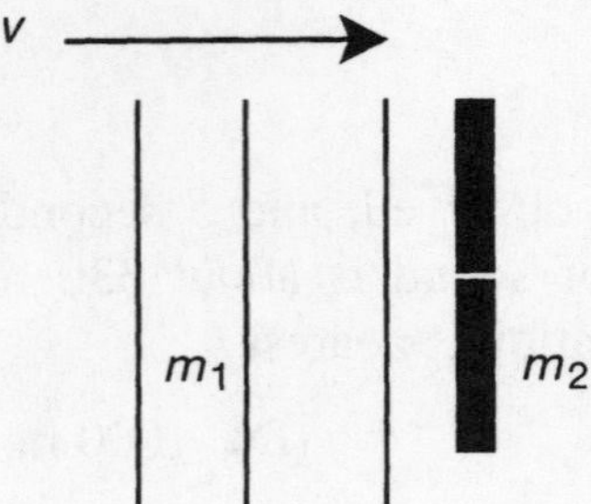

(A) diffracted with no change in wave speed.

(B) diffracted with a change in wave frequency.

(C) diffracted with a change in wave speed.

(D) refracted with a change in wave frequency.

(E) refracted with no change in wave speed.

50. Two pulses with unequal amplitudes and equal widths are traveling on a string in opposite directions as shown. The net amplitude at the point on the string where the pulses coincide is

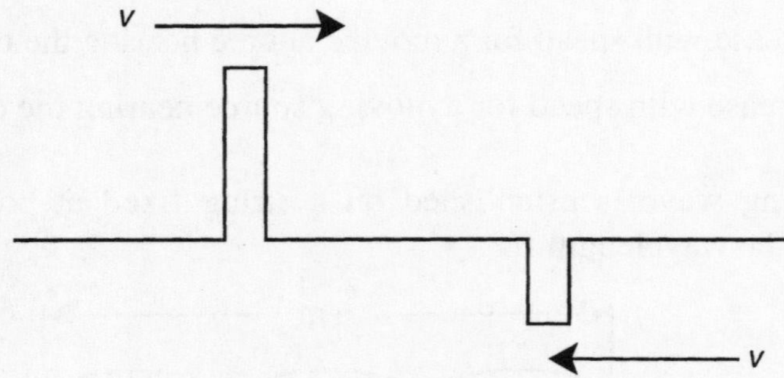

(A) Zero.

(B) the product of the amplitude magnitudes.

(C) the sum of the amplitude magnitudes.

(D) the difference of the amplitude magnitudes.

(E) the sum of the pulse widths.

51. A certain wavelength of light in air is about 600 nm. The corresponding frequency is nearest

(A) 5.0×10^{14} Hz.

(B) 5.0×10^{2} Hz.

(C) 2.0×10^{14} Hz.

(D) 2.0×10^{2} Hz.

(E) 1.0×10^{14} Hz.

Questions 52-53

A light ray is refracted as shown, where θ_1 and θ_2 are diffraction angles in mediums 1 and 2, respectively, where n_1 is the index of refraction in medium 1 and n_2 the index of refraction in medium 2.

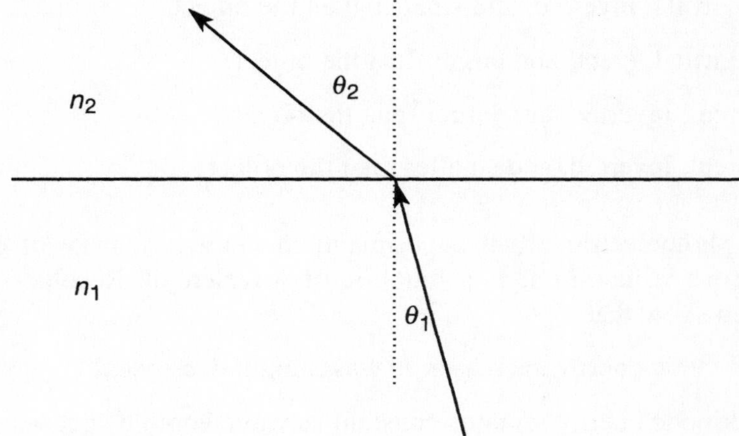

52. If θ_2 is 90°, then sin θ_1 is

(A) n_1/n_2.

(B) n_2/n_1.

(C) $n_1 n_2$.

(D) the difference of n_2 and n_1.

(E) $(n_2/n_1)^2$.

53. If θ_1 is increased beyond the value for which θ_2 is 90 degrees, the incident ray will then be

(A) totally reflected and contained within medium 1.

(B) totally reflected and contained within medium 2.

(C) totally refracted.

(D) totally absorbed by medium 2.

(E) totally absorbed by medium 1.

54. A concave spherical mirror images an object as shown. The object is an upright arrow between the radius of curvature R and the focal length F. The image of the object is

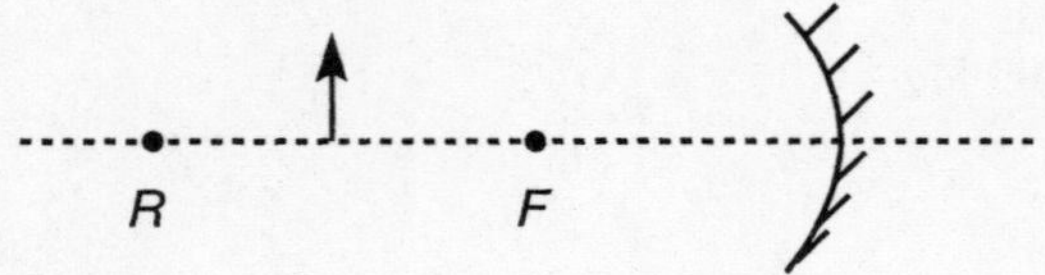

(A) real, erect, and larger than the object.

(B) virtual, inverted, and smaller than the object.

(C) virtual, erect, and larger than the object.

(D) real, inverted, and larger than the object.

(E) real, inverted, and smaller than the object.

55. In a photoelectric effect experiment, the kinetic energy of emitted electrons is measured as a function of wavelength. Results obtained should show that

(A) kinetic energy decreases as wavelength decreases.

(B) kinetic energy remains constant as wavelength decreases.

(C) kinetic energy increases as wavelength decreases.

(D) kinetic energy is zero below the cutoff wavelength.

(E) kinetic energy is greater than zero at the cutoff wavelength.

56. Photon energy for a wavelength of 600 nm is most nearly

(A) 3.1×10^{-19} J.

(B) 6.2×10^{-19} J.

(C) 1.5×10^{-19} J.

(D) 1.0×10^{-19} J.

(E) 3.3×10^{-19} J.

57. In the Bohr model of the atom, emission spectra can be explained as being due to

(A) electron emission resulting from photons returning to lower energy states.

(B) electron emission resulting from photons moving up to higher energy states.

(C) photon emission resulting from nuclear excitation.

(D) photon emission resulting from electrons returning to lower energy states.

(E) photon emission resulting from electrons moving up to higher energy states.

58. According to de Broglie, both photons and mass particles can

(A) sometimes be represented as waves.

(B) never be represented as waves.

(C) undergo fission.

(D) undergo fusion.

(E) be transmuted into nucleons.

59. The momentum of an X-ray photon with wavelength 10 nm is most nearly

(A) 1.0×10^{-26} kg m/s.

(B) 1.5×10^{-26} kg m/s.

(C) 2.2×10^{-26} kg m/s.

(D) 3.0×10^{-26} kg m/s.

(E) 6.6×10^{-26} kg m/s.

60. A fusion reaction could involve

I – a release of energy in the form of gamma-ray photons.

II – combining reactant nuclei to form new product nuclei.

III – triggering a chain reaction that splits nuclei.

(A) II only

(B) I and II

(C) I only

(D) III only

(E) I and III

61. If a proton mass and an electron mass were each converted into energy in accordance with $E = mc^2$, the ratio of proton energy to electron energy would be most nearly

(A) 1.
(B) 1/100.
(C) 100.
(D) 1/1000.
(E) 1000.

62. Which factor(s) do *not* contribute to determining pressure at a given depth in a cylindrical tank filled with a fluid?

I – Fluid density

II – Acceleration of gravity

III – Tank horizontal cross-sectional area A

(A) II and III
(B) II only
(C) I and II
(D) III only
(E) I and III

63. A cylinder with radius r and length L is floating upright in a fluid. L is 10 times longer than r and the density of the cylinder is 9/10 the density of the fluid. The length of the cylinder protruding above the fluid surface is

(A) r.
(B) $2r$.
(C) $3r$.
(D) $r/3$.
(E) $r/2$.

64. An incompressible fluid is flowing through a pipe with varying cross-sectional area as shown. If the flow rate in section 2 is 24 gallons/min, then the flow rate in section 1 is

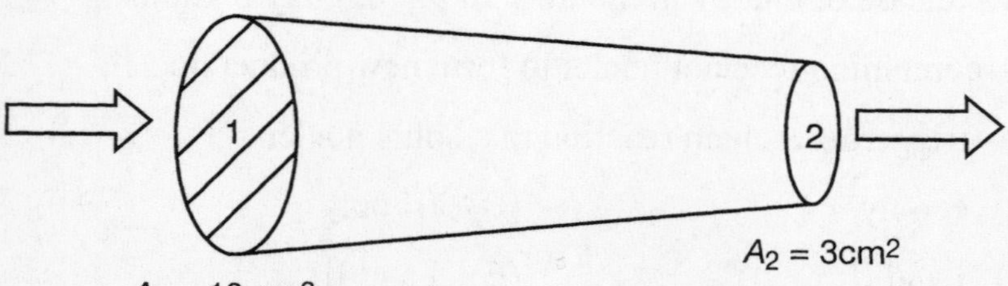

(A) 124 gal/min.
(D) 0.66 gal/min.

(B) 24 gal/min.

(E) 4 gal/min.

(C) 144 gal/min.

65. A bullet moving at speed v with mass m is fired at a concrete wall. If the collision is perfectly inelastic, find the temperature of the bullet material immediately after impact. (Assume that the temperature of the bullet is T before impact and the specific heat of the bullet material is c.)

(A) $(v^2/c) + T$

(D) $(v^2/2c) + T$

(B) $(2c/v^2) + T$

(E) T

(C) $v^2/2c$

66. A steel ring with a linear expansion coefficient of $13 \times 10^{-6}/°C$ has a radius of 5 cm. After the ring is heated from 23° C to 400° C, its radius is nearest to

(A) 5.035 cm.

(D) 5.045 cm.

(B) 5.025 cm.

(E) 4.975 cm.

(C) 5.015 cm.

67. According to the kinetic theory of gases, which of the three statements is/are true?

I – Gas molecule collisions with container walls are inelastic.

II – All molecules in a given sample volume have the same speed.

III – Momentum is conserved in all collisions.

(A) I and III

(D) III only

(B) II and III

(E) II only

(C) I and II

68. According to the first law of thermodynamics, which of these three statements is/are true?

I – Energy is conserved.

II – Work done on or by a system is not involved.

III – Internal energy is a function of absolute temperature only.

(A) II and III
(B) III only
(C) I and III
(D) I and II
(E) I only

69. An ideal gas is at temperature T, pressure p, and volume V. If the temperature is tripled, a possible resulting combination of pressure and volume is

(A) $\sqrt{3}\,p$, $\sqrt{3}\,V$.
(B) $3p$, $3V$.
(C) $p/\sqrt{3}$, $V/\sqrt{3}$.
(D) $3p$, V.
(E) $2p$, V.

70. In general, the specific heat of an ideal gas is

(A) greatest for monatomic gases.
(B) greatest for diatomic gases.
(C) independent of internal energy of the gas.
(D) independent of internal temperature of the gas.
(E) the same at constant volume as it is at constant pressure.

AP PHYSICS B
Test I

Section II

TIME: 90 Minutes
6 Free-Response Questions

DIRECTIONS: Carefully read each question and then make sure to answer *each part* of the question. You must show your work. Crossed out work will not be graded. You will lose credit for incorrect work that is not crossed out.

1. A ball is fired into the air and follows a parabolic trajectory, as shown. Air friction is negligible. The initial velocity (v_0) is 14 m/s and the elevation angle (θ) is 60 degrees from the horizontal.

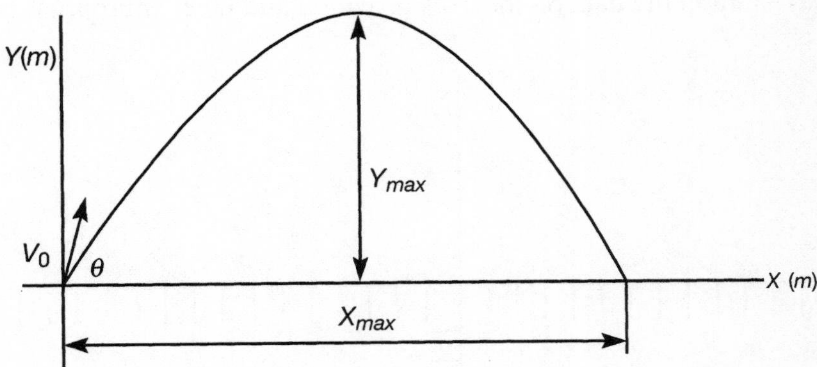

(a) Draw and label a free-body diagram showing all the forces acting on the ball at the highest point of the trajectory. Also, show vectors designating the velocity and acceleration.

(b) Derive an equation for the horizontal component of displacement of the ball in terms of v_0, θ, and t.

(c) Derive an equation for the vertical component of velocity in terms of v_0, θ, and t.

(d) Find the values of X_{max} and Y_{max} in meters.

2. The force acting on a positive test charge ($q = 1.0$ nC) is measured versus distance d from point O along line AB. The results are tabulated as shown. Positive distances are to the right of point O, and negative distances are to the left. The force direction is along the line AB.

F (N × 10^{-9})	d (cm)
36	0
55	25
147	50
560	75
30	– 25
15	– 50
9	– 75

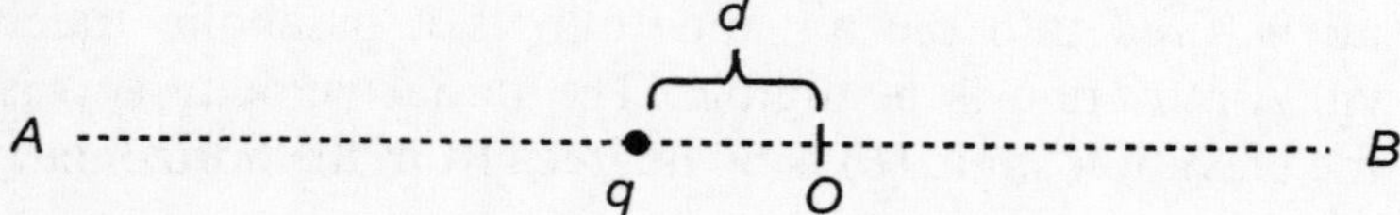

(a) Graph the data on the axes provided and label appropriately.

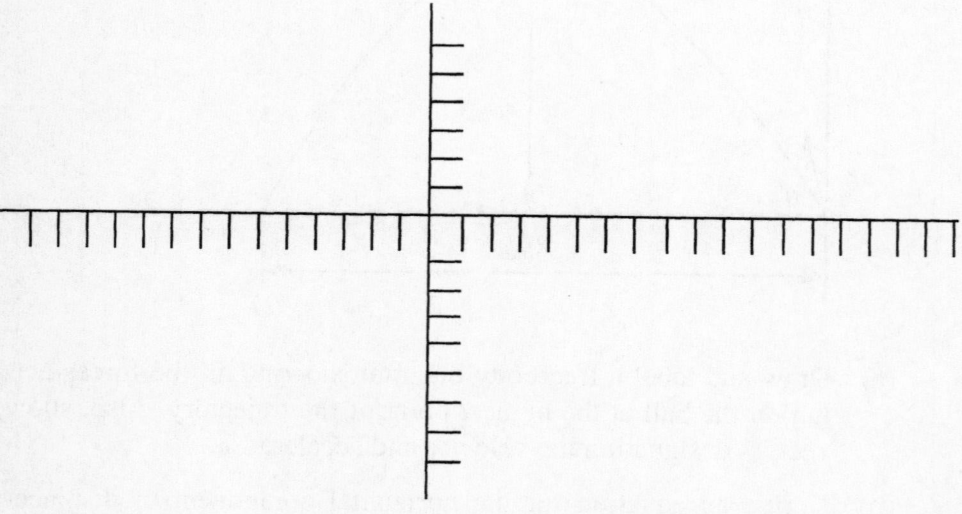

(b) Assume that another point charge on the line to the right of the test charge is the cause of the force on the test charge. If the force acting on the test charge is to the left, what is its polarity?

(c) Using the data in the table, find the approximate location and magnitude of the other charge.

3. An equilateral prism in air (with an index of refraction as given in the accompanying table) is illustrated. A ray of light with wavelength λ = 540 nm enters the prism at side 1 and is refracted. The angle the incident ray makes with the normal N is 42°. A table of refractive index n is shown for various wavelengths.

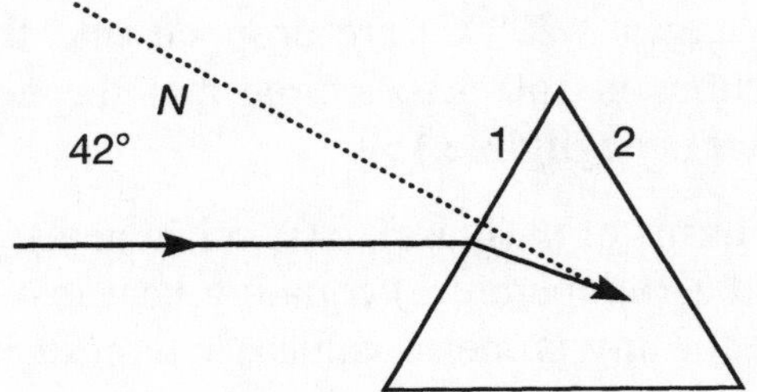

n	λ (nm)
1.7	540
1.8	620
1.9	710
2.0	770

(a) What is the refraction angle with respect to normal N of the ray?

(b) Will the refracted ray internal to the prism be totally internally reflected when encountering side 2 of the prism?

(c) Use the data given in the table to write an equation relating n to λ.

(d) If the prism were immersed in a fluid with n = 1.7, what would the refraction angle be for the incoming ray?

4. A charged particle (q) of unknown mass, charge, and polarity enters a region of a magnetic field, as shown. Its trajectory in the field is that of a semicircular arc.

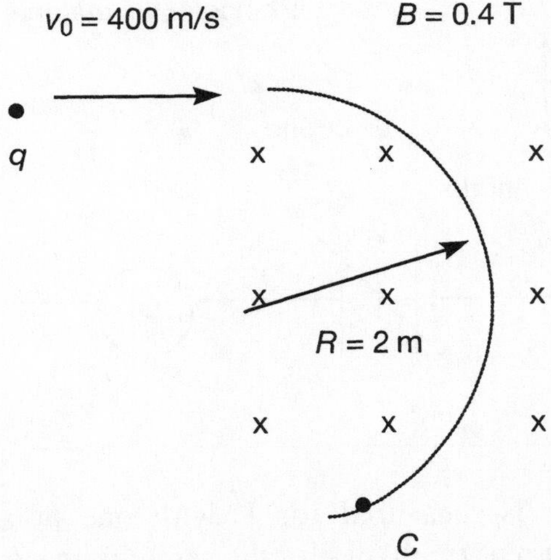

(a) What is the polarity of the charge?

(b) What is the ratio m/q in terms of v, R, and B?

(c) If the magnitude of q is 4.0 nC, what is the value of m?

(d) What is the exit speed of the particle at point C, when it emerges from the region of B?

5. An insulating container is filled with water at 70° C; the water's mass is 500 g. Cubes of ice (at –20° C) are dropped into the container. The mass of the cubes is 150 g. (Assume that the heat loss from the insulated container is negligible.)

(a) Write an equation in terms of m (mass), c (specific heat), L (heat of fusion for ice), and T (temperature) equating heat lost to heat gained. Do not solve for any numeric values, leaving it in algebraic terms.

(b) What is the final temperature of the mixture?

(c) What is the underlying physical principle that allows us to equate heat lost to heat gained?

6. An apparatus for measuring current produced by the photoelectric effect is shown. The battery voltage V can be varied, and the anode (electron collector) and photoelectric material are both sealed within a vacuum enclosure. Light with variable wavelength λ is admitted via a transparent window, as shown. Current is measured with ammeter A.

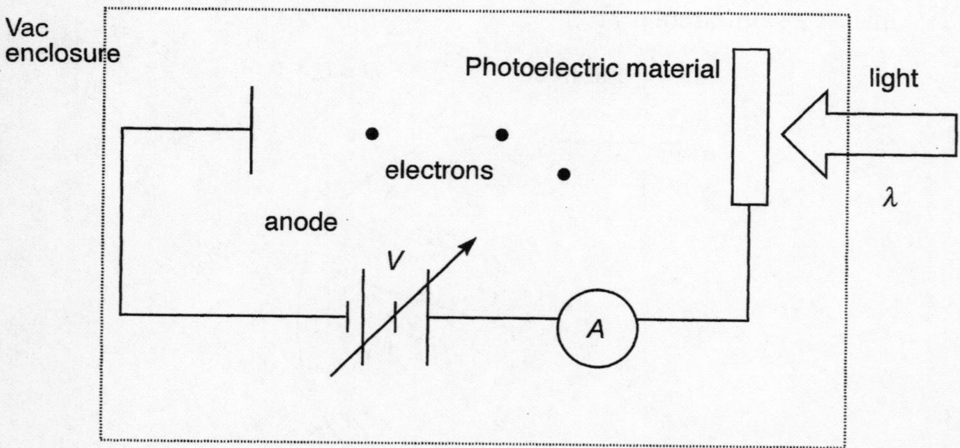

(a) A current is measured for V with one polarity, but a much smaller current (with all else the same) is measured for a reversed polarity. What polarity was the collector with respect to the photoelectric material when the larger current was measured?

(b) The work function for the photoelectric material is 3.0 eV. What is the maximum wavelength of light that will eject electrons from the photoelectric material?

(c) For a photon energy of 4.0 eV, what is the speed of emitted electrons?

(d) What is the magnitude and polarity of V required for the ammeter to read zero when photon energy is 4.0 eV?

AP PHYSICS B
TEST 1
Section I

ANSWER KEY

1. (C)
2. (B)
3. (A)
4. (D)
5. (C)
6. (C)
7. (A)
8. (E)
9. (B)
10. (E)
11. (D)
12. (C)
13. (B)
14. (A)
15. (E)
16. (A)
17. (B)
18. (E)
19. (D)
20. (D)
21. (A)
22. (C)
23. (B)
24. (D)
25. (A)
26. (E)
27. (B)
28. (A)
29. (C)
30. (A)
31. (A)
32. (B)
33. (A)
34. (D)
35. (D)
36. (B)
37. (E)
38. (C)
39. (D)
40. (E)
41. (C)
42. (A)
43. (D)
44. (A)
45. (E)
46. (C)
47. (D)
48. (A)
49. (C)
50. (D)
51. (A)
52. (B)
53. (A)
54. (E)
55. (C)
56. (E)
57. (D)
58. (A)
59. (E)
60. (B)
61. (D)
62. (D)
63. (A)
64. (E)
65. (D)
66. (B)
67. (D)
68. (C)
69. (A)
70. (B)

DETAILED EXPLANATIONS OF ANSWERS

TEST 1
Section I

1. **(C)** The ball's speed is highest when it is closest to the ground. By conservation of energy, the sum of the potential and kinetic energy is constant. Thus, when the ball is near the ground, the potential energy is nearly zero, so the kinetic energy (and therefore speed) is highest.

2. **(B)** The ball's velocity is always tangent to the trajectory, so it is clear that at point B the velocity is in the horizontal direction. Thus, the vertical component of velocity at that point is zero.

3. **(A)** The horizontal component of velocity is $v_0 \cos\theta$ throughout the trajectory; therefore, it is a constant, and the same at points B and A.

4. **(D)** By definition $a_{avg} = \frac{v_f - v_i}{t_f - t_i} = \frac{\Delta v}{\Delta t}$, where v is velocity, t is time, and the subscripts refer to final and initial, respectively.

5. **(C)** Since vectors add in head-to-tail fashion, we can construct the following vector diagram

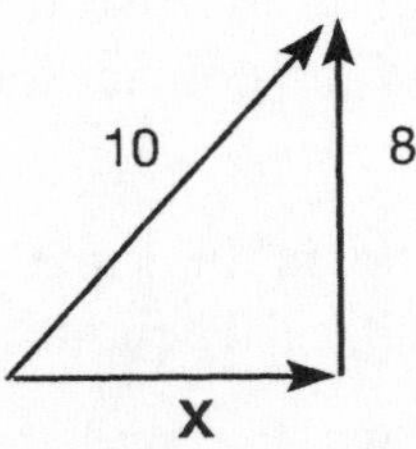

Because **X** is horizontal and 8 is vertical, they form a right angle, and the resultant (10) is the hypotenuse of that triangle. Thus, using the Pythagorean formula, **X** = 6.

6. **(C)** We add the horizontal and vertical vectors (which form a right angle) to obtain $5\sqrt{2}$ N units at 45° in a direction anti-parallel to the third 5-N vector. (The addition is accomplished by use of the Pythagorean theorem, $\sqrt{5^2+5^2} = 5\sqrt{2}$; the direction is determined using trigonometry.) Because this vector and the remaining 5-N vector are pointing in opposite directions, the resultant (R) is given by the difference. Thus, $R = (5\sqrt{2} - 5)$ N.

7. **(A)** We apply Newton's second law to the free-body diagram shown

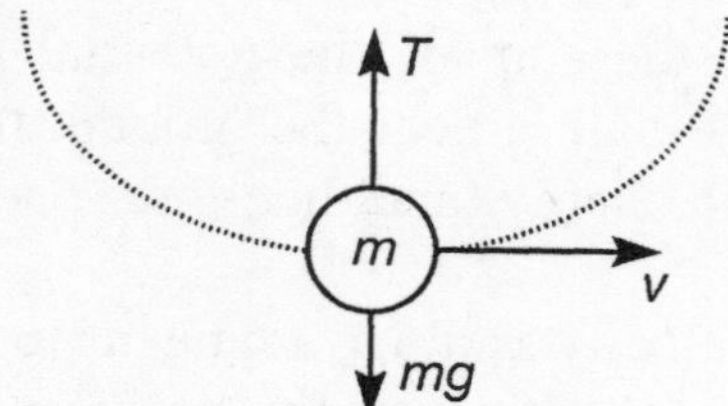

when the ball (mass m) is at the bottom of the circle. T is tension in the string, v is the instantaneous velocity, and mg is the weight. Applying $F = ma$ for centripetal motion, we obtain $T - mg = \dfrac{mv^2}{l} = ml\omega^2$, where we have used $v = r\omega$ (radius r is the length of the string l) on the right-hand side. Solving, we get $T = mg + ml\omega^2 = m(g + l\omega^2)$. Note that the bottom of the circle was selected, as that is where both weight and centripetal force serve to maximize the tension.

8. **(E)** The contact forces between the blocks must be equal and oppositely directed in accordance with Newton's law of action and reaction. The strategy for this problem is to first find the acceleration for both blocks and then use that to find the contact force. Newton's second law ($F = ma$) is used throughout.

The acceleration for both blocks is the same and can be found by considering them as a single mass of 8 kg. Then, $a = F/m = 8/8 = 1$ m/s^2.

Using Newton's second law, we can find the contact force for the 3-kg block: $F = ma = (3)(1) = 3$ N, to the right (e.g., the direction of the acceleration).

Since contact forces are equal and opposite, the contact force on the 5-kg block is 3 N, to the left.

9. **(B)** Average acceleration is given by $a_{avg} = \frac{v_f - v_i}{t_f - t_i} = \frac{\Delta v}{\Delta t} =$

$\frac{25-10}{1} = 15$ m/s^2.

10. **(E)** This problem uses Newton's second law for centripetal motion and the inverse square law for gravitational attraction of two masses.

At radial distance r we can write $mg = \frac{mv_r^2}{r}$, with the left-hand side representing the gravitational force. The symbol v_r is the velocity required to maintain circular motion.

At radial distance $3r$, we write $\frac{mg}{9} = \frac{mv_{3r}^2}{3r}$, with the left-hand side now divided by 9, because in accordance with the inverse square law, the gravitational force must decrease by the inverse square of the distance. Note that v_{3r} is the velocity required to maintain a circular orbit at distance $3r$.

By dividing both equations into one another (or by using substitution) and canceling m's and r's , we get $v_{3r} = \frac{1}{\sqrt{3}} v_r$.

11. **(D)** The formula for vibration frequency for a mass-spring system is $f_m = \frac{1}{2\pi}\sqrt{\frac{k}{m}}$, where k is the spring constant and m is the mass. Doubling of the mass would modify the expression; $f_{2m} = \frac{1}{2\sqrt{2}\pi}\sqrt{\frac{k}{m}}$, or $f_{2m} = \frac{1}{\sqrt{2}} f_m$. Thus, the new frequency is $\frac{5}{\sqrt{2}}$ Hz.

12. **(C)** The approach used here is to find the amount of spring elongation and add it to l, its length when not stretched.

Use is also made of $F = kx$, the force-distance relation for springs, where k is the spring constant and x is the amount of elongation. Refer to the free-body diagram of the block.

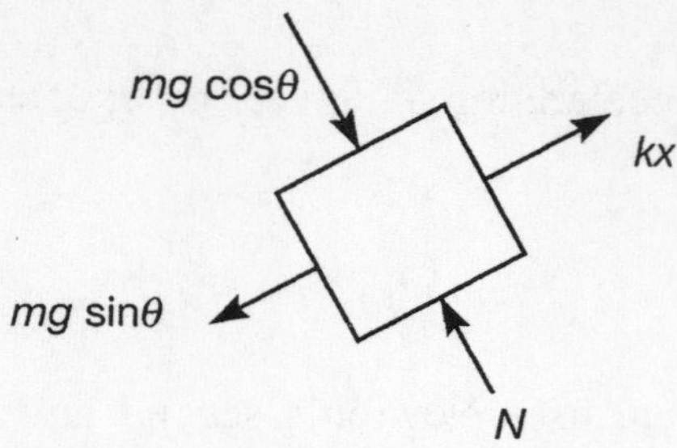

Here, the weight mg has been broken into two components, one parallel to the plane and one perpendicular. N is the normal force.

Since the block is in equilibrium, it is clear that $mg \sin\theta = kx$. Thus, $x = (mg \sin\theta)/k$

Finally, the total displacement is $l + \frac{mg}{k}\sin\theta$.

13. **(B)** Use conservation of energy and set the potential energy equal to the kinetic energy. In equation form, $\frac{1}{2}mv^2 = mgh$; the left side corresponds to the kinetic energy at the base of the plane and the right side corresponds to the potential energy at the point of maximum vertical displacement. The mass m cancels out on both sides, and we get $\frac{1}{2}(2^2) = (9.8)h$, or $h \approx 0.2$ m.

14. **(A)** Refer to problem 13. The fact that the masses cancel indicates that only the velocity matters.

15. **(E)** Using the definition of kinetic energy, we can write $KE = \frac{1}{2}mv^2$, which has units of joules, as does work (W). Evaluating, $KE = W = \frac{1}{2}(5)(2^2) = 10$ J.

16. **(A)** This is an impulse-momentum problem, making use of $F\Delta t = m\Delta v$, where the left side is the impulse and the right side is the change in momentum. F is the applied force, t is time, m is mass, and v is velocity.

Solving for contact time and evaluating, we obtain $\Delta t = \frac{m\Delta v}{F} = \frac{(0.1)(200)}{10{,}000} = 0.002$ s = 2 ms.

17. **(B)** This is a conservation of momentum problem for the case of a perfectly elastic collision.

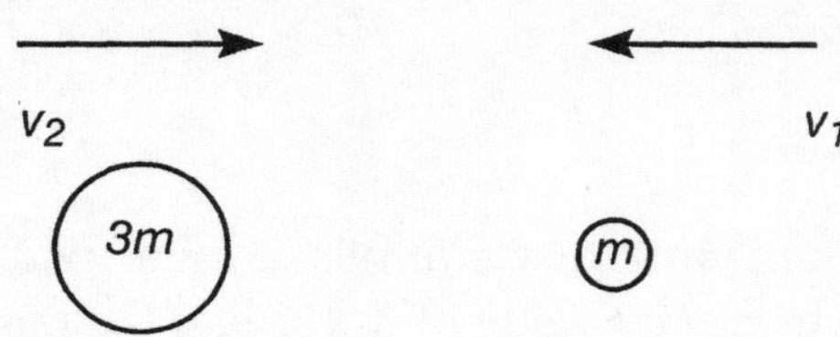

Because of the conservation of momentum, the total momentum before the collision must equal the total momentum after. For this situation, we can write $(3m)v_2 - (m)v_1 = 0$. The left side represents the momentum before the collision and the right side represents the momentum after the collision. Note that the second term on the left is negative because the direction of the small ball is opposite to the direction of the large ball, which was taken as positive. We thus obtain $\frac{v_2}{v_1} = \frac{1}{3}$.

18. **(E)** I is true because both momentum and impulse are vectors. II is incorrect because, for a vector equation to be true, both magnitude and direction must be the same. III is true, as reference to the equation shows. So I and III are true.

19. **(D)** The formula $\omega = \frac{v}{r} = \frac{40}{400} = 0.1$ rad/s gives the answer. Here, the left side is the angular velocity and the right side is the ratio of speed to circular radius.

20. **(D)** I is false because torque is a vector quantity with a direction of either clockwise or counterclockwise. II is true, as evidenced by the formula. III is false; when F and r are parallel, θ is zero degrees and the torque is zero. Thus, only statement II is correct.

21. **(A)** The formula for rotational kinetic energy is $KE = \frac{1}{2}I\omega^2$, where I is moment of inertia and ω is the angular velocity. Thus, $KE = \frac{1}{2}(10)[(2\pi)(6)]^2 = 7100$ J. Note that rev/s must be converted to rad/s, using the factor 2π rad/rev, for the answer to be expressed in joules.

22. **(C)** The sine's maximum value is 1 and it occurs when $8t = \frac{\pi}{2}$, or when $t = \frac{\pi}{16}$.

23. **(B)** Since the maximum value of the sine function is + 1 and the minimum is – 1, the maximum value of X is 5 and the minimum value is – 5. Thus, the magnitude of both the maximum and minimum values of X is 5.

24. **(D)** We use the formula for period T of a pendulum, $T = \frac{1}{2\pi}\sqrt{\frac{l}{g}}$, and apply it to both given situations.

On the Earth's surface, $T = \frac{1}{2\pi}\sqrt{\frac{l}{g}}$.

At a far-removed distance, $\frac{T}{6} = \frac{1}{2\pi}\sqrt{\frac{l}{g_{fd}}}$, where the left side represents the period and the right side includes the acceleration of gravity at the far distance.

Forming a ratio of both equations, the T's, π's and l's all cancel, leaving us with $\frac{6}{1} = \sqrt{\frac{g}{g_{fd}}}$. Thus, the acceleration of gravity at the far distance is $(1/36)g$.

25. **(A)** Referencing Newton's law of universal attraction for two point masses, we have $F = \frac{Gm_1m_2}{r^2}$, where F is the attracting force, G is the universal gravitational constant, the m's represent masses (with subscripts specifying each mass), and r is the distance between the masses. Since no symbol for sphere radius appears in the formula, III is the answer.

26. **(E)** (A) is wrong because taking negatively-charged electrons away from the rod will cause it to become positively charged. (B) is wrong because this is a problem in electrostatics, where nothing is flowing. (C) is incorrect because spontaneous polarization is not an established

physical phenomenon. (D) is wrong because such a transfer would make the rod positive.

27. **(B)** The electron, being negative, will move toward the most positive region, which is to the right. (Recall that electric field lines, by definition, begin at positive charges.) It will accelerate because the force is unbalanced.

28. **(A)** Because the charges are like, the forces must be repulsive. As they are moved closer together, the force must be increased, because the force between two point charges varies as the inverse square of the distance between them.

29. **(C)** I is true; the presence of the positive charge will attract the free electrons in the metal, causing them to accumulate at the surface. II is false because it contradicts I. III is true by convention.

30. **(A)** Using the definition of capacitance (C), we write $C = \frac{Q}{V} = \frac{1\times 10^{-9}}{10} = 100 \times 10^{-12}$ F = 100 pF.

31. **(A)** We use $C = \frac{\epsilon_0 A}{d} = 1\mu\text{F}$, where ϵ_0 is the permittivity of free space, A is the plate area, and d is the spacing between the plates. If A is tripled and the distance between the plates is halved, then we can rewrite the expression as $C_{nv} = \frac{\epsilon_0 3A}{d/2} = 6\left(\frac{\epsilon_0 A}{d}\right) = 6(1\mu\text{F}) = 6\ \mu\text{F}$, where the subscript nv refers to "new value."

32. **(B)** The best approach to solving this problem is to reduce the circuit to a simple series circuit of resistors and add them together. The reduction proceeds in three steps, as follows.

(1) Reduce the three 9-Ω resistors in parallel:

The formula for resistors in parallel is $\frac{1}{R_{eq}} = \sum_i \frac{1}{R_i}$. Applying this to the group of three resistors, we obtain $\frac{1}{R_{eq}} = \frac{1}{9} + \frac{1}{9} + \frac{1}{9} = \frac{1}{3}$. Thus, $R_{eq} = 3\ \Omega$.

(2) Reduce the two 2-Ω resistors in parallel:

Applying the same formula to the group of two we obtain $\frac{1}{R_{eq}} = \frac{1}{2} + \frac{1}{2} = 1$.

Therefore, $R_{eq} = 1\ \Omega$.

(3) Combine the Resistors:

The two parallel equivalents are now series-connected with 1-Ω and 3-Ω resistors. The formula for resistors in series is $R_{eq} = \sum_i R_i$. Applying the formula, we obtain $R_{eq} = 1 + 1 + 3 + 3 = 8\ \Omega$.

33. **(A)** Power dissipation in a resistor is given by $P = IV = RI^2 = V^2/R$. Using the second version of the formula, we obtain $P = (5 \times 10^3)(1 \times 10^{-3})^2 = 5 \times 10^{-3}$ W = 5 mW.

34. **(D)** The current measured is given by the formula $I = \frac{V}{R_{eq}}$, where the numerator is the battery voltage and the denominator is the equivalent resistance of the entire circuit. $R_{eq} = 5\ \Omega$, determined by adding $3 + 1 + 1 = 5\ \Omega$, the middle term being the equivalent to the two 2-Ω resistors in parallel. (See problem 32 for the general formula applying to parallel resistors.) Evaluating, we get $I = \frac{5}{5} = 1$ A.

35. **(D)** The approach used in solving this problem is to reduce the circuit to a parallel combination of capacitors and then add them up. The reduction proceeds in steps as follows:

(1) Combine the 1 μF and 0.5 μF capacitors:

Parallel capacitors can be combined using $C_{eq} = \sum_i C_i$. For these two capacitors, $C_{eq} = 1.0 + 0.5 = 1.5$ μF.

(2) Combine the series combination of 2 μF and 1.5 μF obtained in (1):

Series capacitors can be combined using $\frac{1}{C_{eq}} = \sum_i \frac{1}{C_i}$. For these two capacitors, we write $\frac{1}{C_{eq}} = \frac{1}{2} + \frac{1}{1.5} = 1.16$, so $C_{eq} = 0.9$ μF.

(3) Combine the parallel combination of 1 μF and 0.9 μF (obtained in step 2):

Per the formula given in (1), we add 1.0 and 0.9 to obtain 1.9 μF.

36. **(B)** After a long time, the capacitor is fully charged, so the series circuit can be analyzed as if the capacitor was not there. The three resistors are in series, so the equivalent resistance for the circuit is (5 + 2 + 3) = 10 Ω. The current is given by $I = (V/R)$, where R is the equivalent resistance for the circuit. Evaluating, $I = 10/10 = 1$ A. The capacitor is in parallel with a 2-Ω resistor, so the potential difference across the resistor is equal to the potential difference across the capacitor. Thus, the potential difference is (1)(2) = 2 V.

37. **(E)** The force on a moving charge in a magnetic field is given by $F = qvBI\sin\theta$, where q is the charge magnitude, v is the velocity, and θ is the angle between the velocity and magnetic field vectors. From the expression, it is clear that the magnitude of the force will be the same for equal charges of either polarity, moving either parallel or antiparallel to the given direction. Thus, (A) and (B) are eliminated. (C) is eliminated because all three factors in the formula are nonzero. (D) is eliminated because the force becomes zero under this circumstance. Thus, (E) is the answer because moving the charge in the opposite direction will affect only the sign, not the magnitude of the force.

38. **(C)** By definition, the force is always perpendicular to the plane formed by vectors **v** and **B.** The right-hand rule is then used to establish the sense of the vector.

39. **(D)** (A) is incorrect because the compass needle will rotate 180 degrees only if the field reverses itself. This is not possible unless the current that produces the field changes polarity or direction. (B) is wrong because Earth's magnetic field does not vary in this way. (C) is wrong because heating cannot cause the current, and therefore the field, to alternate. (E) is wrong because an electric field has no interaction with a compass needle.

40. **(E)** Use $\varepsilon = \dfrac{-\Delta\phi}{\Delta t}$ and $\phi = BA$. The former equation gives ε as the negative slope of the ϕ vs. t plot, and the latter gives flux in terms of the product of magnetic field and area.

Substituting the latter into the former, we obtain $\varepsilon = \dfrac{-\Delta BA}{\Delta t} = \dfrac{-A\Delta B}{\Delta t}$.

Evaluating, we get $\varepsilon = \pi(0.01)^2 \frac{1-0}{2-0} = 1.6 \times 10^{-4}$ V, where we have dropped the negative sign, because we are interested in magnitude only.

41. **(C)** Referring to $\varepsilon = \frac{-\Delta BA}{\Delta t} = \frac{-A\Delta B}{\Delta t}$ from the previous problem, we see that ΔB is zero over the 2 to 4 second interval. Therefore, the ε is also zero.

42. **(A)** Lenz's law states that the induced current in a loop will have a polarity opposing the change in flux through the loop. In this case, the flux is into the paper and decreasing, so the current sense will be such that it produces flux that is also into the paper to offset the decrease. A clockwise current tends to produce flux lines that are into the paper, as can be seen by the use of the right-hand rule. Note that only two answers are possible here: clockwise or counterclockwise.

43. **(D)** By definition, the amplitude of a time-varying wave is measured from the time axis to the peak of the waveform. In this case, amplitude = 5 cm.

44. **(A)** By definition, the period of a time-varying wave is measured from any convenient point on the wave to the first point at which the wave repeats itself. In this case, we see that the wave is going upward through zero at $t = 0$ and again at $t = 2$; so, the period is 2 s.

CAUTION: The wave is not repeating itself at $t = 1$, because at that point it is going *downwards* through zero.

45. **(E)** The speed of a wave is given by $v = f\lambda = \frac{\lambda}{T}$, where f is frequency, T is its reciprocal period, and λ is wavelength. Evaluating, we get $v = \frac{\lambda}{T} = \frac{10}{2} = 5$ m/s, where the value of the period was obtained from problem 44.

46. **(C)** The distance is given by $d = vt$, where v is the speed of sound and t is time. Solving, we get $d = (330)(5) = 1650$ m.

47. **(D)** Both (B) and (C) can be eliminated right away, because it is well established that the relative motion between sound source and ob-

server causes frequency or pitch to vary. Moving a source of sound towards a stationary observer causes the wave fronts to reach the ear sooner than would be the case for a stationary source, which is perceived as an increase in frequency. Conversely, moving a source of sound away from an observer causes the wave fronts to reach the ear later. The faster the source moves, the more pronounced the effect. Thus, (D) is the answer.

48. **(A)** The wavelength is the interval of distance over which the standing wave repeats itself. In this case, three half-wavelengths constitute the overall length of 6 m, so the wavelength (λ) is 4 m.

49. **(C)** When passing from one medium to another, a wave cannot change its frequency, so (B) and (D) can be ruled out. (E) is ruled out, even though the wave is refracted, because in going from one medium to another the wave speed will change. This leaves us with diffraction, and because the wave speed will change, eliminating (A), the answer is (C).

50. **(D)** By the principle of superposition, wave amplitudes can be added algebraically at a point in space to obtain the net magnitude. Here, when the pulses coincide, we take the difference of the amplitude *magnitudes* to get the net amplitude. This is equivalent to algebraic addition. Note: It is important to bear in mind that amplitudes above the zero level are taken as positive and amplitudes below the zero level are taken as negative.

51. **(A)** Using the wave equation $c = f\lambda$, where wave speed is the speed of light (c), we solve for frequency (f). We obtain $f = \frac{c}{\lambda} = \frac{3\times10^8}{6\times10^{-7}}$ $= 5 \times 10^{14}$ Hz.

52. **(B)** Using Snell's law, we obtain $n_1 \sin\theta_1 = n_2 \sin\theta_2 = n_2 \sin 90 =$ n_2. Solving, we obtain $\sin\theta_1 = \frac{n_2}{n_1}$.

53. **(A)** Beyond the critical angle (computed in problem 52), a ray in a less dense medium will be reflected at the interface with a denser medium.

54. **(E)** Virtual answers are eliminated because the object would have to be inside the focal length to produce such an image. Real images for convex mirrors are always inverted, so (A) is eliminated. The image is smaller than the object because it is placed between the focal length and

the radius of curvature. It would be larger only if it was placed outside the radius of curvature. So, the image is inverted, real, and smaller than the object.

55. **(C)** The kinetic energy of emitted photoelectrons is given by $E_k = hf - \phi$, where the right side is the difference in photon energy (hf) and the work function (ϕ). An equivalent formula is $E_k = \frac{hc}{\lambda} - \phi$, where c is the speed of light and λ is the wavelength. (The work function is considered to be a constant value in both formulas.) We see from the second expression that E_k increases as the λ decreases. We also see that below the cutoff λ (the wavelength for which the kinetic energy is zero), E_k is always greater than zero.

56. **(E)** Using $E = \frac{hc}{\lambda}$, where h is Planck's constant, c is the speed of light, and λ is the wavelength, we compute the energy as $E = \frac{(6.63\times10^{-34})(3\times10^{8})}{6\times10^{-7}} = 3.3 \times 10^{-19}$ J.

57. **(D)** The Bohr model accounts for quantized energy levels of electrons in atoms and their relation to photon emission. Thus, answers (A) and (B) can be ruled out. In Bohr's model, photon emission is explained as a conservation of energy process, in which photons are emitted when excited electrons return to lower energy states. Photons can also be emitted due to nuclear excitation, but such emissions are beyond the scope of Bohr's theory.

58. **(A)** de Broglie, inspired by the work of others, who showed that light waves could be regarded as particles (photons), wrote a dissertation arguing that matter particles could (under certain circumstances) be regarded as waves. Fission and fusion are nuclear processes, which de Broglie did not address.

59. **(E)** Using the de Broglie relation of $\lambda = \frac{h}{p}$, we solve for momentum, arriving at $p = \frac{h}{\lambda} = \frac{(6.63\times10^{-34})}{1\times10^{-8}} = 6.6 \times 10^{-26}$ kg m/s.

60. **(B)** I is true because the fusion of hydrogen nuclei is known to release photon energy. II is true, as the name fusion implies, with hydrogen nuclei forming helium nuclei in the interior of the sun. III is false because chain reactions are the result of fission, not fusion, reactions.

61. **(D)** We apply Einstein's relationship, $E = mc^2$, twice. For the electron (e), $E_e = m_ec^2$. For the proton (p), $E_p = m_pc^2$. Taking the ratio of energies, the speed of light (c) cancels and we obtain $\frac{E_p}{E_e} = \frac{m_p}{m_e} =$

$$\frac{(1.67\times10^{-27})}{9.11\times10^{-31}} = \frac{1.83\times10^{-3}}{1} \approx \frac{1}{1000}.$$

62. **(D)** The formula for pressure is $p = \rho gh$, where ρ is the fluid density, g is the acceleration of gravity, and h is the height of a column of fluid. Since tank cross-sectional area does not appear in the formula, the answer is III only.

63. **(A)** We use Archimedes' Principle and the property of equilibrium as follows:

(1) The weight of the cylinder is exactly balanced by the buoyant force as illustrated by the equation $AL\rho_{cyl}g = A(L - x)\rho_{fl}g$, where the left side is the weight and the right side is the buoyant force. The ρ's represent density, with the subscripts denoting the densities of the cylinder (*cyl*) and fluid (*fl*). A is the cross-sectional area of the cylinder, L is the total length of the cylinder, and x is the length of the cylinder above the fluid level.

(2) After canceling out the common terms on each side, we substitute $\rho_{cyl} = \frac{9}{10}\rho_{fl}$, to obtain $L\frac{9}{10}\rho_{fl} = (L - x)\rho_{fl}$. Solving, we arrive at $x = \frac{1}{10}L$. And, since $L = 10r$, we get $x = r$.

64. **(E)** For incompressible fluid flow, the mass flow rate must be constant. In equation form, we can write $A_1v_1 = A_2v_2$, where the A's represent cross-sectional areas, the v's represent flow rates, and the subscripts 1 and 2 refer to the respective cross-sections. Evaluating, we obtain $v_1 = \frac{A_2}{A_1}v_2 = \frac{3}{18}(24) = 4$ gal/min. (Note that we need not convert the gal/min to metric quantities in this type of problem; because we are using proportions, the factors common to both sides cancel out.)

65. **(D)** For a perfectly inelastic collision, all the kinetic energy will be conserved as heat, affecting the bullet. In equation form, $\frac{1}{2}mv^2 = mc\Delta T$, where the left side is the kinetic energy before impact and the right side is the heat generated during impact. Therefore, $\Delta T = \frac{v^2}{2c}$, and if we add to this temperature change the temperature before impact we arrive at $T + \frac{v^2}{2c}$.

66. **(B)** The approach here is to find the expanded circumference of the ring and then use $C = 2\pi r$ to get the radius.

The change in the circumference is $\Delta l = \alpha l \Delta t = 2\pi r \alpha \Delta t$, where α is the expansion coefficient, l is the circumference, and Δt is the change in temperature. Solving for the change in circumference length, we get $\Delta l = 2\pi(5)(13 \times 10^{-6})(400 - 23) = 0.15$ cm. Thus, after heating, the radius is 5 + (0.15)/(2)(3.14) ≈ 5.025 cm.

67. **(D)** I is false because gas molecule collisions with the wall are modeled as elastic; i.e., the molecules do not stick to the walls. II is false because the molecule speeds are distributed over a range, having a mean speed in the aggregate. III is true because momentum is always conserved. Thus, only III is true.

68. **(C)** According to the first law of thermodynamics, heat energy either added to or subtracted from a system must be accounted for. In equation form, $\Delta Q = \Delta U + P\Delta V$, where the left-hand side is the change in heat and the right-hand side is the change in internal energy (ΔU) plus the work done by or on the system. Thus, I is true because each term is a form of energy. II is false, because the last $P\Delta V$ term is identified as work. III is true because the ΔU term is a function of temperature only and is energy in potential form. Thus, I and III are true, and (C) is the correct answer.

69. **(A)** The ideal gas law is $pV = nRT$, where the left-side is the product of pressure and volume and the right-side is the product of molar volume n, the universal gas constant R, and the absolute temperature T. If the right side triples, then the left side must also triple. The only combination of p and V that satisfies this condition is $\sqrt{3}\,p$ and $\sqrt{3}\,V$.

70. **(B)** Specific heat is greater for diatomic than for monatomic gases

because the former has rotational modes of storing energy that the latter does not. Thus, it takes more energy to raise the temperature one degree for diatomic gases than monatomic gases. Neither (C) nor (D) is correct because specific heat is a function of internal energy and internal energy is a function of internal temperature. (E) is wrong; for ideal gases, the specific heat at constant pressure is higher than the specific heat at constant volume by the amount R, the universal gas constant.

DETAILED EXPLANATION OF ANSWERS

TEST 1

Section II

1. (a)

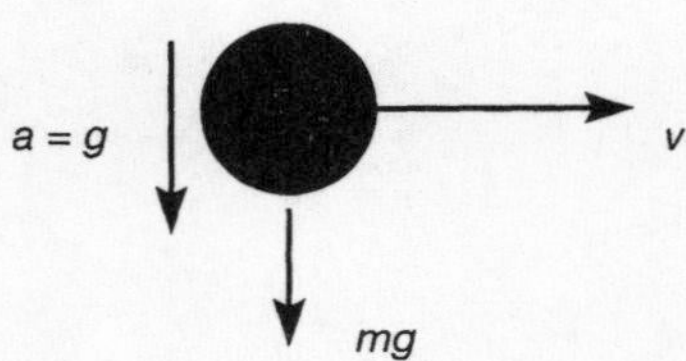

The weight (mg) is the only force acting on the ball. Acceleration (given by g) is parallel to the weight. Velocity (v) at the top of the trajectory is tangent to the curve; thus, v is horizontal.

(b) The horizontal component of displacement X is the product of the horizontal component of velocity and time. In mathematical terms,

$$X = (v_0 \cos\,\theta)t.$$

(c) The vertical component of velocity v_y is derived from the general equation for vertical velocity: $v_y = v_{0y} - gt$, where $v_{0y} = v_0(\sin\theta)$ is the vertical component of velocity at $t = 0$. Thus, $v_y = v_0(\sin\theta) - gt$.

(d) To obtain the value of Y_{max}, use conservation of energy, equating the gain in potential energy to the loss in kinetic energy: $mg\Delta h = (1/2)mv_y^2$. The left side of the equation represents the gain in potential energy and the right side represents the kinetic energy. Note that Δh is identical to Y_{max} and that only the y-component of velocity is used because the x-component does not contribute to increasing h. After canceling the masses and solving for Y_{max}, we obtain:

$$Y_{max} = \frac{v_y^2}{2g} = \frac{(v_0)^2}{2g}(\sin\,\theta)^2 = (14\sin 60)^2/(2)(9.8) = 7.5 \text{ m}.$$

To obtain the value of X_{max}, we can use the equation developed in (b) above, provided the time of flight is known. To obtain the latter, we use the general equation $v_y = v_{0y} - gt$ developed in (c). Here, v_{0y} is the value of the y-component of velocity when $t = 0$. Applying the equation at the top of the trajectory allows us to write $0 = (\sin\theta)v_0 - gt_{top}$, where the subscript (*top*) refers to the time it takes for the ball to reach the top of its trajectory. Because of symmetry, this is half of the time it takes for the ball to reach its maximum range.

Solving for the half-time, we get $t_{top} = \frac{v_0}{g}(\sin\theta) = (14)(\sin 60)/(9.8) = 1.2$ s.

Solving for maximum range, $X = v_0(\cos\theta)(2t_{top}) = (14\cos 60)(2)(1.2) = 16.8$ m.

2. (a) Vertical increments are 60 nN/div and horizontal increments are 5 cm/div.

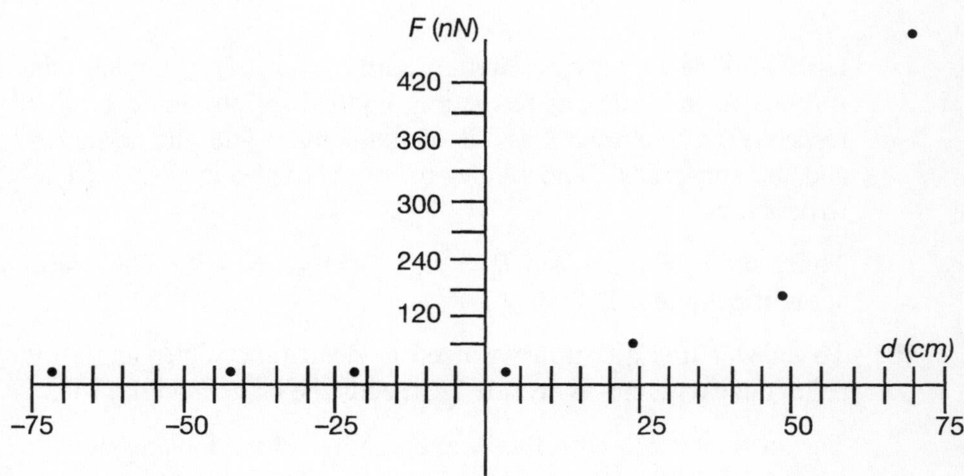

(b) Positive, because the test charge is always assumed to be positive. Since they are repelling, the other point charge must also be positive.

(c) Using Coulomb's law, $F = \frac{kqq_x}{r^2}$, we can calculate the unknown charge q_x. However, r should not be confused with d; r is the separation distance between charges, whereas d is the distance from the test charge to the origin of the coordinate system. To solve the problem, find r and then solve for q_x.

Using $F = \frac{kqq_x}{r^2}$ and the coordinate pair 75 cm and 560 nN, we can write $560 = \frac{kqq_x}{r^2}$, where the numerical value has been substituted for the force and r is taken as the separation distance. Using the same formula and a second coordinate pair (50 cm, 147 nN), we can write $147 = \frac{kqq_x}{(r+0.25)^2}$, since the test charge is now 25 cm farther away. Forming a ratio of the former to the latter, we get $\frac{560}{147} = \frac{(r+0.25)^2}{r^2} = 3.8$, or $r = 0.26$ m.

Plugging this value back into either of the original equations, we can solve for q_x.

$$\text{Thus, } q_x = \frac{Fr^2}{kq} = \frac{(560\times10^{-9})(0.26)^2}{(9\times10^{9})(1\times10^{-9})} = 4.2 \text{ nC.}$$

3. (a) Utilizing Snell's Law, we write $n_a(\sin\theta_i) = n_g(\sin\theta_r)$, where the n refers to the index of refraction, and subscripts a and g refer, respectively, to air and glass. θ refers to angles with the normal N, and the subscripts i and r refer to, respectively, incident and refracted rays.

   Thus, $\sin\theta_r = (n_a/n_g)\sin\theta_i = (1/1.7)\sin 42 = 0.39$. The corresponding angle is 23°.

   (b) To answer this question we need to determine if the angle the refracted ray makes with side 2 exceeds the critical angle.

   The critical angle for this wavelength is found using Snell's Law: $n_a(\sin 90) = n_g(\sin\theta_{cr})$. The equation represents a ray in the glass at the critical angle being totally internally reflected at the air-glass interface, hence the 90-degree value on the left-hand side.

   Solving, $\sin\theta_{cr} = (n_a/n_g) = (1/1.7) = 0.58$, corresponding to an angle of 36°.

   The angle that the ray makes is considerably larger than this, so the ray will be internally reflected. The size of the angle is, in fact, (67 + 60 =) 127 degrees. The first number inside the parentheses is the angle the refracted ray makes with the horizontal and the second is the number of degrees the second side is rotated counterclockwise from the vertical. (In practice, it would likely be easier to make a sketch to scale after figuring out the critical angle, and "eyeball" it to see if the angle made with the normal is much larger.)

(c) Since the data looks like a good fit to a straight line, we write an equation equating slope to a ratio of differences in coordinates:

$$\text{Slope} = \frac{\Delta n}{\Delta \lambda} = \frac{(2.0-1.7)}{(770-540)} = \frac{0.3}{230} = \frac{n-1.7}{\lambda-540}.$$

In point-slope form, we have $n = (0.0013)\lambda + 1.0$.

(d) In order for the ray to be straight, the refraction angle would be the same as the incident angle.

4. (a) The right-hand rule for a positive particle produces a force acting perpendicular to the velocity and pointing toward the top of the page. But such a force would cause the particle to travel in a counterclockwise direction, so the polarity must be negative.

(b) Using Newton's second law and the Lorentz force law, we equate forces' F_{mag} and F_{cent}, recognizing that the magnetic force is identical to the centripetal force. Equivalently, $(qv_0 \sin 90)B = qv_0B = (mv_0^2)/R$. Thus, the ratio m/q is equivalent to BR/v_0.

(c) Substituting values, we obtain $m = [(4 \times 10^{-9})(0.4)(2)]/400 = 8 \times 10^{-12}$ kg = 8 ng.

(d) The exit speed is the same as the entrance speed. The magnetic force does not alter the tangential speed, it only accelerates the particle in the radial direction. This is the nature of centripetal force.

5. (a) The heat lost by the hot water must equal the heat gained by the ice.

$Q_w = Q_i$, where the left-hand side is the heat lost by the water and the right-hand side is the heat gained by the ice. In general, $Q = mc\Delta T$ (for substances being heated and not undergoing a phase change) and $Q = mL$ (for substances being heated and undergoing a phase change). Note that the phase change is independent of temperature, occurring at a fixed temperature.

Thus, we can rewrite the loss/gain equation as

$$m_w c_w(70 - T_f) = m_i c_i(20) + m_i L + m_i c_w(T_f - 0),$$

where w subscripts refer to water, i subscripts refer to ice, and T_f refers to the final temperature. The three terms on the right side of the equation correspond, respectively, to (a) heating the ice to 0° C, (b) melting it into water, and (c) warming the water to T_f. Note that the w subscript in $m_i c_w(T_f - 0)$ is not a misprint, because the ice has changed into water.

(b) Substituting values into the equation obtained in (a),

$$(0.5)(4190)(70 - T_f) = (0.15)(2220)(20) + (0.15)(333{,}000) + (0.15)(4190)T_f.$$

Solving, $T_f = 33°$ C.

(c) Conservation of Energy. Energy is neither destroyed nor created.

6. (a) Positive. Under these conditions, the collector attracts the negative electrons rather than repelling them.

(b) Einstein's photoelectric equation will allow us to answer this question. In general form, it is $K = hf - \phi$, where the left-hand side represents the kinetic energy of ejected photoelectrons and the right-hand side represents the difference of the photon energy and work function. A second form is $K = hc/\lambda - \phi$, where h is Planck's constant, c is the speed of light, and λ is the wavelength.

At the maximum wavelength for emission (also known as the "cut-off" wavelength), the kinetic energy of the photoelectrons is zero. Thus, we can write

$$\lambda_{max} = hc/\phi = (1.24 \times 10^3)/3.0 = 410 \text{ nm}.$$

(c) Using $K = hc/\lambda - \phi$ again, we see that $K = 1.0$ eV. Equating this energy to $(1/2)mv^2$, we can solve for v:

$$(1/2)mv^2 = (1.0)(1.6 \times 10^{-19}) \text{ J}.$$

Here, we have converted the electron-volts into joules using a conversion factor. Plugging in the electron mass of an electron, $m_e = 9.11 \times 10^{-31}$ kg, and solving for v, we obtain $v = 5.9 \times 10^5$ m/s.

(d) Because the emitted energy of photoelectrons is 1.0 eV, it follows that the magnitude of the "stopping-potential" is 1.0 V. Its polarity is such that the collector is negative with respect to the photoelectric surface.

AP PHYSICS B

Test 2

AP PHYSICS B
Test 2

Section I

TIME: 90 Minutes
70 Questions

DIRECTIONS: Each of the questions or incomplete statements below is followed by five answer choices or completions. Select the one that is best in each case.

Questions 1-3

Three vectors are as shown; both **B** and **C** are parallel to the x-axis.

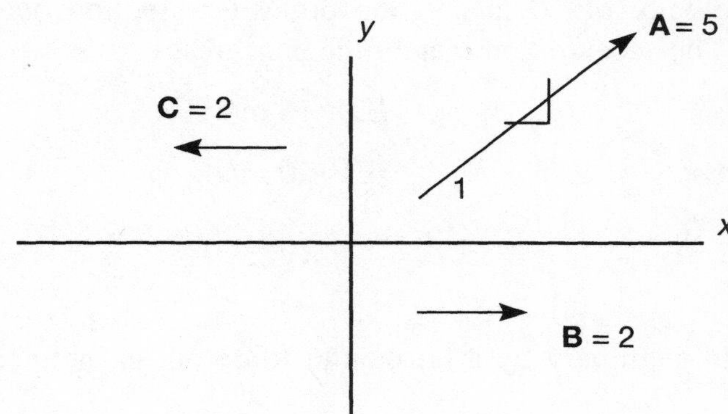

1. The vector sum of **A, B,** and **C** has a magnitude nearest

(A) 9.
(B) 5.
(C) 1.
(D) 6.
(E) 4.

2. The vector sum of **C** and **A** has an x-component nearest

(A) 2.5.
(B) 3.5.
(C) 5.5.
(D) 2.0.
(E) 1.5.

3. If **B** were increased to a length of 4, the resultant of **A** + **B** + **C** would create an angle with the x-axis of

(A) less than 45 degrees.
(B) more than 45 degrees.
(C) 45 degrees.
(D) 0 degrees.
(E) 90 degrees.

4. A particle is traveling in a straight line and accelerating uniformly at 4.0 m/s^2. If the initial velocity is opposite in direction to the acceleration and has a magnitude of 2.0 m/s, the net displacement after 5 s is nearest

(A) 40 m.
(B) 90 m.
(C) 50 m.
(D) 30 m.
(E) 5 m.

5. A particle is uniformly accelerated from an initial velocity of 2 m/s to a final velocity of 10 m/s in the opposite direction over a 60-cm distance. The acceleration magnitude is nearest

(A) 8 m/s^2.
(B) 40 m/s^2.
(C) 80 m/s^2.
(D) 16 m/s^2.
(E) 20 m/s^2.

Questions 6-8

A block is held stationary by a horizontal force on an inclined plane, as shown.

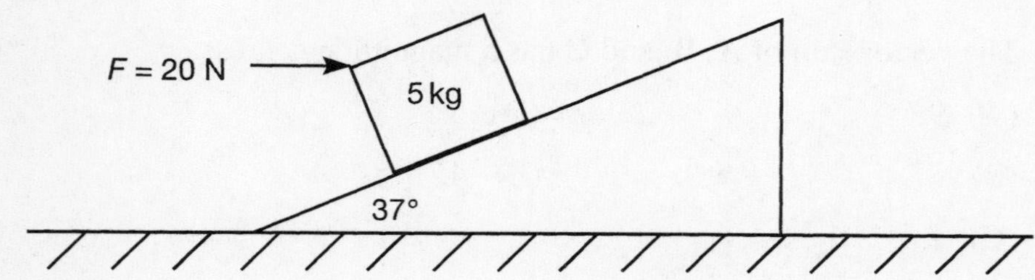

6. The normal force exerted by the plane on the block is

(A) 0 N.
(B) 28 N.
(C) 12 N.
(D) 52 N.
(E) 40 N.

7. The frictional force on the block is

(A) 14 N.
(B) 46 N.
(C) 25 N.
(D) 7 N.
(E) 35 N.

8. The coefficient of friction for the block and plane surfaces is about

(A) 0.01.
(B) 0.10.
(C) 0.47.
(D) 0.88.
(E) 0.27.

9. Which of the following statements regarding centripetal force are correct for circular motion of a point-like object with mass m?

I – Its magnitude is directly proportional to the instantaneous velocity of the object.

II – Its direction is tangent to the circular path at any given time.

III – Its magnitude is proportional to the mass of the object.

(A) I and III
(B) III only
(C) II and III
(D) II only
(E) I and II

10. A car traveling at 30 m/s skids to a halt over a distance of 50 m on a horizontal roadway. If its mass is 2000 kg and the deceleration is assumed to be uniform, the frictional force acting on the car is

(A) 18,000 N.
(B) 36,000 N.
(C) 9,000 N.
(D) 50,000 N.
(E) 100,000 N.

11. Which of the following statements is/are *not* true regarding contact forces when kicking a soccer ball?

I – The net force on the ball at time of impact is zero.

II – The force acting on the ball is equal and opposite to the force acting on the foot.

III – In general, the magnitude of acceleration of the foot during contact is not equal to the magnitude of acceleration of the ball.

(A) I and II
(B) I only
(C) II only
(D) III only
(E) II and III

Questions 12-13

The block shown moves on a horizontal surface at constant speed.

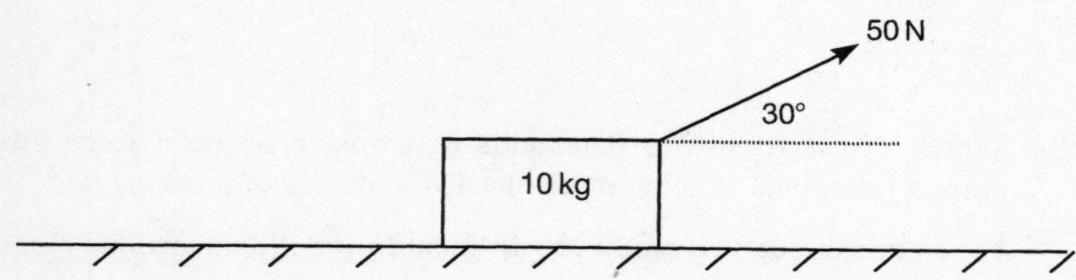

12. The work done over a 10-m distance to overcome friction is nearest

(A) 425 J.
(B) 250 J.
(C) 500 J.
(D) 0 J.
(E) 4 J.

13. The coefficient of friction between the block and the plane is about

(A) 1/3.
(B) $\sqrt{3}$.
(C) $\sqrt{3}/4$.
(D) $\sqrt{3}/5$.
(E) $\sqrt{3}/3$.

14. Which of the following statements about average power is/are correct?

I – It is a vector quantity.

II – It is defined as the ratio of total work done to the time taken to do that work.

III – It is defined as the ratio of total work done to the distance over which the work was done.

(A) II and III
(B) III only
(C) I and III
(D) II only
(E) I and II

15. A mass and spring oscillate in a vertical direction. If frictional losses are negligible, the energy stored in the spring is

(A) zero at either vertical extreme.
(B) maximum at both vertical extremes.
(C) maximum at the upper vertical extreme only.
(D) maximum at the lower vertical extreme only.
(E) maximum when the block is at maximum velocity.

16. Two boxcars with masses m_1 and m_2 are moving in the same direction on the same track at the respective velocities of v_1 and v_2. One overtakes the other and couples to it. The speed of the coupled pair is expressed by

(A) $(m_1v_1 - m_2v_2) / (m_1 + m_2)$.
(B) $(m_1v_1 + m_2v_2) / (m_1 - m_2)$.
(C) $(m_1v_1 - m_2v_2) / (m_1 - m_2)$.
(D) $(v_1 + v_2)$.
(E) $(m_1v_1 + m_2v_2) / (m_1 + m_2)$.

17. A ball with mass 100 g is struck by a force (with duration as shown in the graph). The initial speed of the ball after impact is

(A) 50 m/s.
(B) 0.05 m/s.
(C) 5 m/s
(D) 100 m/s.
(E) 200 m/s

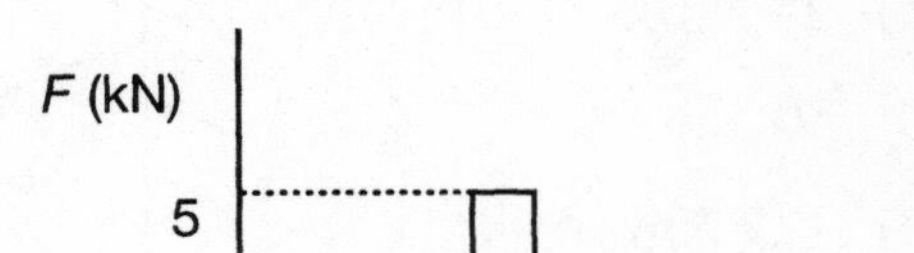

18. Which of the following statements regarding totally inelastic collisions is/are *not* true?

I – Total momentum is conserved.

II – Total kinetic energy is conserved as kinetic energy.

III – Kinetic energy is converted to heat.

(A) I and III
(B) III only
(C) II only
(D) II and III
(E) I and II

Questions 19-20.

A wheel rotating at 200 rev/min is uniformly braked to a halt in 10 s.

19. The magnitude of the angular acceleration is

(A) 2 rad/s.
(B) 120 rad/s.
(C) 1 rad/s.
(D) 10 rad/s.
(E) 20 rad/s.

20. The total angle turned through while braking is nearest

(A) 50 radians.
(B) 100 radians.
(C) 200 radians.
(D) 75 radians.
(E) 25 radians.

21. A beam is pivoted at O and held in position by a tether, one end of which is attached to the end of the beam and the other to the wall, as shown. The beam's weight is 500 N. The net torque about an axis perpendicular to the plane of the paper and through O is

(A) 100 Nm.
(B) 25 Nm.
(C) 50 Nm.
(D) 125 Nm.
(E) 0 Nm.

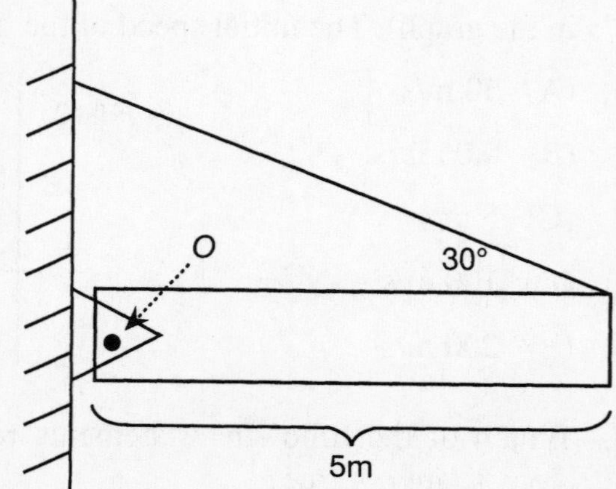

22. The period of a repetitive signal is 10 μs. Its frequency is

(A) 100 kHz.
(B) 10 kHz.
(C) 100 Hz.
(D) 1 MHz.
(E) 1000 Hz.

23. The mass of an object is 4 grams. Its weight on the Earth's surface is

(A) 0.4 N.
(B) 4.0 N.
(C) 0.04 N.
(D) 0.004 N.
(E) 9.8 N.

24. Consider two objects of differing masses, separated by a distance d. Which of the following statements about gravitational attraction between them is/are true?

I – Gravitational force decreases inversely with the distance.

II – Gravitational force increases directly with the product of the masses.

III – Gravitational force increases directly with the square of the distance.

(A) I and II
(B) II only
(C) II and III
(D) III only
(E) I and III

25. Identify the expression that correctly relates the following: g = acceleration of gravity, M = mass of the Earth, G = universal gravitational constant, and R = radius of the Earth.

(A) $g = (R^2/GM)$
(B) $g = \sqrt{GM/R^2}$
(C) $g = (GM/R^2)^2$
(D) $g = (GM/R^2)$
(E) $g = (GM/R)$

26. Which of the following statements regarding simple harmonic motion is/are false?

    I – The restoring force is proportional to, and opposite the direction of, the displacement.

    II – The restoring force is proportional to, and in the same direction as, the displacement.

    III – The motion is periodic, but not sinusoidal.

    (A) II and III
    (B) II only
    (C) I and II
    (D) I and III
    (E) III only

27. A mass is hung from a spring, elongating it by 5 mm. If the mass is 200 kg, the spring constant k is

    (A) 4×10^6 N/m.
    (B) 4×10^2 N/m.
    (C) 4 N/m.
    (D) 4×10^5 N/m.
    (E) 2.5×10^{-6} N/m.

28. According to Kepler's third law, which one of the following expressions is constant for planetary motion in the solar system? (T = planet period and R = radial distance from the sun.)

    (A) $(R/T)^3$
    (B) $(R/T)^2$
    (C) T/R
    (D) T^2/R^3
    (E) T^2/R^2

29. Which of the following statements about electrical potential is/are correct?

    I – It is a vector field quantity.

    II – The zero-potential level is arbitrary.

    III – Equipotential lines can never cross.

    (A) I and II
    (B) I and III
    (C) II and III
    (D) I, II, and III
    (E) II only

30. A negative charge $-Q$ has a magnitude of 3.2 μC. The number of electrons required to produce this charge is

(A) 2×10^5.
(B) 2×10^{19}.
(C) 2×10^{13}.
(D) 2×10^{14}.
(E) 2×10^{21}.

31. Two identical positive point charges are equidistant from straight line *AB*, as shown. The potential along line *AB* is

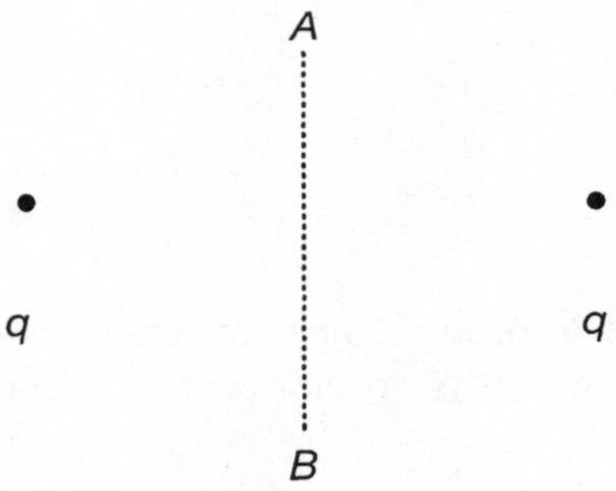

(A) zero at all points.
(B) negative for all points, with the magnitude a maximum at the point of intersection of *AB* and a line joining the charges.
(C) negative and constant for all points on line *AB*.
(D) positive and constant for all points on line *AB*.
(E) positive for all points, with the magnitude a maximum at the point of intersection of *AB* and a line joining the charges.

32. Refer to the diagram given in question 31. The electric field at any point on line *AB*

(A) has a zero component in a direction perpendicular to *AB*.
(B) has a zero component in a direction parallel to *AB*.
(C) is zero.
(D) has the same direction as it would with both charges made negative.
(E) has the same direction as it would with one charge made negative.

33. An array of charges is distributed as shown, with a pair of $2Q$ charges and a pair of Q charges both equidistant from q. A third Q charge is collinear with q and $2Q$ and is a units distant from q. The net force on q is

(A) kQ/a^2.

(B) $2kQq/a^2 + kQ^2/a^2$.

(C) $8kQ^2/a^2 + kQq/a^2$.

(D) kQ/a.

(E) kQq/a^2.

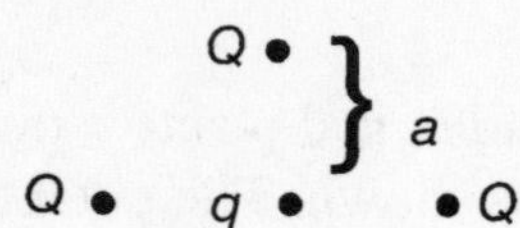

34. A positive charge is brought near an infinite metal sheet. Which of the following statements is/are *not* correct regarding the lines of force produced?

I – The lines of force terminate at the metal sheet.

II – The lines of force bunch together near the charge and separate far from it.

III – The lines of force originate at the charge.

(A) I only

(B) II only

(C) I and II

(D) III only

(E) All of the statements are correct.

35. A hollow metal sphere is charged by transferring a negative charge of Q C. The electric field inside the sphere is

(A) the same as at the surface, with the radial direction inward.

(B) the same as at the surface, with the radial direction outward.

(C) half that at the surface, with the radial direction outward.

(D) zero.

(E) half that at the surface, with the radial direction inward.

36. A capacitor is charged to 1 nC by 100 V. The capacitance *C* is

(A) 10 pF.
(B) 1 μF.
(C) 100 pF.
(D) 10 μF.
(E) 1000 pF.

37. Which of the following statements about parallel-plate capacitors is/are true?

I – Capacitance is inversely proportional to the separation distance of the plates.

II – Capacitance is inversely proportional to the area of the plates.

III – Capacitance is directly proportional to the dielectric constant of the material between the plates.

(A) II only
(B) II and III
(C) I and III
(D) I and II
(E) I only

38. A wire has a current flowing in it. If 8 μC of charge are known to circulate through the wire every 10 s, the current in the wire is nearly

(A) 8 μA.
(B) 0.8 μA.
(C) 0.8 mA.
(D) 1.2 μA.
(E) 0.12 mA.

39. What is the essential difference between a good electrical conductor and a good insulator?

(A) Conductors have mobile nuclei and insulators do not.

(B) Electrons flowing in insulators collide with other electrons, interfering with their movement, but in conductors this cannot happen.

(C) There are free valence electrons in insulators, but not in conductors.

(D) The length and area of conductors determine conductivity, but the same cannot be said for insulators.

(E) There is an abundance of free valence electrons in conductors compared to insulators.

40. A 25 kΩ resistor has a potential difference of 50 V across it. What is the power dissipated in the resistor?

(A) 100 W
(B) 0.1 W
(C) 1.0 W
(D) 2.5 W
(E) 1.3 W

Questions 41-44

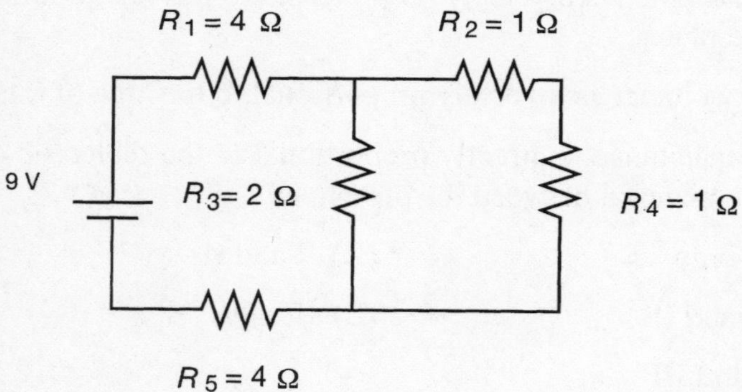

41. A single resistor that could replace the entire network is

(A) 8 Ω.
(B) 2 Ω.
(C) 5 Ω.
(D) 7 Ω.
(E) 9 Ω.

42. In which resistor pair does the current have equal value?

(A) R_1 and R_3
(B) R_3 and R_5
(C) R_1 and R_5
(D) R_1 and R_2
(E) R_4 and R_5

43. The total current flowing out of the battery is nearly

(A) 1.0 A.
(B) 0.5 A.
(C) 0.3 A.
(D) 2.0 A.
(E) 1.5 A.

44. The voltage drop or potential difference across R_2 is

(A) 0.75 V.
(B) 0 V.
(C) 0.25 V.
(D) 0.5 V.
(E) 1.0 V.

45. The total energy stored in the capacitor network is

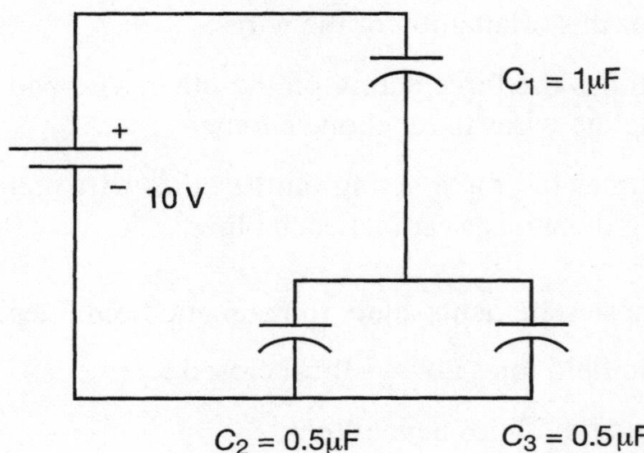

(A) 50 μJ.
(B) 25 μJ.
(C) 12.5 μJ.
(D) 100 μJ.
(E) 75 μJ.

46. Which of the following factors is/are *not* significant when considering the Lorentz force acting on a charged particle in a magnetic field?

I – The velocity of the particle

II – The magnitude of particle charge

III – The mass of the particle

IV – The direction of the particle relative to the direction of the magnetic field

(A) I and III
(B) I, II, and III
(C) III only
(D) I and IV
(E) I, II, and IV

47. Two long wires are parallel and have currents of I and $3I$ flowing through them, both in the same direction. The force acting on the wire with $3I$ is

(A) the same as the force acting on the other wire and in a direction causing the wires to repel one another.

(B) the same as the force acting on the other wire and in a direction causing the wires to attract each other.

(C) zero for this orientation of the wires.

(D) three times the force acting on the other wire and in a direction causing the wires to repel one another.

(E) three times the force acting on the other wire and in a direction causing the wires to attract each other.

48. Which of these statements apply to magnetic field lines?

I – Magnetic field lines always form closed loops.

II – Magnetic field lines never cross.

III – Tangents to magnetic field lines show the direction of force acting upon a charged particle moving through the magnetic field.

(A) I only

(B) II only

(C) I and II

(D) II and III

(E) I and III

Questions 49-50

A copper rod of length L is moved at constant velocity v through a region of magnetic field B, as shown. The rod lies in the plane of the paper. The velocity is 10 m/s, magnetic field strength (B) = 2 T, and the rod's length (L) is 15 cm.

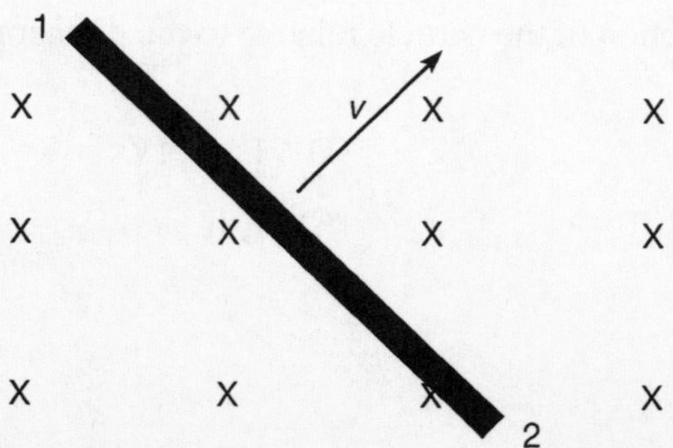

49. The magnitude of the ε developed across the rod is

(A) 300 V.
(B) 0.75 V.
(C) 7.5 V.
(D) 75 V.
(E) 3 V.

50. The polarity of end 1 relative to end 2 is

(A) negative.
(B) positive.
(C) alternately positive and negative.
(D) the same as end 2.
(E) indeterminate.

51. Which of the following plots of magnetic flux (ϕ) versus time (t) could produce the ε versus t shown for a rectangular loop of wire placed within a field?

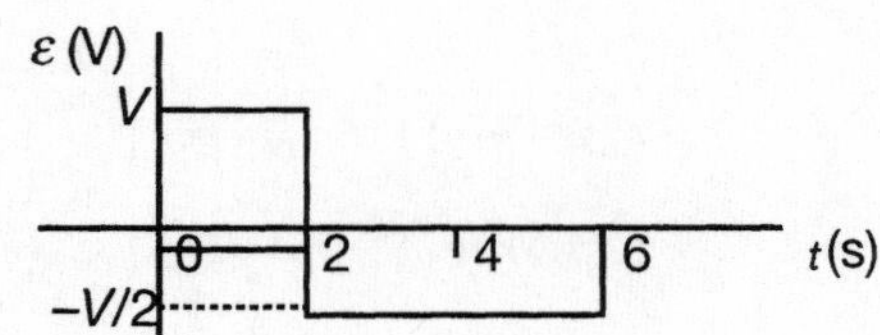

(A)

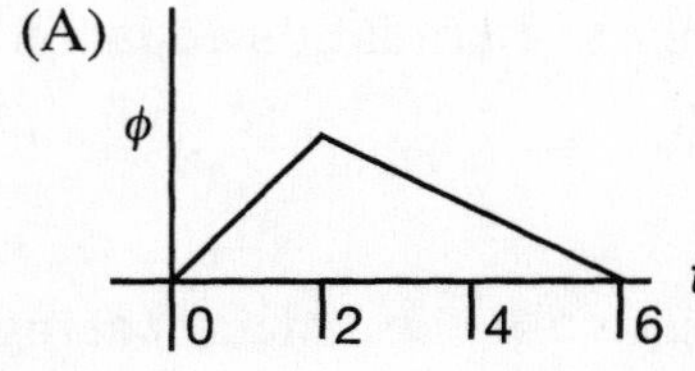

(D)

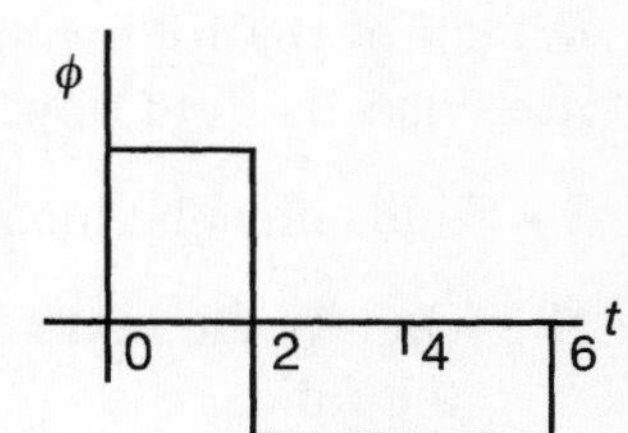

(B)

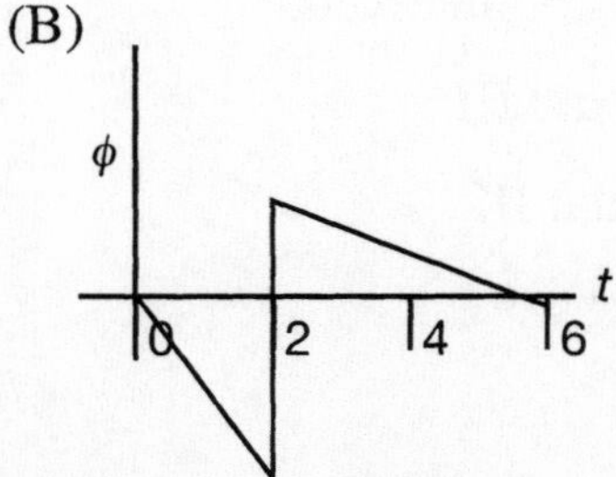

(E)

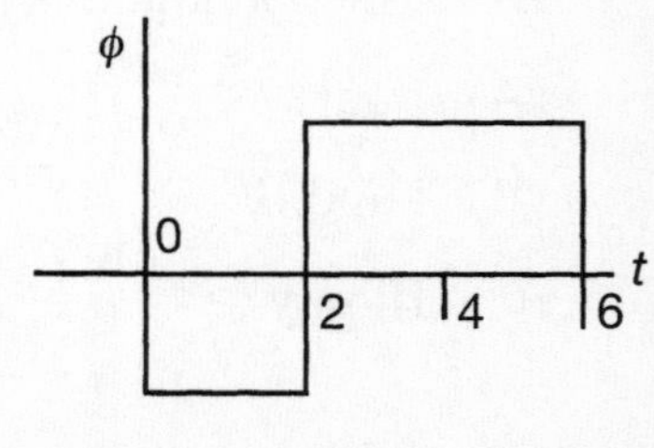

(C)

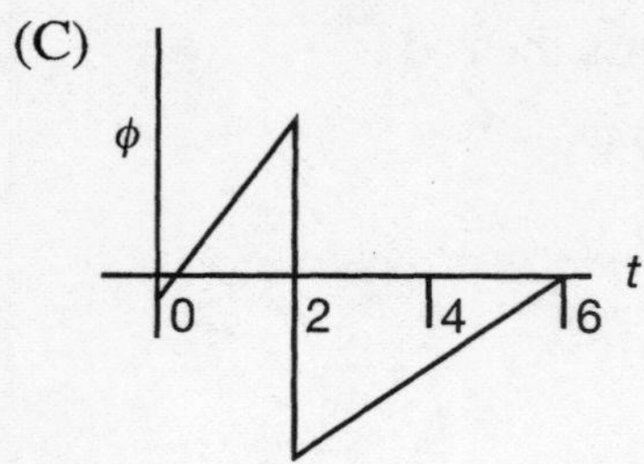

52. A circular lid on a large pipe, closed at the other end, is held in place by atmospheric pressure P_a. If the cross-sectional area of the pipe is A and a force F is required to remove the lid, what is the pressure inside the pipe?

(A) $P_a - (F/A)$

(B) $P_a + (F/A)$

(C) F/A

(D) $F - P_a$

(E) Zero

53. A solid sphere with mass m and density ρ_1 is suspended by a string and immersed in fluid with density ρ_2. The tension in the string is expressed by

(A) $mg(\rho_2/\rho_1)$.

(B) mg.

(C) $mg[1 + (\rho_1/\rho_2)]$.

(D) $mg[1 - (\rho_1/\rho_2)]$.

(E) $mg[1 - (\rho_2/\rho_1)]$.

54. Which of the following statements apply to Bernoulli's equation for non-viscous fluid flow?

I – Fluids must be incompressible.

II – One of the equation's terms accounts for the kinetic energy of the fluid.

III – The potential energy of the fluid is not involved.

(A) I only

(B) I and II

(C) II only

(D) II and III

(E) I and III

55. A water tower tank is L meters above ground level and filled with water of density ρ. What will be the pressure at a water tap $L/3$ meters above ground level? (Neglect depth of water in the tank.)

(A) ρgL

(B) $5\ \rho gL/9$

(C) $4\ \rho gL/9$

(D) $\rho gl/3$

(E) $2\ \rho gL/3$

56. A metal cube has a linear temperature expansion coefficient of α and length of side L. What is the approximate increase in surface area of the cube when heated from T_1 to T_2?

(A) $24\alpha L^2(T_2 - T_1)$

(B) $8\alpha L^2(T_2 - T_1)$

(C) $3\alpha L^2(T_2 - T_1)$

(D) $12\alpha L^2(T_2 - T_1)$

(E) $2\alpha L^2(T_2 - T_1)$

57. Which of the following statements is/are correct regarding the heat of fusion for ice?

I – It is greater than the heat of vaporization for water.

II – It varies with the temperature of the ice.

III – Each unit mass of ice releases an amount of heat equal to the heat of fusion upon freezing.

(A) III only

(B) I and III

(C) I and II

(D) II and III

(E) I only

58. An ideal gas fills a closed container. If its absolute temperature is tripled, the root-mean-square speed of the molecules changes by a multiplying factor of

(A) 3.

(B) $\sqrt{3}$.

(C) 9.

(D) $1/\sqrt{3}$.

(E) 1/3.

59. Which of the following is *not* an explicit factor in the expression for the ideal gas law?

I – Pressure

II – Volume

III – Temperature

IV – Internal energy

(A) IV only

(B) II only

(C) I only

(D) I and IV

(E) II and IV

60. The universal gas constant (R) is a measure of the

(A) energy contained in 1 gram of gas at 0 degrees K.

(B) energy required to heat 1 mole of gas 1 degree K.

(C) energy required to heat 1 gram of gas 1 degree K.

(D) energy required to heat 1 liter of gas 1 degree K.

(E) energy contained in 1 mole of gas at 0 degrees K.

61. An adiabatic volume change for an ideal gas takes place. The pressure (P), volume (V), and ratio of molar heat capacities (γ) are related by

(A) $(PV)^\gamma =$ constant.

(B) $PV^\gamma =$ constant.

(C) $PV = \gamma$.

(D) $PV\gamma =$ constant.

(E) $P/V^\gamma =$ constant.

62. A Carnot cycle for a heat engine consists of

(A) two adiabatic processes alternating with two constant volume processes.

(B) two adiabatic processes alternating with two constant pressure processes.

(C) one adiabatic process alternating with two isothermal processes.

(D) one isothermal process alternating with two adiabatic processes.

(E) two adiabatic processes alternating with two isothermal processes.

63. A heat engine utilizing a Carnot cycle has a high temperature of 600° C during one process and a low temperature of 300° C during another process. The engine efficiency is nearest

(A) 52%.
(B) 18%.
(C) 34%.
(D) 66%.
(E) 75%.

64. Which of the following statements about photons is correct?

I – Photon energy increases with wavelength.

II – Photon energy increases with frequency.

III – The ratio of photon energy to frequency is equal to Planck's constant (h).

IV – The ratio of photon energy to wavelength is equal to Planck's constant (h).

(A) II only
(B) II and III
(C) III only
(D) I and II
(E) II and III

65. A photon has energy of 3 eV. The corresponding wavelength is

(A) 625 nm.
(B) 200 nm.
(C) 500 nm.
(D) 820 nm.
(E) 400 nm.

66. Which of the following statements about the work function of a metal is/are correct?

I – The work function is a vector quantity.

II – When electron emission takes place under photon irradiation, the work function is always greater than the photon energy.

III – The work function for metals is generally larger than for nonmetals.

(A) None
(B) I and II
(C) II only
(D) III only
(E) II and III

67. The Heisenberg uncertainty principle applied to an electron with position uncertainty of 1 μm implies a momentum uncertainty of no less than

(A) 6.6×10^{-31} kgm/s.
(B) 6.6×10^{-34} kgm/s.
(C) 6.6×10^{-28} kgm/s.
(D) 1.1×10^{-34} kgm/s.
(E) 3.3×10^{-28} kgm/s.

68. Sound waves are

(A) longitudinal, propagating only in a medium.
(B) transverse, propagating only in a medium.
(C) longitudinal, propagating in a medium and vacuum.
(D) transverse, propagating in a medium and vacuum.
(E) longitudinal, with direction of propagation perpendicular to wave amplitude.

69. The speed of sound in a medium depends on which of the following factors?

I – Index of refraction of the medium

II – Elasticity of the medium

III – Density of the medium

(A) I and II
(B) I and III
(C) II only
(D) III only
(E) II and III

70. Light in air is incident, as shown on a glass slab having an index of refraction (n) of 1.5. The angle the refracted ray makes with the normal (N) is about

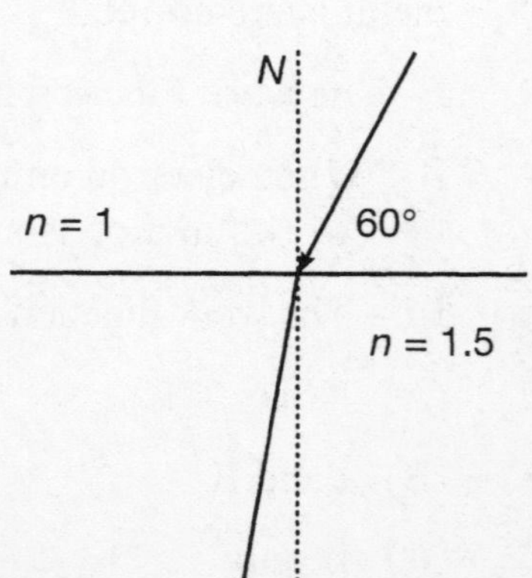

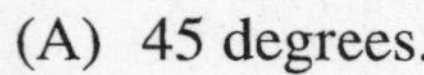
(A) 45 degrees.
(B) 30 degrees.
(C) 60 degrees.
(D) 37 degrees.
(E) 19 degrees.

AP PHYSICS B
Test 2

Section II

TIME: 90 Minutes
6 Free-Response Questions

DIRECTIONS: Carefully read each question and then make sure to answer *each part* of the question. You must show your work. Crossed out work will not be graded. You will lose credit for incorrect work that is not crossed out.

1. A puck is fired along a horizontal surface with an initial velocity of 15 m/s. After traveling a distance of 75 m, it comes to rest. The puck weight is 2 N.

   (a) What is the puck's initial kinetic energy?

   (b) What is the frictional force acting on the puck?

   (c) How long does it take for the puck to come to rest?

   (d) What is the coefficient of friction for the surface material?

2. Four charges are arranged in rectangular array as shown, where q_1 = 2 nC, q_2 = 5 nC, q_3 = –2 nC, and q_4 = –5 nC.

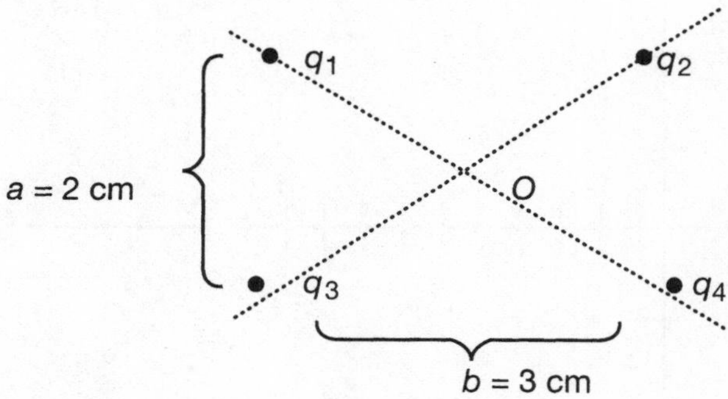

   (a) Draw a free-body diagram showing vectors that indicates all the forces acting on q_2.

   (b) Calculate the force on q_2 due to q_1 only.

   (c) Calculate the electrical potential V at point O.

   (d) Calculate the electric field **E** at point O, and indicate its direction.

(e) Calculate the electric potential at a point midway between q_2 and q_4.

3. A rectangular loop of wire with an area 0.25 m^2 is contained in a region of a magnetic field B as shown. The loop can be rotated about its long axis as shown.

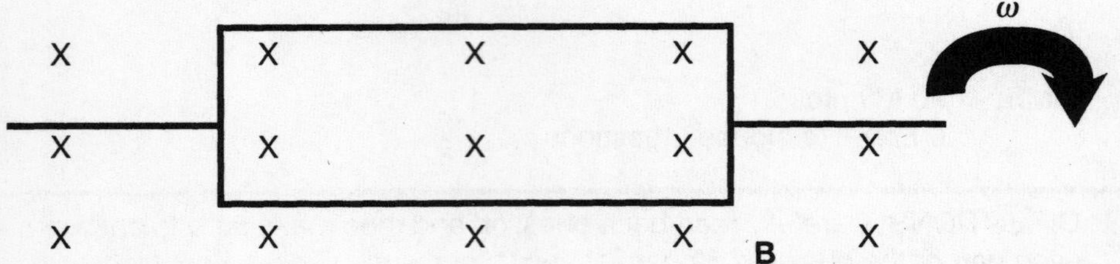

(a) When the loop is stationary and with magnetic field B constant, what is the emf (ε) induced in the loop?

(b) With the loop held stationary and **B** varying as shown in the graph, plot the emf (ε) obtained.

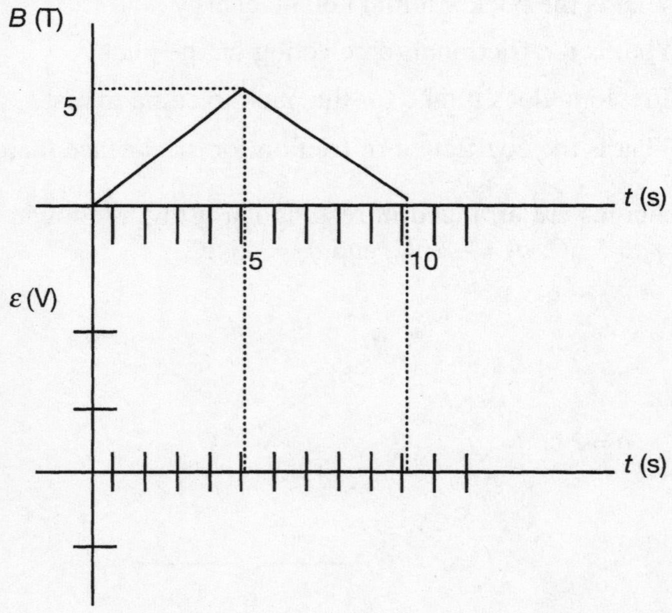

(c) If the loop is rotated 45 degrees from the position given above and then held in place, what will ε be for the same B variation?

(d) If the loop is spun at a constant speed of ω, what general shape of waveform will be produced? Make a sketch of the shape and indicate the period in terms of ω.

4. A compound metal bar of uniform cross-sectional area $A = 50\ \text{cm}^2$ is composed of two different materials welded together as shown. The ends of the bar are maintained at 0° C and 200° C. The thermal conductivity for the 10-cm section is $k_{10} = 400$ W/m K°, and the thermal conductivity of the 30-cm section is $k_{30} = 800$ W/m K°.

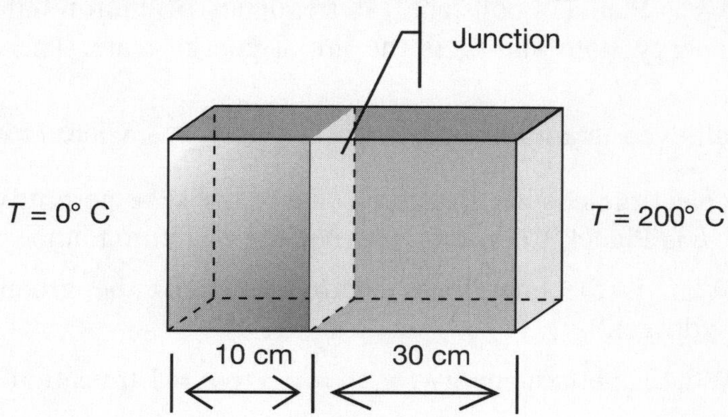

(a) What is the direction of heat flow?

(b) Develop an expression for the junction temperature T_j in terms of cross-sectional area A, length L, and thermal conductivities k_{10} and k_{30}. Do not solve for a numerical value.

(c) Determine the numerical value of T_j.

(d) On the axes provided, graph temperature versus distance measured from the right end of the bar. Label the axes with T and d. Show T_j clearly on graph.

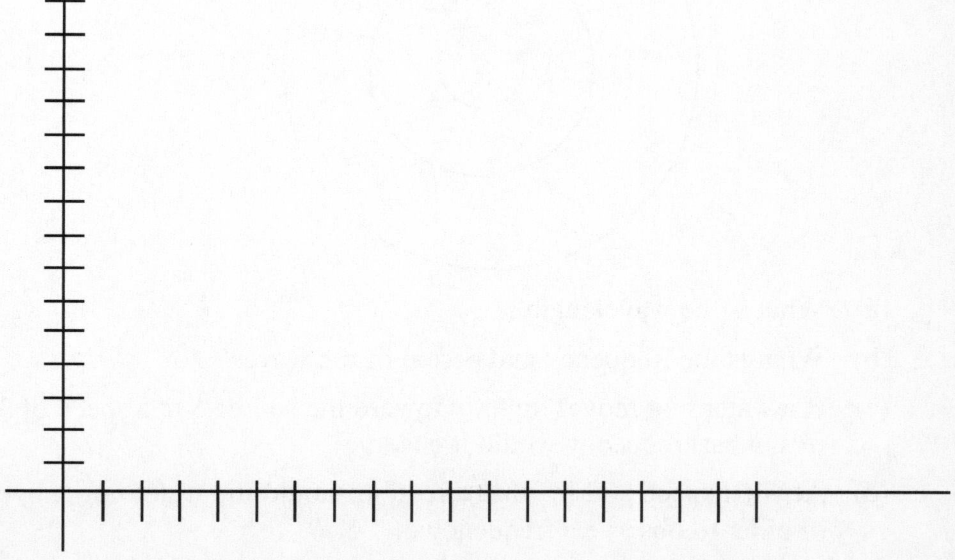

(e) What effect would increasing k_{10} have on T_j with all else held constant?

5. The Bohr model of the hydrogen atom quantized energy in multiple ways. The energy of an emitted photon is given by $hf = E_f - E_i$, where h is Planck's constant, f is frequency of photon light, E_f is the final energy state and E_i is the initial energy state. The energy for each allowed quantum state is $E = -\frac{me^4}{8\epsilon_0^2 h^2}\frac{1}{n^2}$, where m is the mass of the electron, e is the electronic charge, ϵ_0 is the permittivity of free space, h is Planck's constant, and n is the quantum number.

(a) What is the energy in electron-volts for the ground state of hydrogen?

(b) What is photon energy for an $n = 3$ to $n = 1$ transition?

(c) What is the corresponding wavelength for this transition?

(d) What is the maximum energy level permitted by Bohr's model, and what is the corresponding quantum number?

6. A source S generates circular waves on the surface of a pool. The pattern of wave crests is as shown. The speed of the waves is 7 m/s and crest separation is 1.2 m.

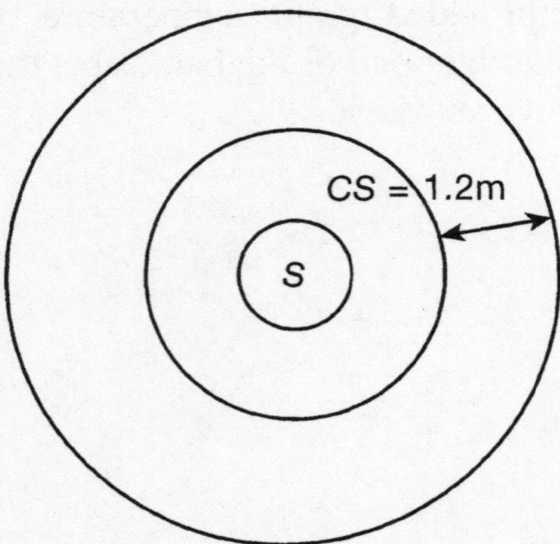

(a) What is the wavelength?

(b) What is the frequency and period of the waves?

(c) If a water bug moves directly toward the source S at a speed of 3 m/s, what frequency would it observe?

(d) At what speed and in what direction should the water bug move in order to observe a frequency of 1 Hz?

AP PHYSICS B
TEST 2

Section I

ANSWER KEY

1.	(B)	19.	(A)	37.	(C)	55.	(E)
2.	(E)	20.	(B)	38.	(B)	56.	(D)
3.	(A)	21.	(E)	39.	(E)	57.	(A)
4.	(A)	22.	(A)	40.	(B)	58.	(B)
5.	(C)	23.	(C)	41.	(E)	59.	(A)
6.	(D)	24.	(B)	42.	(C)	60.	(B)
7.	(A)	25.	(D)	43.	(A)	61.	(A)
8.	(E)	26.	(A)	44.	(D)	62.	(E)
9.	(B)	27.	(D)	45.	(B)	63.	(C)
10.	(A)	28.	(D)	46.	(C)	64.	(B)
11.	(B)	29.	(C)	47.	(B)	65.	(E)
12.	(A)	30.	(C)	48.	(C)	66.	(A)
13.	(C)	31.	(E)	49.	(E)	67.	(C)
14.	(D)	32.	(A)	50.	(B)	68.	(A)
15.	(B)	33.	(E)	51.	(A)	69.	(E)
16.	(E)	34.	(E)	52.	(A)	70.	(E)
17.	(A)	35.	(D)	53.	(E)		
18.	(C)	36.	(A)	54.	(B)		

DETAILED EXPLANATIONS OF ANSWERS

TEST 2
Section I

1. **(B)** Vectors **C** and **B** cancel one another out in the summation, leaving only **A**.

2. **(E)** The vector sum of **A** and **C** has an x-component equal to the sum of the each vector's x-components. So, $\mathbf{A}_x + \mathbf{C}_x = 5\cos 45 + (-2) = 1.5$.

3. **(A)** Increasing **B**'s length beyond 2 will cause the resultant to rotate more toward the x-axis as **B**'s length increases. (Imagine what the resultant would look like if **B** = 100,000!) Thus, the angle will be less than 45 degrees.

4. **(A)** The problem is solved using a general formula for straight-line motion $x = v_0t + (1/2)at^2$, where the v represents velocity, a is acceleration, t is time, and x is displacement. The subscript "0" denotes initial velocity.

Evaluating, we have $x = -2(5) + (1/2)4(5)^2 = 40$ m.

5. **(C)** We use the equation for straight-line motion, $v^2 = v_0^2 + 2ax$, where v represents velocity and x represents displacement. The subscript 0 denotes initial velocity.

Evaluating $(-10)^2 = (2)^2 + 2a(-0.6)$ and solving for a, we obtain $a = -80$ m/s^2. Note that the displacement was made negative in the equation because the object not only decelerated, but was displaced in a direction opposite to the initial velocity, which was taken as positive.

6. **(D)** We utilize the free-body diagram shown here.

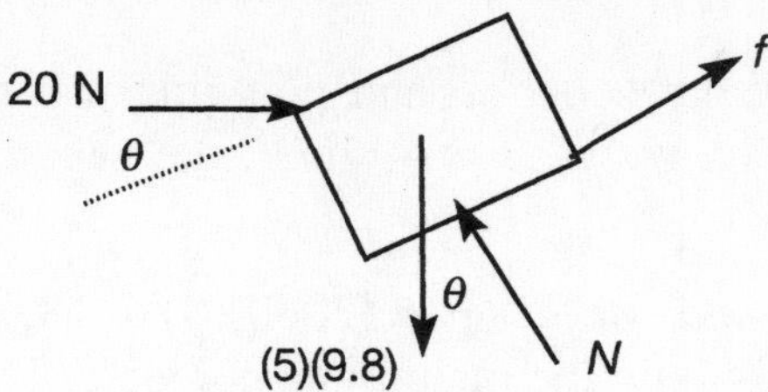

Here, N is the normal force, f is the frictional force, and the angle $\theta = 37°$.

We make use of equilibrium and sum the forces to zero in a direction perpendicular to the plane.

Thus, $N - (5)(9.8)\cos 37 - 20\sin 37 = 0$. Here we have taken the direction of N to be positive, so the components of the other two forces perpendicular to the plane are negative. Solving, we obtain $N = 51.2$ N (52 N if 10 is used as an approximation instead of 9.8).

7. **(A)** Refer to the free-body diagram of problem 6.

We make use of equilibrium and sum the forces to zero in a direction parallel to the plane.

Thus, $f - (5)(9.8)\sin 37 + 20\cos 37 = 0$. Here we have taken the direction of f to be positive, so the components of the other two forces along the plane have appropriate signs. Solving, we obtain $f = 14$ N.

8. **(E)** By definition, the coefficient of friction is computed: $\mu = f/N = 14/52 = 0.27$.

9. **(B)** Referring to the defining expression for centripetal force, $F_c = \dfrac{mv^2}{R}$, we see that its magnitude is proportional to m, so the answer must contain III, ruling out (D) and (E). However, the force is proportional to the square of velocity, not velocity, so any answer containing I is wrong, ruling out (A) and (E). The direction of the force is radial and inwards, so II is wrong, and the answer is III only (B).

10. **(A)** We make use of $F = ma$ and $v^2 = v_0^2 + 2ax$. The former is Newton's second law and the latter is one of the kinematic equations for straight-line motion, in which a represents uniform acceleration, v repre-

sents velocity, and x represents displacement. The subscript 0 denotes initial velocity.

Working with the second equation and plugging in numbers, we get $0 = (30)^2 - 2a(50)$. Solving, we get $a = -9$ m/s^2, the negative value indicating deceleration.

Substituting into $F = ma$, we get $F = (2000)(9) = 18{,}000$ N. We dropped the minus sign because only the magnitude is required.

11. **(B)** The net force on the ball at impact cannot be zero; it would never leave the foot if it were. I and any answers containing it are possibilities, ruling out (C), (D), and (E). II is a restatement of Newton's law of action and reaction and is true, so the answer cannot contain it. III is, in general, true; with equal and opposite forces acting on unequal masses (ball and foot), the acceleration magnitudes will differ in accordance with Newton's second law. Thus, the answer is I only.

12. **(A)** We use $W = (F\cos\theta)x$ to calculate the work done. Here, F is the applied force, θ is the angle between the force and the displacement, and x is the displacement.

Evaluating, we obtain $W = (50)\dfrac{\sqrt{3}}{2}(10) = 433$ J.

13. **(C)** By definition, the coefficient of friction (μ) is f/N, where f is the friction force and N is the normal force. But f is (in magnitude) equal to the horizontal component of F, the block being in equilibrium, as indicated by the constant velocity. N is in this instance equal to the weight, so $\mu = f/N \approx 50\dfrac{\sqrt{3}}{2}\dfrac{1}{(10)(10)} = \dfrac{\sqrt{3}}{4}$, where we have used 10 instead of 9.8 for the acceleration of gravity.

14. **(D)** The definition of average power is $P = (W_f - W_i)/(t_f - t_i)$, where the numerator is the work done in the time interval given in the denominator. The subscripts f and i refer to, respectively, final and initial. From the definition, it is clear that power is not a vector because the ratio is of two scalars, work and time. So, I is ruled out. II is the verbal equivalent of the definition, so it must appear in the answer, ruling out (B), (C), and (E). III contradicts the definition, so it is wrong, ruling out (A), (B), and (C). Only (D) is left.

15. **(B)** This is a problem in conservation of energy. Use is made of the fact that the total energy is constant and equal to the energy stored in the spring (potential) plus the kinetic energy of the block. At the vertical extremes of motion, the kinetic energy is zero because the block's velocity is zero. Thus, it is clear that all the energy is stored in the spring at both extremes, so the energy stored in the spring is at its maximum.

16. **(E)** We use conservation of momentum for an inelastic collision to solve this problem as follows.

We write $m_1v_1 + m_2v_2 = (m_1 + m_2)v$, where the left side represents momentum before the collisions and the right side represents momentum after the collision. The v represents the velocity of the coupled boxcars. Solving, we get $v = (m_1v_1 + m_2v_2)/(m_1 + m_2)$.

17. **(A)** This is an impulse-momentum problem involving $F\Delta t = m\Delta v$. The left side of this equation represents the impulse and the right side represents the change in momentum. Solving for the change in velocity we get, $\Delta v = (F\Delta t)/(m)$, where F is the force, Δt is the time interval of the impact, and m is the mass. Evaluating, we get $\Delta v = \dfrac{(5\times10^3)(1\times10^{-3})}{(0.1)} =$ 50 m/s. Because the initial velocity was zero, the change in velocity is the final velocity.

18. **(C)** I is true for all types of collisions (elastic or inelastic), so answers (A) and (E) can be ruled out. II is not true, so the answer must contain it, narrowing the possible correct answers down to (C) and (D). III is true, so (D) is eliminated, leaving only (C).

19. **(A)** We use $\omega = \omega_0 + \alpha t$, where the left-hand side is the angular velocity at time t and the right-hand side is the sum of the initial angular velocity and the angular acceleration-time product. Solving for α, we get $\alpha = \dfrac{\omega - \omega_0}{t} = \dfrac{-\omega_0}{t}$, since the final velocity is zero. Evaluating, we obtain $\alpha = \dfrac{-\omega_0}{t} = \dfrac{-(200)(2\pi)}{(60)(10)} \approx -2$ rad/s. We disregard the minus and note that the presence of the factor $\dfrac{2\pi}{60}$ is required to convert rev/min to rad/s.

20. **(B)** We use $\theta = \omega_0 t + (1/2)\alpha t^2$, where the left side is the angle turned through in time t and the right side is the sum of an angular velocity and an angular acceleration term. The subscript 0 denotes the initial angular velocity. Evaluating, we obtain $\theta = \frac{2\pi}{60}(200)(10) - (1/2)(2)(10)^2$, where the minus has been introduced because the wheel is decelerating. Thus, θ is nearly 100 radians.

21. **(E)** The net torque is zero because the beam is in static equilibrium. There is no need for analysis.

22. **(A)** By definition, frequency and period are reciprocals of one another, $f = 1/T$. For this problem, $f = (1/T) = \frac{1}{1\times10^{-5}} = 1 \times 10^5$ Hz = 100 kHz, since 1 kHz = 1000 Hz.

23. **(C)** Weight is given by mg, where m is in kg; so, it is (0.004)(9.8) $\approx$ 0.04 N.

24. **(B)** The gravitational force magnitude for differing masses is given by $F = (Gm_1m_2)/d^2$, where G is the universal gravitational constant, the m's are masses, d is the distance separating them, and the subscripts 1 and 2 differentiate the masses. From the equation it is clear that the gravitational force decreases inversely with the *square* of the distance. Therefore, I is wrong and answers (A) and (C) can be eliminated. Also, gravitational force does increase with the product of the masses; therefore, II is correct and the answer must include it, thereby eliminating (D). III is wrong because force does not increase with distance. Thus, only II is correct.

25. **(D)** This problem can be worked by utilizing $F = ma$ and Newton's law of universal gravitation, $F = (Gm_1m_2)/d^2$. Equating the expressions, we obtain $F = (Gm_1M)/d^2 = m_1a = m_1g$, where the subscript 1 refers to the mass of object 1. But Earth's mass (M) can be treated as a point mass located at a distance R (Earth's radius) from m_1. After canceling out m_1's, we obtain $g = GM/R^2$.

26. **(A)** I is true and is the defining characteristic of harmonic motion, thereby eliminating answers (C) and (D). II contradicts I, so it must appear in the answer, thereby narrowing the choices to (A) and (B). III is also

incorrect because a consequence of I is that sinusoidal and periodic motion is obtained. Thus, the answer is (A).

27. **(D)** We use the equation for a force due to a spring, $F = kx$, where the left side is the force and the right side is the product of spring constant k and elongation x. Solving for the spring constant, we obtain $k = (F/x) = \frac{(200)(9.8)}{(5 \times 10^{-3})} \approx 4 \times 10^5$ N/m.

28. **(D)** A planet's orbit about the sun can be closely approximated as circular. Under such conditions the centripetal force can be set equal to the gravitational force given by Newton's universal law of gravitation.

In mathematical terms, $mv^2/R = GmM/R^2$, where m is the mass of the plant, R is the sun-planet distance, M is the mass of the sun, v is orbital velocity, and G is the universal gravitational constant. Also, $v = 2\pi R/T$, where T is the period (year) of the planet. Substituting this equation into the first equation and rearranging terms, we obtain $R^3/T^2 = (2\pi)^2 GM$, the right-hand side a constant. The reciprocal of both sides also yields a constant.

29. **(C)** Electric potential is by definition a scalar quantity; so, I is incorrect, ruling out answers (A), (B), and (D). II is correct because the zero-level is routinely assigned to points of convenience; it is the difference in potential that is usually important in calculations. Thus, II must appear in the remaining answers. III is correct because crossing equipotentials would suggest that two different values of potential can exist for a given point in space, a physical impossibility. Thus, statements II and III are correct.

30. **(C)** Charge Q and the charge e on a single electron are related by $Q/e = N$, where N is the number of electrons comprising charge Q. For this problem, $N = \frac{(3.2 \times 10^{-6})}{(1.6 \times 10^{-19})} = 2.0 \times 10^{13}$.

31. **(E)** The expression $V = kQ/r$ gives the potential V for a point charge Q at a distance r. In this case, it would be applied twice and both outcomes would be added together in accordance with the superposition principle. Since the points on line AB are at variable distances from the charges, it follows that (A), (C), and (D) can be eliminated because the

potential cannot be constant. (E) is the answer, because V is positive for all points and its value is maximum when r is minimum (i.e., on the line connecting the two charges).

32. **(A)** For any point on line AB, the electric field will be determined by adding the two E-vectors associated with each charge, as shown in the following sketch.

A
E_q E_q
B

From the geometry of the figure, we see that components of E_q perpendicular to AB will cancel out and that the net field will be nonzero, consisting of the sum of the components parallel to AB. Thus, (A) is the answer, and all the others are false.

33. **(E)** The net force on q is the vector sum of five forces, one each due to the surrounding five charges. However, due to the symmetry and equality of certain charge-pairs, four of the forces cancel out, leaving only the force due to the third Q charge. Specifically, the force pair due to the equal charge pair Q-Q cancels, as does the force pair due to equal charge pair $2Q$-$2Q$. Coulomb's law can then be used to compute the force as $F_{net} = kQq/a^2$.

34. **(E)** I is true because electric field lines do terminate at a metal interface. II is true because the lines of force are dense where the field is strong. III is also correct because, by convention, positive charges are taken as the source of electric field lines. Thus, all of the statements are true.

35. **(D)** The interior of a hollow metal object is always a field-free region.

36. **(A)** By the definition of capacitance, $C = Q/V = \dfrac{1\times10^{-9}}{100} = 1\times10^{-11}$ F $= 10$ pF.

37. **(C)** We use the capacitance formula $C = \frac{k\epsilon_0 A}{d}$, where k is the dielectric constant, A is the plate area, d is the plate separation distance, and ϵ_0 is the permittivity of free space. I is seen to be confirmed by the formula, so (A) and (B) are eliminated. II is not confirmed by the formula, so (D) is eliminated. III is confirmed by formula; so, statements I and III are true.

38. **(B)** Current is given by the expression $I = q/t = \frac{(8\times10^{-6})}{10} = 8 \times 10^{-7}$ A = 0.8 μA.

39. **(E)** (A) is wrong because nuclei for both conductors and insulators are not mobile. (B) is wrong because electron collisions in conductors are numerous, but they do not affect the conductivity. (C) is wrong because it reverses the correct attribution of properties to conductors and insulators. (D) is wrong because the length and area (in addition to material type) determine the conductivity of both insulators and conductors. (E) is a correct statement of the microscopic properties of insulators and conductors.

40. **(B)** $P = V^2/R = \frac{(50)^2}{(25\times10^3)} = 0.1$ W.

41. **(E)** Resistors R_2 and R_4 are in series, so they can be replaced with a single resistor $R_{24} = 1 + 1 = 2\ \Omega$. This resistor is in parallel with R_3, so the parallel combination of R_3 and R_{24} can be replaced by $\frac{R_{24}R_3}{R_{24}+R_3} = \frac{(2)(2)}{2+2} = 1\ \Omega$. Finally, the resulting series combination of resistors can be added together to obtain $R_{eq} = R_1 + \frac{R_{24}R_3}{R_{24}+R_3} + R_5 = 4 + 1 + 4 = 9\ \Omega$.

42. **(C)** Without analyzing the circuit, it is apparent that R_1 and R_5 each have the total battery current flowing through them, the former on the outgoing side and the latter on the incoming side. None of the other combinations can be guaranteed to have equal currents flowing through them.

43. **(A)** The total current is given by $I = V/R_{eq} = 9/9 = 1$ A.

44. **(D)** The voltage drop or potential difference across R_2 is given by $V_2 = I_2R_2$. Recalling from problem 41 that R_{24} and R_3 can be represented by two 2-Ω resistors in parallel, we see that the battery current splits into two equal parts, each 0.5 A. Thus, we can write $V_2 = I_2R_2 = (0.5)(1) = 0.5$ V.

45. **(B)** The potential energy stored in a capacitor is given by $U_C = (1/2)CV^2$. Applying this to the given circuit, we note that C_2 and C_3 are both in parallel, so they can be replaced by an equivalent capacitor of $C_2 + C_3 = 1.0$ μF. This leaves two capacitors of equal value in series; therefore, the voltage drop across each is one-half of the battery volts, or 5 V. The energy can now be computed as $U_C = (1/2)C_1V_1^2 + (1/2)\,C_{23}\,V_{23}^2 = (1/2)(1 \times 10^{-6})(5)^2 + (1/2)(1 \times 10^{-6})(5)^2 = 25 \times 10^{-6}$ J $= 25$ μJ. Here we have used the notation C_{23} to denote the equivalent of the parallel capacitors.

46. **(C)** The Lorentz expression for the magnetic force on a charged particle is $F = qv\sin\theta$, where q is the charge, v is the velocity, and θ is the angle between the force and velocity vectors. This expression illustrates that I, II, and IV are significant factors, while III is not (mass not appearing in the expression).

47. **(B)** The expression relating force to current for two parallel wires is $F = \dfrac{\mu_0 I_1 I_2}{2\pi d}$, where F is the force, μ_0 is the permeability of free space, I is the current, and d is the separation distance between the wires. The subscripts 1 and 2 are used to differentiate the two wires. The force magnitude is the same on *both* wires, as the expression suggests. The direction of each force is such that the wires attract, which can be seen from the use of the right-hand rule as applied to this diagram.

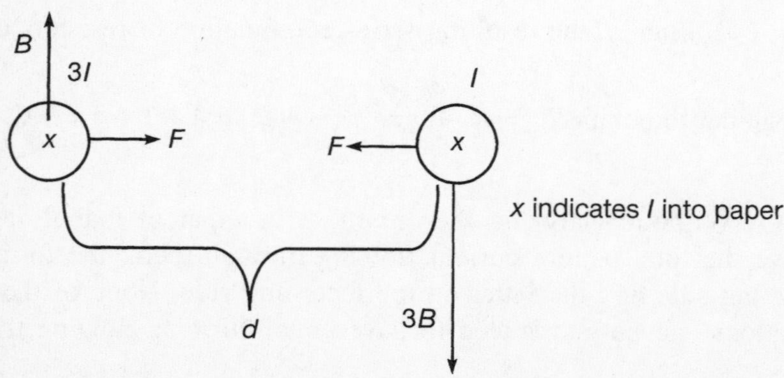

Note that the left wire (with $3I$) produces a B-field three times larger at the right wire than is produced by the right wire (with I) at the left wire. The magnitude of F remains equal because one of the currents is associated with the current in the wire under consideration (wire a), while the other is associated with the field produced by wire b. In both cases, the product is the same.

Regarding direction, application of the right-hand rule to a current vector into the paper (with the **B**-vector as drawn) must produce the F directions shown.

48. **(C)** I is true because there are no magnetic monopoles. The elemental magnetic unit is the dipole, which has field lines starting on the N and ending on the S in closed loops. II is true; if they did cross, there would be two different directions for the magnetic field at the same point at the same time; this is a physical impossibility. III is incorrect; tangents to the magnetic field give the direction of the field, not the direction of the force acting upon a charged particle. Thus, I and II are both true.

49. **(E)** The magnitude of ε developed in a conductor of length L is given by $\varepsilon = BLv\sin\theta$, where B is the magnetic field, v is the velocity, and θ is the angle between the field and velocity vectors. For this problem, we can write $\varepsilon = BLv\sin\theta = (2)(0.15)(10)\sin 90 = 3$ V.

50. **(B)** The rod can be considered a collection of free electrons moving through a magnetic field. As such, we can apply the right-hand rule to any one of them to find out which way all of them are being pushed. In this case, the right-hand rule would cause positive particles to move to end 1; however, since electrons are negative, the reverse situation will be obtained, with electrons moving to end 2, leaving end 1 positive with respect to end 2. Answers (C), (D), and (E) are nonsense answers because only reversal of velocity could cause alternation, and the mobility of free electrons in metals guarantees that charging will happen.

51. **(A)** Use is made of $\varepsilon = -\Delta\phi/\Delta t$, where f is flux and t is time. For this problem, the right side is interpreted as the slope of the flux-time plot. (D) and (E) can be eliminated because zero slopes cannot produce nonzero ε. (B) and (C) are eliminated because both of these plots have the same sign of slope in the 0 to 2 s and 2 to 4 s regions, which cannot produce the bipolar ε required. Thus (A), with its alternation of slope polarity, is the answer.

52. **(A)** Using equilibrium, we sum the forces on the lid when it is removed.

$F + P_iA - P_aA = 0$, where F is the force, A is the area, P_i is the internal pressure, and P_a is the atmospheric pressure. Note that the internal pressure and the force both have the same sign because both are acting in a direction tending to remove the lid.

Solving, we obtain $P_i = P_a - F/A$.

53. **(E)** A free body diagram of the sphere is shown:

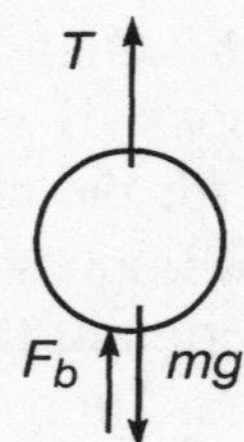

Here, T is the tension, F_b is the buoyant force, and mg is the weight. Since the sphere is in equilibrium, we can sum the vertical forces and write $T + F_b - mg = 0$. Solving, we obtain $T = mg - F_b$. But, by Archimedes' principle, F_b is equal to $gV\rho_2$, where V is the sphere volume and the subscript 2 refers to the fluid density. Also, $\rho_1 = m/V$, where the subscript 1 refers to sphere material density. Eliminate V by using the last expression, and we obtain $F_b = mg\frac{\rho_2}{\rho_1}$. Finally, substitute this back into the expression for T to get $T = mg - mg\frac{\rho_2}{\rho_1} = mg(1 - \frac{\rho_2}{\rho_1})$.

54. **(B)** One form of Bernoulli's equation is $P + (1/2)\rho v^2 + \rho gy$ = a constant. Here, the P-term is pressure, ρ is fluid density, v is fluid velocity, and y is elevation above some reference level. The equation was developed for incompressible fluid flow, so I is true. The second term accounts for kinetic energy of the flow, so II is true. The third term is associated with potential energy, so III is not true. Thus, the answers are I and II.

55. **(E)** Utilize $P = \rho gh$, with the left-hand side representing pressure and the right-hand side the product of density, acceleration of gravity, and depth. For this problem, we are given the height above ground level ($L/3$),

so the corresponding depth is $2L/3$. Plugging this in and solving, we obtain $P = 2\rho gL/3$.

56. **(D)** Since there are six sides to a cube, we must find the increase for one side and then multiply by six. The change in area for one side is the expanded area minus the unexpanded area. In equation form, $\Delta A = A_{T_2} - A_{T_1}$, where A represents area and the subscripts refer to the two temperatures. Area is given by the product of the edge length, and the expanded length is $L + \alpha L(T_2 - T_1)$. Given this, we can write, $\Delta A = [L + \alpha L(T_2 - T_1)]^2 - L^2$. After squaring the first term this reduces to $\Delta A = 2\alpha L(T_2 - T_1)$, as the L-squared terms cancel and the other squared term is negligibly small. Finally, the cube's area increase is six times this amount, or $12\alpha L(T_2 - T_1)$.

57. **(A)** I is not correct; the heat of vaporization of water is much higher than the heat of fusion. II is not correct; although ice must reach a certain temperature to melt (0° C), once it gets there the heat of fusion is independent of temperature. III is correct; if it takes a certain input of heat to melt the ice, that heat must be released when the reverse process of freezing occurs. Thus, only III is correct.

58. **(B)** The root-mean-square speed for molecules comprising an ideal gas is given by $v_{rms} = \sqrt{\frac{3RT}{M}}$, where R is the universal gas constant, T is the absolute temperature, and M is the molecular mass, which is the product of molecule mass and Avogadro's number. Reference to the formula indicates that tripling T will increase the speed by a factor of $\sqrt{3}$.

59. **(A)** The ideal gas law is given by $PV = nRT$, where P is pressure, V is volume, n is molar amount of gas, R is the gas constant, and T is absolute temperature. IV (internal energy) is the only parameter not explicitly cited in the expression.

60. **(B)** The units of R = 8.31 J/mol°K reveal that it is the energy required to heat one mole of gas one degree K.

61. **(A)** The correct answer is $(PV)^{\gamma}$ = a constant, an equation that can be derived from the first law of thermodynamics and the ideal gas law.

62. **(E)** By definition, a Carnot cycle consists of two adiabatic processes and two isothermal processes.

63. **(C)** The formula for efficiency (e) for a Carnot Engine is $e = (T_H - T_C)/T_H$, where all temperatures are in degrees K and the H and C subscripts refer to hot and cold, respectively. Evaluating, we have $e = (873 - 573)/873 = 0.34$. In terms of percent, the answer is 34%.

64. **(B)** I is incorrect because photon energy increases with frequency not wavelength, in accordance with $E = hf$ (the left-hand side representing photon energy and the right-hand side the product of Planck's constant and the frequency f). II is correct per the formula. III is correct, as demonstrated by $h = E/f$. Finally, IV is incorrect per the formula. Thus, II and III are correct.

65. **(E)** Using Einstein's photoelectric equation ($E = hf$) and the wave equation ($f = c/\lambda$), we obtain $\lambda = hc/E = (1.24 \times 10^3)/3 \approx 400$ nm.

In $E = hf$, the left-hand side represents photon energy and the right-hand side represents the product of Planck's constant and the frequency f. In $f = c/\lambda$, c represents the speed of light and λ, the wavelength.

66. **(A)** I is not true; the work function has the units of joules or electron-volts, both scalars. II is not true; for electron emission to occur, the photon energy must be larger than the work function. III is not true; metals generally have smaller work functions than non-metals, the alkali metals of Na and K being prominent examples. Thus, none of the statements are true.

67. **(C)** The uncertainty principle expressed in mathematical terms is $\Delta x \Delta p \approx h$, which means that the product of the momentum (p) and position (x) uncertainties (the Δ's) cannot be smaller than h, Planck's constant.

For this problem, the uncertainty in p is $\Delta p \approx h/\Delta x = \dfrac{6.63 \times 10^{-34}}{1 \times 10^{-6}} \approx 6.6 \times 10^{-28}$ kgm/s.

68. **(A)** Sound waves are longitudinal; they require a medium for propagation and have their direction of propagation parallel to the wave amplitude variations.

69. **(E)** The speed of sound is related to media properties by $v_s = \sqrt{\dfrac{B}{\rho}}$, where the left side is the speed of sound and the right side is the square root of the bulk modulus of the medium divided by the media density. The

bulk modulus is a measure of media elasticity. Thus, the answers are II and III.

70. **(E)** Note that only one of the answers is smaller than 30 degrees. Since the incident ray is passing from a less dense to a denser optical media, it will be bent toward the normal and thus be less than 30 degrees. Therefore, we can say the answer is 19 degrees with no calculations required.

DETAILED EXPLANATIONS OF ANSWERS

TEST 2

Section II

1. (a) Kinetic energy is given by $KE = \frac{1}{2}mv^2 = \frac{1}{2}\left(\frac{2}{9.8}\right)(15)^2 = 23$ J.

(b) All of the kinetic energy is eventually dissipated as work done by friction, so we can set the work done equal with the kinetic energy.

Thus, $W = F_f d = KE$, where F_f is the frictional force and d is the distance covered. Solving, $F_f = KE/d = 23/75 = 0.31$ N.

(c) Using $v = v_0 + at$ and $F = ma = F_f$, we proceed as follows:

Solving the second equation for a and plugging it into the first, we get

$$v = v_0 + \left(\frac{F_f}{m}\right)t.$$

Plugging in numbers gives us $0 = 15 + \left(\frac{-0.31}{2/9.8}\right)t.$

Solving, we get $t = 9.9$ s. Note that F_f was made negative in the above expression because its direction is opposite to the velocity.

(d) By definition, the coefficient of friction μ is given by the ratio of frictional force to normal force, or $\mu = F_f/N$, where N is the weight. Thus, $\mu = 0.31/2 = 0.16$.

2. (a)

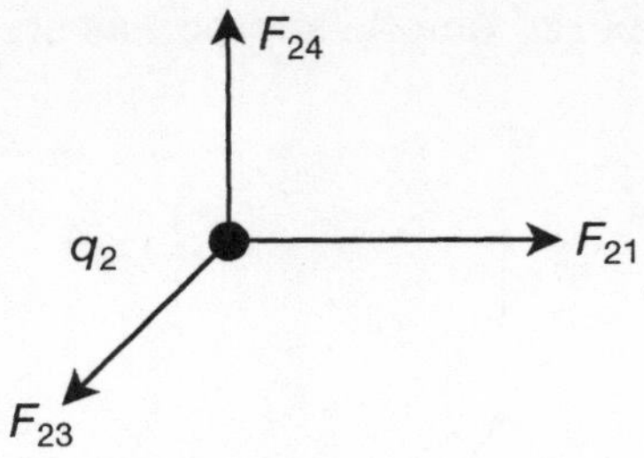

Note that the vector lengths are not to scale in this diagram. The sense of the vectors indicates attraction between like and repulsion between unlike charges. Direction is established as the line between the two charges. The first subscript number indicates the charge under consideration (2), and the second subscript number indicates the charge producing the force on charge number 2.

(b) This involves using Coulomb's Law for electrostatic force between two point charges.

In equation form: $F = \dfrac{kq_iq_j}{r^2}$, where the subscripts refer to the ith and jth charge, r is the distance between them and k is the electrostatic constant = (9×10^9) Nm²/C².

For this problem, we write $F = \dfrac{kq_1q_2}{r^2} =$

$$\frac{(9\times10^9)(5\times10^{-9})(2\times10^{-9})}{(9\times10^{-4})} = 0.0001 \text{ N}.$$

(c) The formula for potential is $V = \dfrac{kQ}{r^2}$ for a single point charge Q, where K is the electrostatic constant = (9×10^9) Nm²/C² and r is the distance from the charge to the point of interest. In principle, we can use superposition and find the potential for each of the four charges at point O and take the algebraic sum. However, the symmetry of the arrangement and value of the charges make this unnecessary. If the charges are viewed as equal and opposite pairs, it is clear that the potential from one charge cancels the potential from the other. Thus, by symmetry, the potential is 0.

(d) This problem is best solved by considering the vector diagram of the four forces acting on the test charge q. (Note that F_1 and

F_2 are superimposed on one another, as are F_3 and F_4, for a total of four vectors.)

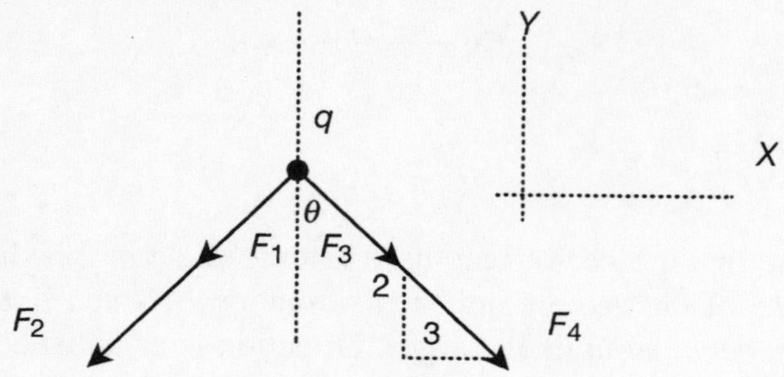

Note that the subscripts refer to the charge number at each corner and each force is understood to be acting upon a test charge q. The symmetry of the arrangement is such that the x-components all cancel. Thus, applying $\mathbf{E} = \mathbf{F}/q$ and using superposition, we are led to

$E = \dfrac{\Sigma F}{q} = \dfrac{F_1\cos\theta + F_2\cos\theta + F_3\cos\theta + F_4\cos\theta}{q}$, where θ is the angle between each vector and the y-axis. But, by Coulomb's law, $F = \dfrac{kq_iq}{r^2}$, where the subscript i refers to the ith charge.

Substituting into the summation, $E = \dfrac{kq_1q(2/\sqrt{13})}{r_1^2q} + \dfrac{kq_2q(2/\sqrt{13})}{r_2^2q} + \dfrac{kq_3q(2/\sqrt{13})}{r_3^2q} + \dfrac{kq_4q(2/\sqrt{13})}{r_4^2q}$, where $\cos\theta = \dfrac{2}{\sqrt{13}}$ was obtained from the geometry of the figure. Note that all the q's cancel.

Evaluating, we get $E = \dfrac{k(2/\sqrt{13})}{1}\left[\dfrac{q_1}{r_1^2} + \dfrac{q_2}{r_2^2} + \dfrac{q_3}{r_3^2} + \dfrac{q_4}{r_4^2}\right]$.

Using $k = (9 \times 10^9)$, $q_1 = 2$ nC, $q_2 = 5$ nC, $q_3 = 2$ nC, $q_4 = 5$ nC, and all the r-distances $= 1.8 \times 10^{-2}$ m, we can obtain a numerical value. Please note that the *magnitudes* of the charges are used, because the sign of the charges in producing either repulsion or attraction was taken into account by means of vector directions. Since all the y-components were seen to be additive, all the terms in this expression must also be additive.

Evaluating, we get $E = \dfrac{(9\times10^{9})(2/\sqrt{13})(2+5+2+5)(1\times10^{-9})}{(1.8\times10^{-2})^2}$

$= 2.2 \times 10^5$ V/m, which has a direction along the negative x-axis.

(e) The potential is zero because both of the q_1-q_3 and q_2-q_4 pairs are equidistant from the midway point with equal and opposite charges.

3. (a) The ε is zero because it is equal to the rate of change of flux, or $\varepsilon = \dfrac{\Delta\phi}{\Delta t}$. The ratio will be zero unless **B** is made to vary, either by rotating the loop or by causing **B** itself to change. Note that $\phi_m = BA$ in this instance, where A is the area enclosed by the loop.

(b)

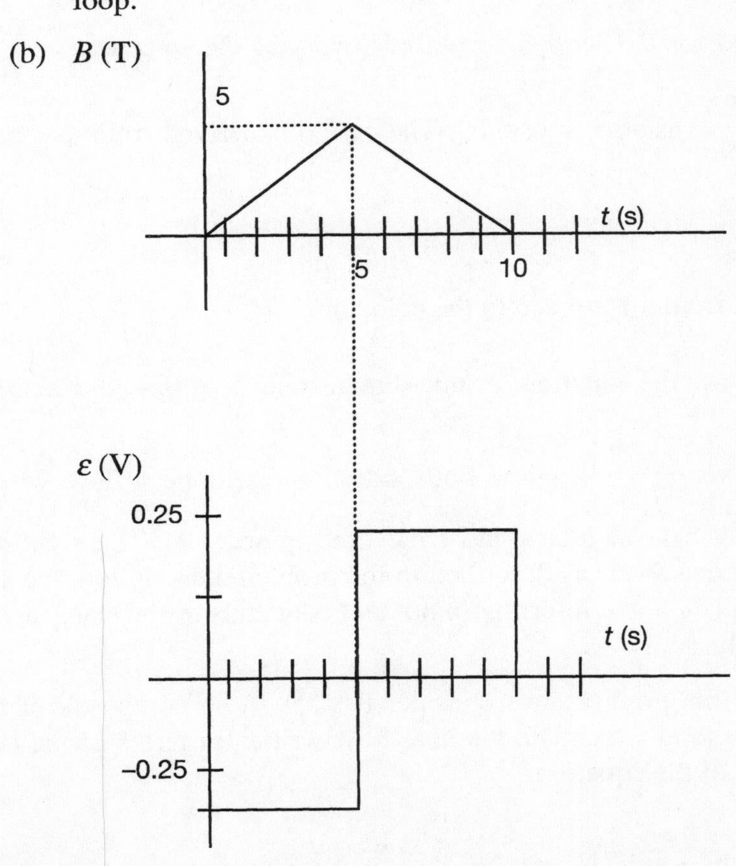

Using $\varepsilon = \frac{\Delta\phi}{\Delta t} = \frac{\Delta(BA)}{\Delta t}$, we obtain (0.25)(5 – 0)/5 = 0.25 for the 0 to 5 s region and (0.25)(0 – 5)/(10 – 5) = –0.25 for the 5 to 10 s region. The polarities are switched in the graph because the induced ε always opposes the change in flux in accordance with Lenz's law.

(c) ε will be reduced by a factor of $\frac{1}{\sqrt{2}} = 0.71$, because $\phi = BA\cos\theta$, where θ is the angle between **B** and a normal to the plane of the area. Thus, $\phi = BA\cos 45 = \frac{BA}{\sqrt{2}}$.

(d) It will be a sine wave with a period of $T = \frac{2\pi}{\sqrt{2}}$. The shape is known from $\phi = BA\cos\theta = BA\cos\omega t$, where ωt has been substituted for θ. Clearly, $\Delta\phi$ will also vary as the sine, so $\varepsilon = \frac{\Delta\phi}{\Delta t} = \frac{\Delta(BA)}{\Delta t}$ is also sinusoidal. The period is derived from $\omega = 2\pi f = \frac{2\pi}{T}$.

4. (a) It is from the hot end to the cold end.

(b) We use the equation for one-dimensional heat flow in a slab, $\frac{Q}{t} = kA\left[\frac{T_h - T_c}{L}\right]$, where both sides represent heat flow with Q being heat in joules and t the time in seconds. The right side contains terms as described in the problem description, the subscripts h and c referring to hot and cold ends of the slab, respectively.

For this problem, we consider the bar to be composed of two slabs, and we equate the heat flow written in terms of the right side of the equation.

Thus, $\frac{k_{30}A}{0.3}(200 - T_j) = \frac{k_{10}A}{0.1}(T_j - 0)$.

After canceling out the A's and solving, we arrive at $\frac{k_{30}}{3}(200 - T_j) = \frac{k_{10}}{1} T_j$, or $T_j = \frac{200}{\left(1 + \frac{3k_{10}}{k_{30}}\right)}$.

(c) $T_j = \frac{200}{\left(1 + \frac{3(400)}{800}\right)} = (200)/(2.5) = 80° \text{ C}.$

(d)

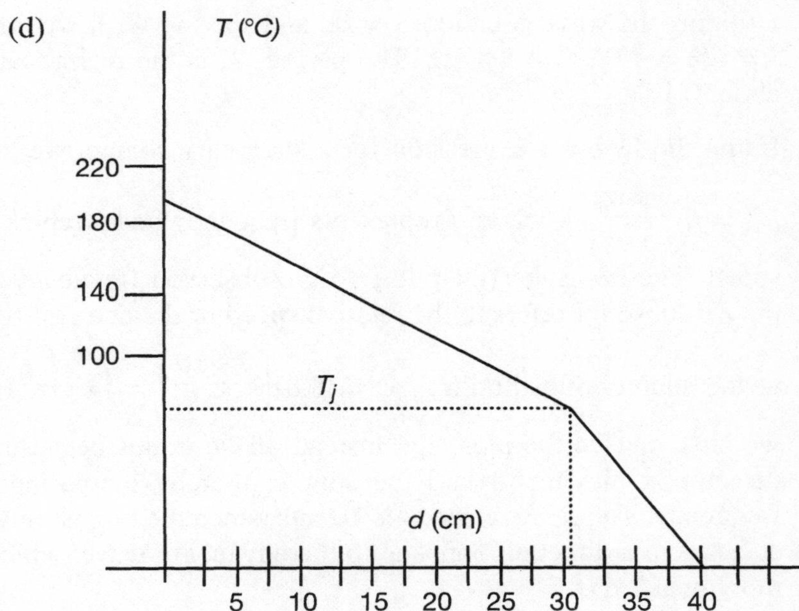

(e) Increasing k_{10} would decrease T_j, as reference to the expression developed for T_j in part (b) clearly indicates.

5. (a) The ground state corresponds to the $n = 1$ state. Utilizing parameters given and an h value of 4.14×10^{-15} eV, we get $E_1 = \frac{-(9.11 \times 10^{-31})(1.6 \times 10^{-19})^2}{8(8.85 \times 10^{-12})^2(4.14 \times 10^{-15})^2}\left(\frac{1}{1^2}\right) = -13.6$ eV. Note that, in general, $E_n = \frac{-13.6}{n^2}$.

(b) For this transition, we have $hf = E_3 - E_1 = \frac{-13.6}{3^2} - \left(\frac{-13.6}{1^2}\right) =$ 12 eV.

(c) According to Einstein's photoelectric theory, photon energy is $hf = \frac{hc}{\lambda}$, where λ in the denominator denotes wavelength. Solving for $\lambda = \frac{hc}{12} = \frac{(4.14\times10^{-15})(3\times10^{8})}{12} = 1.1 \times 10^{-7}$ m = 110 nm.

(d) The maximum energy occurs when n approaches ∞; so, in the limit, the maximum energy is zero.

6. (a) The wavelength is equal to the crest separation of 1.2 m.

(b) Utilizing the wave equation, $v = f\lambda$, and solving for f, we obtain $f = v/\lambda = 7.0/1.2 = 5.8$ Hz. The period, T, is the reciprocal, or about 0.17 s.

(c) Using the Doppler expression for a stationary source, we write $f_{obs} = f\left(\frac{v \pm v_{rel}}{v}\right)$, where f represents frequency and v represents speed. The *obs* subscript refers to the observed frequency and the *rel* subscript refers to the relative speed of the detector (bug) to the source. Substituting, $f_{obs} = (5.8)\left(\frac{7+10}{7}\right)$ = 14 Hz. Here we have chosen the plus sign instead of the minus because the detector is moving toward the source, thereby increasing the frequency. The relative speed is 10 m/s, since the bug is moving at 3 m/s in a direction opposite to the advancing wave, which is moving at 7 m/s.

(d) We again use the Doppler Expression $f_{obs} = f\left(\frac{v \pm v_{rel}}{v}\right)$. In this case, we alter the expression as follows: $1 = (5.8)\left(\frac{7 - v_{rel}}{7}\right)$. Here the left side is made equal to the required outcome and the minus is chosen, because the bug must be swimming *away* from the source in order for the frequency to decrease.

Solving, we get $v_{rel} = 7 - \frac{7}{5.8} = 5.8$ m/s. But this is a *relative* velocity; since the bug is swimming in the same direction as the advancing wave, we must take the difference, getting (7.0 – 5.8) = 1.2 m/s.

AP PHYSICS C

Test 3

AP PHYSICS C
Test 3: Electricity and Magnetism

Section 1

Time: 45 Minutes
35 Questions

DIRECTIONS: Each of the questions or incomplete statements below is followed by five answer choices or completions. Choose the best answer to each question.

1. Assume that $N_e > N_p > N_n$, where N is the number of charges. The net charge in coulombs produced by assembling N_e electrons, N_p protons, and N_n neutrons is

   (A) $(N_e - N_p)\ e$ and positive.

   (B) $(N_e - N_p)\ e$ and negative.

   (C) $(N_e + N_p)\ e$ and positive.

   (D) $(N_e + N_p)\ e$ and negative.

   (E) $(N_e - N_p - N_n)\ e$ and negative.

2. For the rectangular arrangement of charges shown, the equal charges q_1 on diagonal AB are each doubled, and the equal charges q_2 on diagonal CD are each tripled and made negative. The electric field **E** at the intersection of the diagonals is then

   (A) unchanged and greater than zero.

   (B) unchanged and less than zero.

   (C) changed and greater than zero.

   (D) unchanged and equal to zero.

   (E) changed and less than zero.

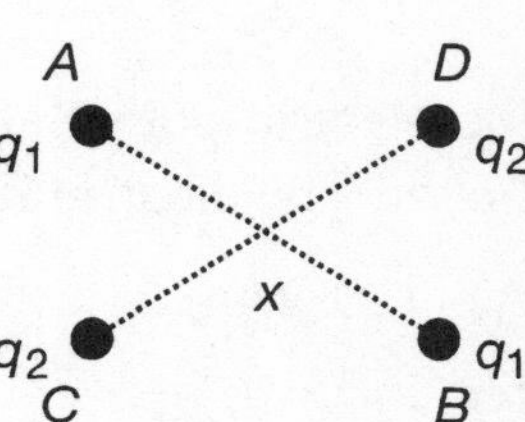

3. A 5-nanocoulomb charged particle with mass of 1 microgram is placed in a region of a vacuum with a uniform electric field of $E = 10$ V/m. After 10 seconds, the speed of the particle is

(A) 500 m/s.
(B) 700 m/s.
(C) 2500 m/s.
(D) 250 m/s.
(E) 125 m/s.

4. Which of the following statements pertaining to Gauss's law is (are) correct?

I – Any closed imaginary surface can be utilized to calculate the flux produced by a charge distribution.

II – Outward flux is proportional to the net charge enclosed by a closed surface.

III – Inward flux is proportional to the net charge outside a closed surface.

(A) I and II only
(B) I, II, and III
(C) I and III
(D) II only
(E) III only

5. A spherical metal shell of radius r is in a vacuum, carrying a charge of Q. The electric field E near its inner surface is

(A) $Q/4\pi\epsilon_0 r^2$ radially outward.
(B) $Q/4\pi\epsilon_0 r$ radially outward.
(C) $Q/4\pi\epsilon_0 r$ radially inward.
(D) zero.
(E) $Q/4\pi\epsilon_0 r^2$ radially inward.

6. The electric potential V as a function of distance r in a region is as shown. The electric field in the interval from 6 to 12 cm is

(A) 120 V/m.
(B) –120 V/m.
(C) 4 V/m.
(D) 400 V/m.
(E) –400 V/m.

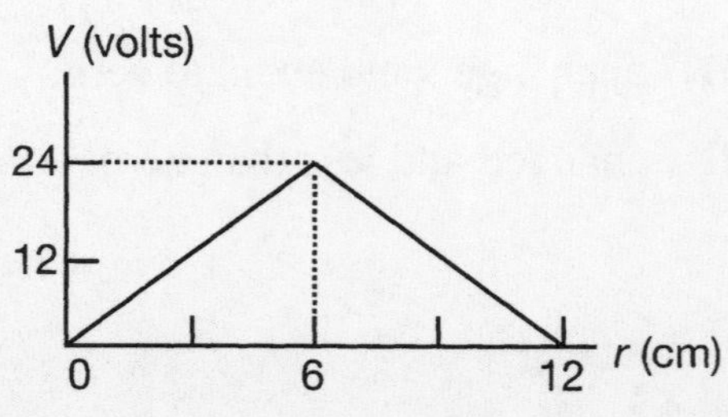

7. Four point charges lie in a straight line as shown, each separated by distance a. If the potential V midway between q_3 and q_2 is zero, then the charge q_3 is nearest

(A) 2.5 nC.

(B) 1.3 nC.

(C) –1.3 nC.

(D) –2.5 nC.

(E) –3.0 nC.

$q_4 = -5$ nC q_3 $q_2 = 3$ nC $q_1 = 4$ nC

8. The equivalent capacitance of the network shown is

(A) 3/7 μF.

(B) 7/3 μF.

(C) 4/7 μF.

(D) 7/4 μF.

(E) 1 μF.

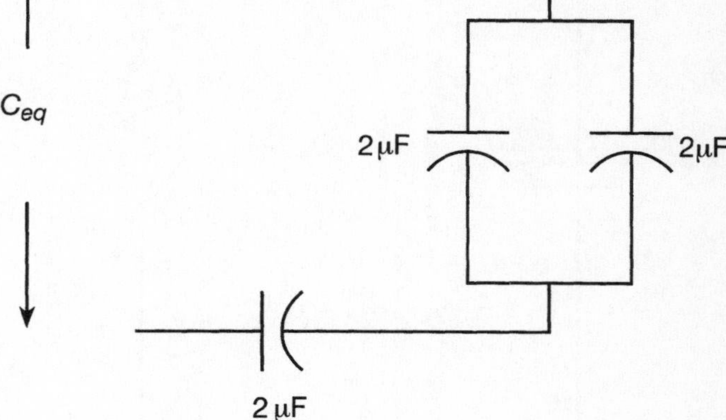

9. 100 volts is applied to the capacitive network as shown. The energy stored in all three capacitors is nearly

(A) 0.03 J.

(B) 0.01 J.

(C) 0.05 J.

(D) 0.07 J.

(E) 0.10 J.

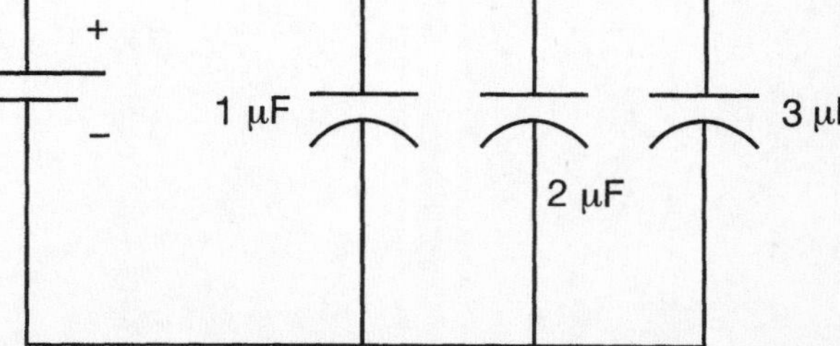

10. A parallel-plate capacitor in vacuum is charged by a battery. The space between the plates is then filled with a liquid dielectric with dielectric constant κ. The charge on the capacitor plates will

    (A) decrease by a factor of κ.

    (B) increase by a factor of κ.

    (C) remain the same.

    (D) decrease by a factor of κ^2.

    (E) increase by a factor of κ^2.

Refer to this circuit for problems 11, 12, and 13.

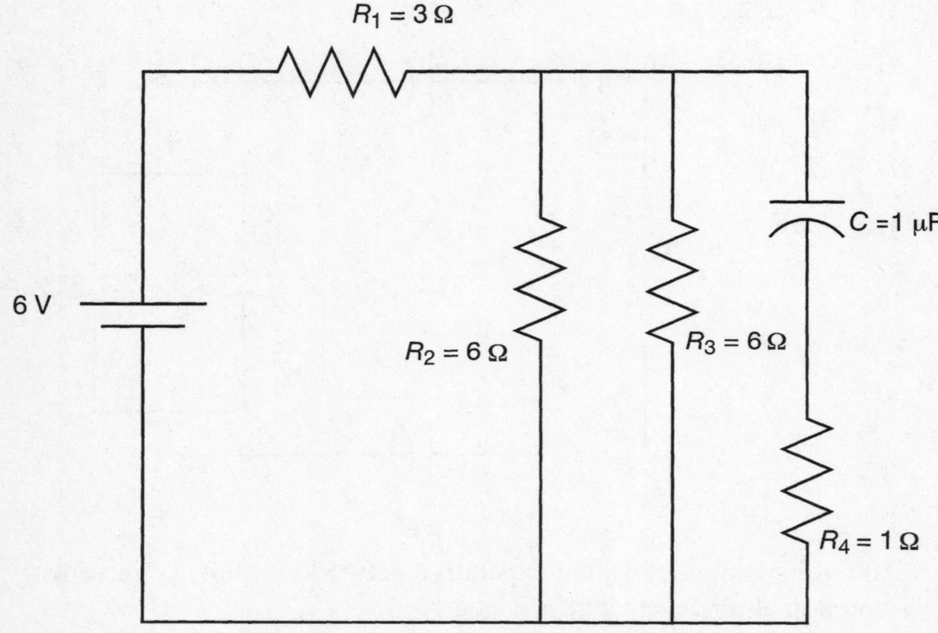

11. The steady-state current flowing out of the positive terminal of the battery is nearest

    (A) 0.5 A.

    (B) 2 A.

    (C) 1 A.

    (D) 1.5 A.

    (E) 3 A.

12. The potential difference across R_2 is nearest

(A) 3 V.
(B) 2 V.
(C) 1 V.
(D) 5 V.
(E) 0 V.

13. After a long time, the current through R_4 will be nearest

(A) 2.0 A.
(B) 1.5 A.
(C) 0.5 A.
(D) 0 A.
(E) 1.0 A.

Refer to the schematic shown for problems 14 and 15.

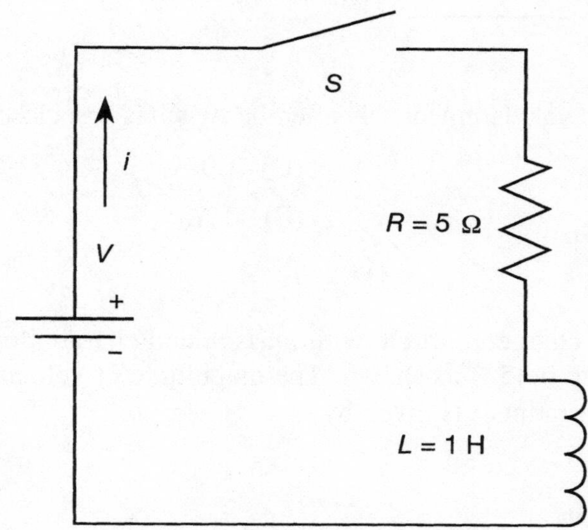

14. Determine which of the following general shapes of current (I) versus time (t) plots is correct. (Assume that switch S is closed at $t = 0$.)

(A) 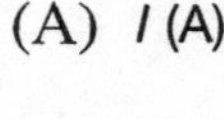

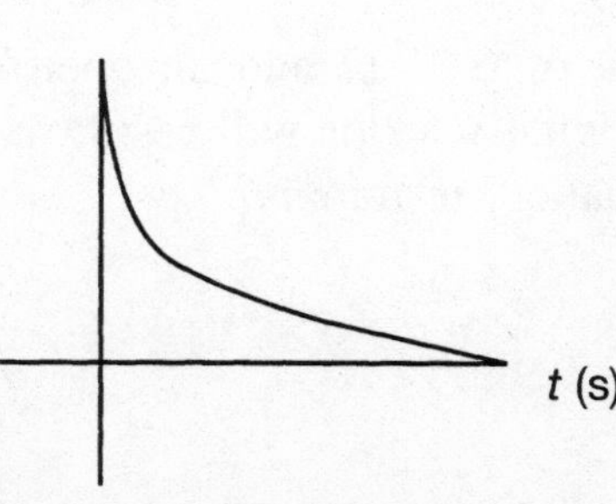

(D) 

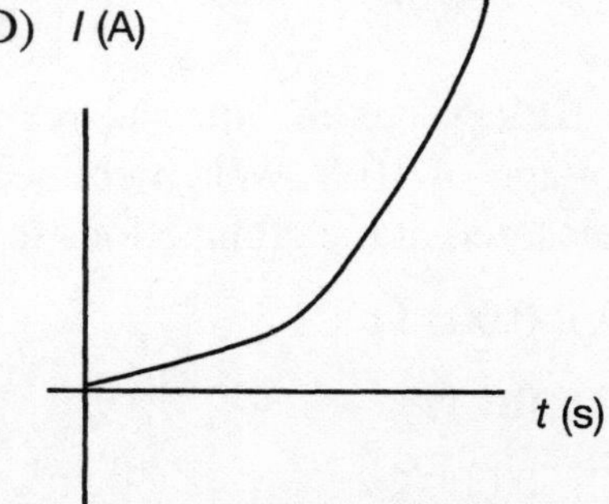

(B) I (A)

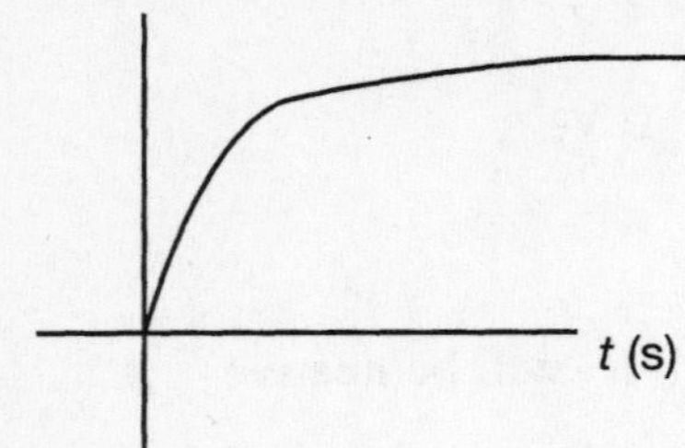

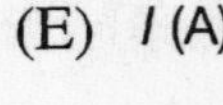

(E) I (A)

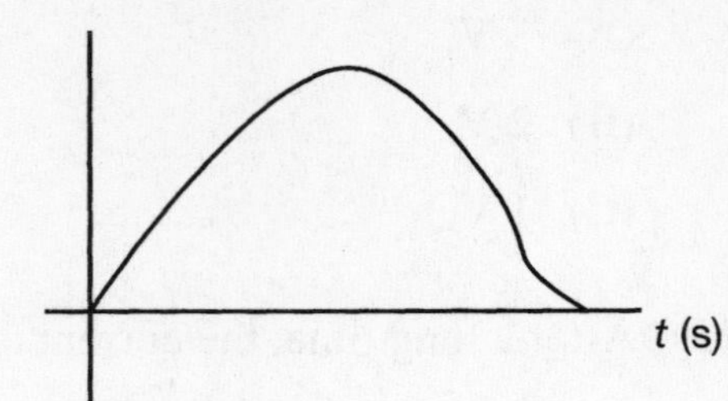

(C) I (A)

t (s)

15. The current value immediately after the switch is first closed is nearest

(A) 2.0 A.
(B) 10 A.
(C) 5.0 A.
(D) 1.0 A.
(E) 0 A.

16. A moving charged particle with mass m and charge q enters a region of magnetic field **B** as shown. The magnitude of velocity, v, required for circular radius r is given by

(A) m/qBr.
(B) $2qBr/m$.
(C) qBr/m.
(D) $qBr/2m$.
(E) $2m/qBr$.

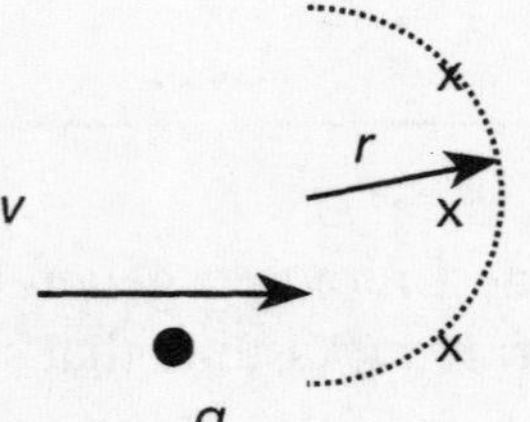

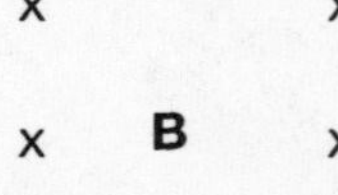

17. A battery has an internal resistance of 0.01 Ω and an open circuit voltage of 10 V. When connected, what resistor will result in 9.9 V measured at the connections to the battery terminals?

(A) 0.001 Ω
(B) 0.1 Ω
(C) 0.009 Ω
(D) 0.99 Ω
(E) 9.9 Ω

18. Two parallel wires are separated by a distance r, and each carries current I flowing in opposite directions. If the distance between the wires is halved and the current doubled, the force acting on each wire will then be

(A) 8 times larger and mutually repulsive for both wires.

(B) 8 times larger and mutually attractive for both wires.

(C) 4 times larger and mutually repulsive for both wires.

(D) 4 times larger and mutually attractive for both wires.

(E) 16 times larger and mutually attractive for both wires.

19. Which of the following statements is (are) correct regarding the magnetic field of a long current-carrying wire?

I – The field forms closed loops of flux around the wire.

II – The field strength is directly proportional to radial distance from the wire.

III – The field strength is directly proportional to the square of the current.

(A) I and II

(B) I only

(C) I and III

(D) II only

(E) III only

20. A toroidal solenoid with radius r and N turns has an internal magnetic field B produced by current I flowing in its windings. The value of the current is

(A) $2\pi Br/N^2$.

(B) $2\pi Br$.

(C) $2\pi BrN$.

(D) $2\pi Br/\mu_0 N$.

(E) $2\pi BrN^2$.

21. A spherical capacitor has a formula for its capacitance value $C = 4\pi\epsilon_0 \frac{ab}{b-a}$, where a and b represent the radii of the spherical surfaces. (Assume that $b > a$). Which of the following statements is (are) true?

I – Decreasing b will increase C.

II – Increasing b will increase C.

III – Decreasing a will increase C.

(A) II only
(B) III only
(C) II and III
(D) I only
(E) None of these

22. The total magnetic flux cutting through a loop is given by $\phi_m = 6t^2 + 4t - 3$. The magnitude of induced EMF in the loop at $t = 4$ s is

(A) 116 V.
(B) 52 V.
(C) 49 V.
(D) 24 V.
(E) 66 V.

23. Which of the following statements about Lenz's law is (are) NOT true?

I – The direction of induced current flow in a closed conducting loop always opposes the flux change that produced it.

II – The direction of induced current flow in a closed conducting loop always supports the flux change that produced it.

III – Lenz's law is an alternative statement of the conservation of energy.

(A) II only
(B) I only
(C) All are true
(D) I and III
(E) III only

24. An inductor of $L = 3$ mH has a steady-state current of 12 A flowing through it. The energy stored in the associated magnetic field is about

(A) 0.16 J.
(B) 0.04 J.
(C) 0.07 J.
(D) 0.22 J.
(E) 0.46 J.

25. Which of the following statements is (are) true regarding flux lines for electric fields?

I – Flux lines bunch together where the field is strongest.

II – Flux lines never cross.

III – Flux lines originate on negative charges and terminate on positive charges.

(A) I only
(B) II only
(C) I and III
(D) II and III
(E) I and II

26. Two nonconducting balls, each of mass m and charged to q_1, are suspended from threads as shown. The balls are mutually repelling one another and in static equilibrium. The separation distance between centers is r, thread length is L, and the separation distance is small compared to L. Identify the expression that is equal to r.

(A) 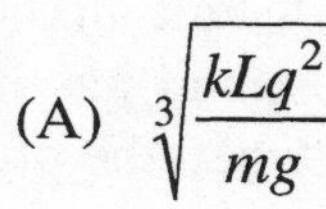

(B) $(kmq^2)/L^2$

(C) 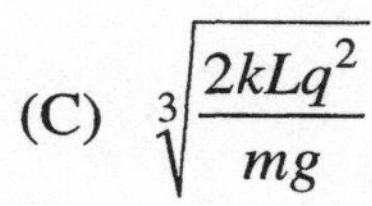

(D) $(kmq^2)/L$

(E) $(kmq^2)/2L^2$

27. A 500 Ω resistor has a potential difference of 50 V across its terminals. The power dissipated is nearly

(A) 5 W.
(B) 1 W.
(C) 10 W.
(D) 2.5 W.
(E) 7 W.

28. A current of 8 mA is flowing in a wire. The number of electrons passing through the wire's cross section each second is nearly

(A) 3×10^{14}.
(B) 3×10^{19}.
(C) 5×10^{12}.
(D) 5×10^{19}.
(E) 5×10^{16}.

29. A cube is oriented and totally immersed in a magnetic field region as shown. The magnetic field **B** is parallel to the cube's top-face diagonal AC as shown. The net flux cutting face $CDEF$ is

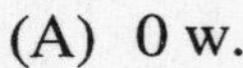
(A) 0 w.

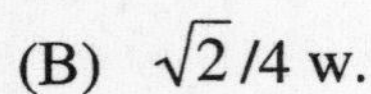
(B) $\sqrt{2}/4$ w.

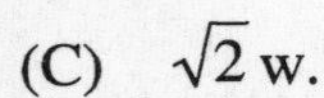
(C) $\sqrt{2}$ w.

(D) $2/\sqrt{2}$ w.

(E) $\sqrt{2}/2$ w.

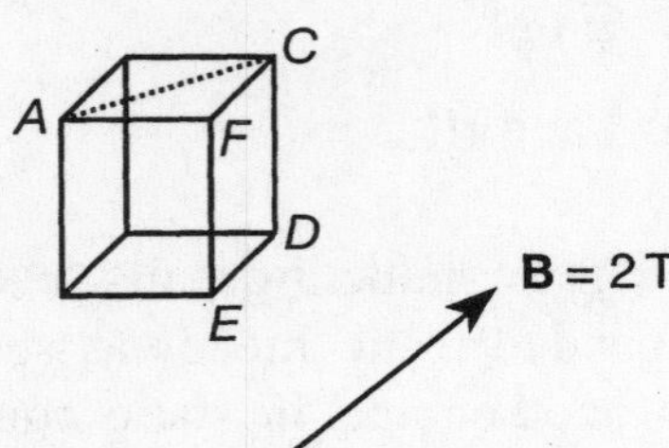

30. A proton is moving in a straight line, approaching a distant unknown positive fixed charge Q. If the proton starts from rest and has mass m_p, the separation distance between the two particles when the proton slows to a stop is

(A) $\sqrt{\dfrac{2ekQ}{m_p v^2}}$.

(B) $\dfrac{m}{2ekQ}$.

(C) $\dfrac{2ekQ}{m}$.

(D) $2ekQ$.

(E) $\dfrac{2ekQ}{m_p v^2}$.

31. Which of the following statements is (are) correct?

I – A magnetic field can be produced by a time-varying electric field.

II – A magnetic field can be produced by any electric current.

III – A magnetic field can be produced by any electric field.

(A) II only

(B) I and II

(C) III only

(D) II and III

(E) I and III

32. A capacitor is charged to 0.04 μC by an 8 V battery. The capacitance is nearly

(A) 2 pF.
(B) 5 pF.
(C) 2 nF.
(D) 5 nF.
(E) 5 μF.

33. A 10-mH inductor has a current of $I = 10 \sin(40t)$ passing through it. The magnitude of the peak potential difference across L is

(A) 4 V.
(B) 40 V.
(C) 0.1 V.
(D) 1.0 V.
(E) 10 V.

34. The combination of units equivalent to a tesla (T) is

(A) N/Am.
(B) N/A.
(C) N/Cm.
(D) Am/N.
(E) A/N.

35. 20 W of power are dissipated in an 80 Ω resistor. The potential difference across the resistor is

(A) 20 V.
(B) 40 V.
(C) 10 V.
(D) 80 V.
(E) 100 V.

AP PHYSICS C
Test 3: Electricity and Magnetism

Section II

TIME: 45 Minutes
3 Free-Response Questions

DIRECTIONS: Carefully read each question and then make sure to answer *each part* of the question. You must show your work. Crossed out work will not be graded. You will lose credit for incorrect work that is not crossed out.

1. A spherical volume charge distribution is given by $\rho = k_1 r^{2/3}$, where r is the radial distance from the distribution center and k_1 is a constant. The distribution is valid for the region $0 < r < R$, where R is the cutoff point beyond which the charge density is zero.

   (a) Find the total charge enclosed in a sphere with radius R.

   (b) Develop an expression in terms of r and R for the electric field E for $r > R$.

   (c) Develop an expression in terms of r and R for the electric potential V for $r > R$.

   (d) Develop an expression in terms of r and R for the electric field E for $0 < r < R$.

   (e) On the axes provided, graph E for both regions of r. Indicate the value of E when $r = R$ on the graph. Also, indicate values when $r = 0$ and when $r = \infty$.

2. A circuit consisting of an inductor L, a capacitor C, a resistor R, a battery V, and two switches $S1$ and $S2$ is as shown. Initially, both $S1$ and $S2$ are in the open position as shown, and the capacitor is uncharged.

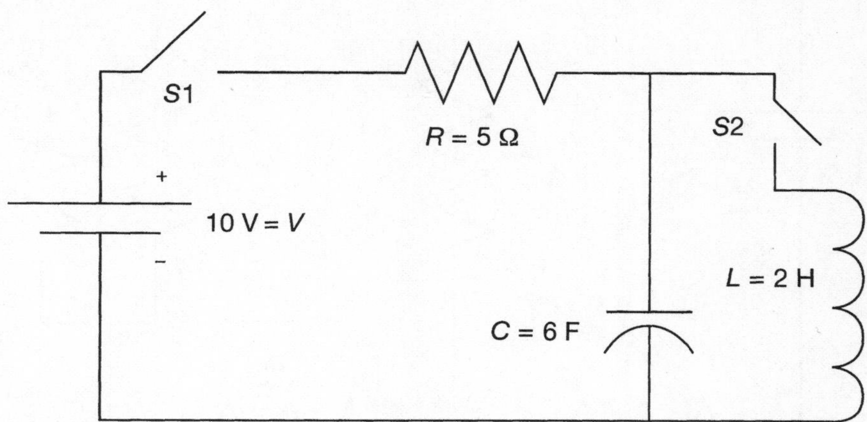

(a) With $S1$ closed and $S2$ open, what is the initial current through the capacitor?

(b) With $S1$ closed and $S2$ open, what is the current through the 5 Ω resistor after one hour?

(c) With $S1$ closed and $S2$ open, what is the current through R and C in terms of V, R, C, and time t?

(d) With $S1$ closed and $S2$ open, calculate the time required for the current to reach 0.5 A.

(e) With C fully charged, $S1$ is opened. $S2$ is then closed. Describe the circuit behavior in terms of the voltage across the parallel combination of L and C.

3. A circuit consisting only of resistors is as shown. The symbols and names for a variety of instruments and circuit elements are also shown in the accompanying table.

Instrument/Element	Symbol
Voltmeter	—(V)—
Ammeter	—(A)—
Shorting Lead	————
Switch	__S__

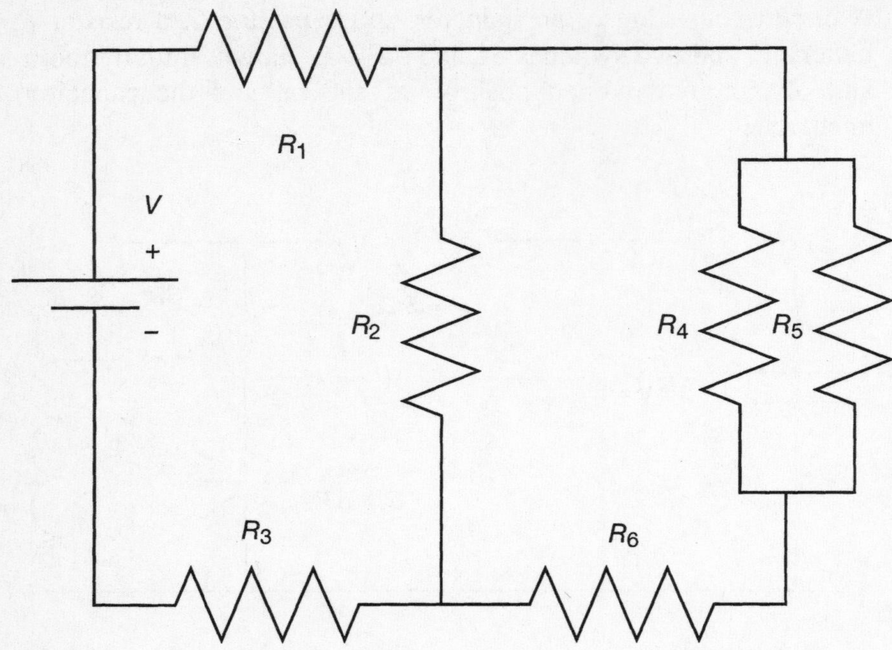

(a) Draw a sketch of how you would connect an instrument of your selection to measure the battery voltage V.

(b) Draw a sketch of how you would connect an instrument of your selection to measure *total* battery current.

(c) Which resistors are known for sure to have equal currents?

(d) Draw a sketch or describe how you would modify the circuit so as to interrupt the current flow through R_2 only.

(e) The table shown below gives known values of current, voltage drop, and resistance for each resistor in the circuit. From these values, calculate the values of the missing table entries. Also determine battery voltage V.

Resistor ID	Volt Drop (V)	Current (mA)	Resistance (kΩ)
R_1		2.1	1.0
R_2	3.6		
R_3	4.2		
R_4		0.45	2.0
R_5		0.45	
R_6	2.7		3.0

Battery Voltage = ____________

AP PHYSICS C
TEST 3

Section I

ANSWER KEY

1.	(B)	10.	(B)	19.	(B)	28.	(E)
2.	(D)	11.	(C)	20.	(D)	29.	(D)
3.	(A)	12.	(A)	21.	(D)	30.	(E)
4.	(A)	13.	(D)	22.	(B)	31.	(B)
5.	(E)	14.	(B)	23.	(A)	32.	(D)
6.	(D)	15.	(E)	24.	(D)	33.	(A)
7.	(D)	16.	(C)	25.	(E)	34.	(A)
8.	(C)	17.	(D)	26.	(C)	35.	(B)
9.	(A)	18.	(A)	27.	(A)		

DETAILED EXPLANATIONS OF ANSWERS

TEST 3
Section I

1. **(B)** Neutrons have no charge, so answer (E), which includes the number of neutrons, is incorrect. Since electrons and protons have equal and opposite charges, they will cancel one another, leaving a surplus charge (in this case, of electrons, which are negative).

2. **(D)** Before any changes are made, the field at point x is zero. It is clear if the like charges are considered in pairs that a test charge at point x will have no net force on it, since the like charges will produce equal and opposite force pairs. Superposition allows us to do this analysis, adding the effect of each charge pair to get the total effect. The doubling and tripling (along with negation of the latter) does not change the argument. The net force is still zero, so the field must be zero in accordance with $\mathbf{E} = \mathbf{F}/q$, the defining equation for electric field.

3. **(A)** Since $F = ma$, substitute for F in $E = \dfrac{F}{q} = \dfrac{ma}{q}$. In $v = v_0 + at$, $v_0 = 0$ and, solving for a, we find that $a = v/t$. Plugging this into the above equation, we obtain $E = \dfrac{mv}{qt}$.

Solving for v, we get $v = \dfrac{qEt}{m} = \dfrac{(5\times10^{-9})(10)(10)}{(1\times10^{-9})} = 500$ m/s.

4. **(A)** III is ruled out because an exterior charge produces no net flux for a closed Gaussian surface. Since flux is directly proportional to the enclosed charge and any shape of closed surface can be used, both I and II are true.

5. **(E)** Use Gauss's law as follows: $\oint \mathbf{E} \bullet d\mathbf{A} = Q/\epsilon_0$. The left side indicates that flux is computed according to the dot product of **E** and unit-vectors to the surface elemental areas. The right side indicates that the flux is equal to the total enclosed charge Q divided by the permittivity of free space. For this problem, we choose a concentric spherical Gaussian surface only slightly larger than the metal sphere that encloses the total charge Q. Thus, the left side becomes $E\oint dA = E(4\pi r^2)$, E being numerically constant everywhere and the term under the integral being the surface area of the sphere. Setting this equal to the right side, we obtain $E(4\pi r^2) = Q/\epsilon_0$. Solving for E, we get $E = Q/4\pi\epsilon_0 r^2$. Its direction is inward because a positive test charge would be attracted to the spherical charge distribution and point towards the center.

6. **(D)** The relationship between E and V is $E = -dV/dr$: the electric field is given by the negative of the potential function's slope. For this problem, the slope in the 6 to 12 cm region is $-(24/6) = -4$ V/cm, or -400 V/m. Negating this result yields the answer 400 V/m.

7. **(D)** The approach here is to use the formula $V = \frac{1}{4\pi\epsilon_0}\sum_i \frac{q_i}{r_i} = k\sum_i \frac{q_i}{r_i}$ and solve for the unknown charge. Letting $V = 0 = \frac{kq_1}{(1.5)a} + \frac{kq_2}{(0.5)a} + \frac{kq_3}{(0.5)a} + \frac{kq_4}{(1.5)a}$. After canceling out k's and a's, and multiplying both sides by 1.5, we are left with $V = 0 = \frac{q_1}{1} + \frac{3q_2}{1} + \frac{3q_3}{1} + \frac{q_4}{1}$. Substituting the charge values, we obtain $V = 0 = 4 + 3 + q_3 - 5$. Therefore, $q_3 = 5 - 7 = -2$ nC, which is nearest -2.5 nC.

8. **(C)** The circuit can be reduced to three capacitors in series. These are C_1, C_{23}, and C_4. C_{23} represents the parallel combination of C_2 and C_3, and equals 4 μF. To find the equivalent capacitance of these three series capacitors we use $\frac{1}{C_{eq}} = \sum_i \frac{1}{C_i}$. For this (reduced) circuit, three terms are involved as follows: $\frac{1}{C_{eq}} = \frac{1}{1} + \frac{1}{4} + \frac{1}{2} = \frac{7}{4}$. Therefore, the equivalent capacitance is 4/7 μF.

9. **(A)** Because all the capacitors are in parallel, they each have 100 volts applied. We then use $U_C = \frac{1}{2}CV^2$ for each capacitor and sum the results. (U_C is the energy in joules.) Thus, $U_C = \frac{1}{2}(1 \times 10^{-6})(10^4) + \frac{1}{2}(2 \times 10^{-6})(10^4) + \frac{1}{2}(3 \times 10^{-6})(10^4) = 0.03$ J.

10. **(B)** The capacitance for capacitors is given by two formulas. The first relates capacitance to electrical parameters and is $C = Q/V$, where Q is the charge on the plates and V is the potential difference across the plates. The second formula relates capacitance to physical parameters and is $C = \kappa\epsilon_0 A/d$, where κ is the dielectric constant of the fill material, ϵ_0 is the permittivity of free space, A is plate area, and d is separation distance. For this problem, we make use of both as follows.

Before filling with dielectric, we can write $C = \epsilon_0 A/d = Q_b/10$, where the voltage of 10 has been plugged in and the subscript b represents charge conditions before adding the dielectric. Note that κ in this instance has a value of 1.

After filling with dielectric, we can write $C = \kappa\epsilon_0 A/d = Q_a/10$, where the subscript a represents the charge after filling with dielectric. If the latter equation is divided on both sides by the former, it is clear that the charge must increase by a factor of κ, i.e., $\frac{Q_a}{Q_b} = \kappa$.

11. **(C)** Under "steady-state" conditions in this circuit, one can consider the capacitor to be completely charged, so the branch containing the 1 μF capacitor and 1 Ω resistor does not enter into the calculation. The circuit can then be reduced to two resistors in series, which in turn can be added to find the equivalent resistance of the entire circuit. This, in turn, can be used to find the current by Ohm's law. First, to find the resistance of the parallel combination of 6-Ω and 6-Ω, we utilize $\frac{1}{R_{23}} = \sum_i \frac{1}{R_i} = \frac{1}{6} + \frac{1}{6} = \frac{1}{3}$. Thus, $R_{23} = 3\ \Omega$. Then, to find the resistance of the series combination of R_1 and R_{23}, we add 3 and 3 to get $R_{eq} = 6\ \Omega$. Finally, to find the total current, we use Ohm's law and divide $R_{eq} = 6\ \Omega$ into 6 V, arriving at 1 A.

12. **(A)** The voltage drop, or potential difference, across the resistor R_2 is given by $V_2 = I_2R_2$. Solving, we get $V_2 = (0.5)(6) = 3$ V. The value for a current of 0.5 A is obtained by noting that the battery current splits into two equal parts in the 6 Ω resistors.

13. **(D)** After a long time, the capacitor in the branch containing it will have completely charged (a "long time" being a time much longer than the RC time-constant of the series combination). Thus, no current will be flowing in the branch, and the answer is zero.

14. **(B)** We use $\varepsilon = -L\frac{dI}{dt}$ to solve this problem. (This is the expression relating inductor voltage to inductance (L) and current rate of change (dI/dt). The presence of the negative sign indicates that the voltage is in opposition to the product of $L\frac{dI}{dt}$.)

When the switch is closed, the derivative term is maximum, causing 10 V of polarity opposite the battery to appear across L. Thus, the current is zero at that time. This observation rules out (A) and (C). At a much later time, the derivative term is zero, so the voltage drop across L is zero. This means that all 10 V are dropped across the 5 Ω resistor, and a DC current of 2 A flows in the circuit. Inspection of the remaining choices shows that only (B) satisfies the conditions.

15. **(E)** See discussion for problem 14.

16. **(C)** We use the Lorentz force expression $\mathbf{F}_M = q\mathbf{v} \times \mathbf{B}$. The magnitude of $\mathbf{F}_M$ is $qvB \sin 90° = qvB$. But this is also a centripetal force and, according to Newton's second law, $F_c = \frac{mv^2}{r}$. Equating qvB to the right side of the second equation and solving for v, we get $v = (qBr)/m$.

17. **(D)** In order for 9.9 V to appear across the load, the voltage drop across the internal resistance must be 0.1 V. This implies a battery current of $I = V/R = 0.1/.01 = 10$ A. Thus, the smallest resistance that can be connected to the battery is $R = V/I = (9.9)/10 = 0.99$ Ω.

18. **(A)** We make use of the formulas $\mathbf{F} = \int I d\ell \times \mathbf{B}$ and $B = \frac{\mu_0 I}{r}$. The former provides the force F exerted on a wire section $d\ell$, carrying current

I due to field **B**. The latter provides the field as a function of distance r for a wire carrying current I. It is clear from the second equation that doubling the current will double the field. Halving the distance will also double the field. Since both are done, the field is increased by a factor of 4. However, the current was also doubled in the other wire, so the net increase in force is 8 times. As for direction, use of the right hand rule for parallel currents in opposite directions shows that the force is repulsive.

19. **(B)** Statement I is correct, so it must be contained in the answer, eliminating (D) and (E). Neither II nor III are correct, as the relation between B, distance from the wire, and current is given by $B = \mu_0 I/r$. Thus, B varies inversely with distance and directly with current, not the square of current.

20. **(D)** Use is made of Ampere's law $\oint \mathbf{B} \bullet d\ell = \mu_0 I$ by taking a line integral around a circular path along the toroid's axis. Because the **B** and the $d\ell$ vectors are everywhere parallel on this path, in taking the dot product the left side becomes $B\oint d\ell = B(2\pi r)$. On the right side, I is interpreted as the net current enclosed by the amperian loop. For this problem, it is NI. Solving for I, we obtain $I = 2\pi rB/\mu_0 N$.

21. **(D)** It is helpful to rewrite the expression for C as follows: $C = 4\pi\epsilon_0 \frac{a}{1-\frac{a}{b}}$. (To obtain this expression, divide both numerator and denominator of the rightmost term by b.) In considering I and II, we see that a decrease in b will make the denominator smaller, so C will increase. Conversely, an increase in b will decrease C. Thus I will increase C, but II will not. By dividing both the numerator and denominator on the right side of the original formula by a, we arrive at a similar expression. By testing III, we see that decreasing a will make the denominator larger, thereby decreasing C. Thus, the answer is (D).

22. **(B)** We make use of Faraday's law, which states that the induced voltage in a loop is equal in magnitude to the time derivative of the flux cutting the loop. Taking the derivative of the flux function, we obtain $\frac{d\phi_m}{dt} = 12t + 4$. Plugging in $t = 4$ s, we get 52 V.

23. **(A)** Lenz's law states that the polarity of the induced voltage produced by a change in magnetic flux is always such that it opposes the

change in flux. I summarizes this statement, so it can be ruled out. II contradicts it, so the answer must contain II. III is true, because if the induced polarity change were such that it supported the change in flux, a regenerative spiral of increasing current/flux would result, violating the conservation of energy. Thus, only II is incorrect.

24. **(D)** The energy stored in an inductor is given by $U_L = \frac{1}{2}LI^2$. For this problem, the calculation is $U_L = \frac{1}{2}(3 \times 10^{-3})(144) = 0.22$ J.

25. **(E)** Flux lines cannot cross; if they did, there would be two different directions of E at a single point, which is physically impossible. By definition, they bunch together where the field is strongest, but they originate on positive, not negative, charges.

26. **(C)** Refer to the free-body diagram of one of the balls.

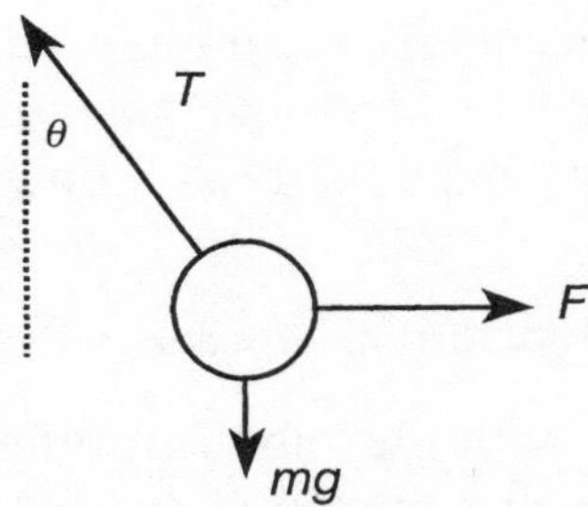

Since the ball is in equilibrium, we can write equations in both the vertical and horizontal direction. In the vertical direction, $T \cos \theta = mg$. In the horizontal direction, $T \sin \theta = F$. Taking the ratio of horizontal forces to vertical forces, we obtain $(\sin \theta)/(\cos \theta) = \tan \theta = \frac{F}{mg}$. But, since θ is small, it can be approximated by $\theta \approx \frac{r/2}{L}$, where r is the separation distance and L is length of string. Using Coulomb's law, the force F is given by $F = \frac{kq^2}{r^2}$, where k is a constant. Substituting this for F in the equation obtained earlier, we arrive at $\frac{r}{2L} = \frac{kq^2}{mgr^2}$. Solving, we get $r = \sqrt[3]{\frac{2Lkq^2}{mg}}$.

27. **(A)** The formula for power dissipation is $P = I^2R = V^2/R = IV$. Using the second version, we get $P = 2500/500 = 5$ W.

28. **(E)** By definition, current $I = dQ/dt$, which has units of amperes or coulombs/second. Also, the electronic charge e^- is 1.6×19^{-19} C. Thus, if I is 8 mA, then the number of electrons passing a given point in the circuit in one second is $\dfrac{8 \times 10^{-3}}{1.6 \times 10^{-19}} = 5 \times 10^{16}$.

29. **(D)** Flux is computed by using the formula $\phi_m = \int \mathbf{B} \cdot d\mathbf{A}$, where B is the magnetic field strength and A is the area. For this problem, the magnitude of the dot product under the integral is everywhere $B \cos 45°$ $dA = \dfrac{BdA}{\sqrt{2}}$. Thus, the flux is given by $\phi_m = \dfrac{B}{\sqrt{2}} \int dA$, because B is constant. But the integral term is simply the area of face $CDEF$ and equal to 1 m^2. Thus, the total flux is $\phi_m = (2/\sqrt{2})(1) = 2/\sqrt{2}$ webers.

30. **(E)** At the point of closest separation, all of the proton's kinetic energy has been converted to electrical potential energy. By equating these energies, the distance can be found as follows.

At the point of smallest separation, we can write $\frac{1}{2}m_pv^2 = eV$. The left side is the kinetic energy, with the subscript referring to the proton. The right side is the product of proton charge and potential, which equals the potential energy. But the potential itself can be written as $V = \dfrac{kQ}{r}$, where k is a constant, Q is the fixed charge, and r is the separation distance. Plugging this into the above equation, we arrive at $\frac{1}{2}m_pv^2 = \dfrac{ekQ}{r}$. Solving for r, we obtain $r = \dfrac{2ekQ}{m_pv^2}$.

31. **(B)** A magnetic field can be produced by either a time-varying electric field or an electric current. These observations are outcomes of Maxwell's equations, with the former attributable to Maxwell's law of induction and the latter to Ampere's law. However, a magnetic field cannot be produced by any electric field, a static **E**-field being the prime example. Thus, only I and II are correct.

32. **(D)** Using $C = \frac{Q}{V}$ and substituting the numbers given, we get $C = \frac{4 \times 10^{-8}}{8} = 5 \times 10^{-9}$ F or 5 nF.

33. **(A)** Faraday's law states that $\varepsilon = -L\frac{dI}{dt}$. Taking the derivative magnitude, we get $E = (1 \times 10^{-2})(400\cos 40t)$. The peak occurs when the cosine term is one. Thus, the peak voltage is 4 V.

34. **(A)** This is a problem in unit conversion. From the Lorentz expression for force on a charged particle moving through a magnetic field of $B = F/qv$, we can obtain units for the tesla, which is the measure of magnetic field B. In terms of units, we have T = N/(C m/s) = N/Am, as by definition an A is equivalent to C/s.

35. **(B)** The formulas for power dissipation in a resistor are $P = I^2R = V^2/R = IV$. Choosing the second version, we write $20 = V^2/80$. Solving, we get $V = 40$ V.

DETAILED EXPLANATION OF ANSWERS

TEST 3

Section II

1. (a) Choosing a spherical shell as a differential volume element, we can write $dq = 4\pi r^2\ (k_1 r^{2/3})dr$. We then integrate this expression over the radial distance to obtain $Q_{tot} = \int_0^R 4\pi r^2 (k_1 r^{2/3})dr =$

$4\pi k_1 \int_0^R r^{8/3}dr = 4\pi k_1 \left(\frac{3}{11}\right) R^{11/3} = \frac{12\pi k_1 R^{11/3}}{11}$.

(b) For a spherical distribution, all the charge can be considered to be concentrated into a point charge at the center of the sphere. Use can then be made of $E = \frac{kQ}{r^2}$ as follows: $E = \frac{k(12\pi k_1 R^{11/3})}{11r^2}$,

where $k_1 = \frac{1}{4\pi\epsilon_0}$.

(c) Similarly, the potential can be derived from all the charge considered as a point charge at the center of the sphere by using $V = \frac{kQ}{r}$. Thus, $E = \frac{k(12\pi k_1 R^{11/3})}{11r}$.

(d) Using Gauss's law, we choose a spherical surface concentric with the distribution of charge with radius $r < R$. Mathematically, we write $\oint \mathbf{E} \bullet d\mathbf{A} = Q/\epsilon_0$, where the dot product summed by the integral represents total flux and the right-hand side is the charge enclosed by the sphere divided by the permittivity of free space.

For this problem, we write $E(4\pi r^2) = \frac{1}{\epsilon_0}\int_0^r 4\pi k_1 r^{8/3}dr =$

$\frac{4\pi k_1}{\epsilon_0}\frac{3}{11}r^{11/3}$. After rearranging and canceling out 4π on both sides, we are left with $E = \dfrac{12k_1r^{5/3}}{(11)(4\pi)\epsilon_0} = \dfrac{12\pi}{11}kk_1r^{5/3}$, since $\dfrac{1}{4\pi\epsilon_0} = k$.

We note in passing that the expression developed under (b) above yields an identical result when $r = R$, as it must.

(e)

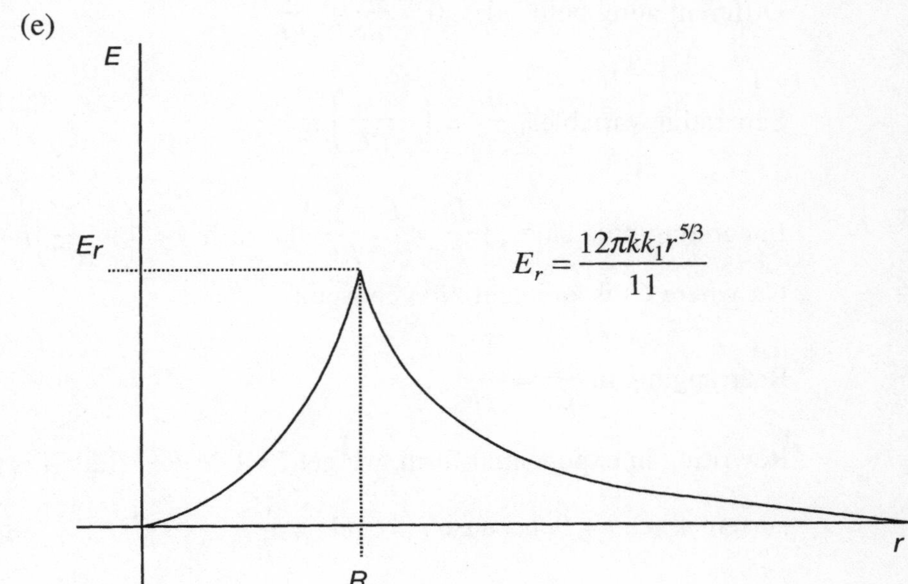

2. (a) Applying Kirchhoff's law to the circuit loop, we obtain $V = IR + \dfrac{1}{C}\int Idt$. But right after the switch is closed, no charge has accumulated on the capacitor, so the integral term is zero. Thus, all of the battery volts are dropped across R. Therefore, the current is $I = \dfrac{V}{R} = 10/5 = 2$ A.

(b) The time constant of the above circuit is $\tau = \dfrac{1}{RC} = \dfrac{1}{(5)(6)} = 0.03\ \text{s}^{-1}$, so the time for it to completely charge the capacitor will be no greater than $5RC$*, or about 150 seconds. This is much less than 1 hour = 3600 seconds, so the capacitor is completely charged. Thus, the current is zero.

(c) Applying Kirchhoff's law to the loop, we obtain $V = IR + \frac{1}{C}\int I dt$.

Differentiating both sides, $0 = \frac{dI}{dt} + \frac{1}{RC}I$.

Separating variables, $\frac{dI}{I} = \left(-\frac{1}{RC}\right)dt$.

Integrating both sides, $\int \frac{dI}{I} = \left(-\frac{1}{RC}\right)\int dt$ or $\ln I = \left(-\frac{1}{RC}\right)t + \ln C_1$, where C_1 is an integration constant.

Rearranging, $\ln \frac{I}{C_1} = -\frac{t}{RC}$.

Rewriting in exponential form, we get $I = C_1 e^{-t/RC}$. But C_1 is the current when $t = 0$, because $I = C_1(1) = \frac{V}{R}$.

Finally, $I = \frac{V}{R}e^{-t/RC}$.

(d) Substituting 0.5 A into the expression derived in (c), we get $0.5 = \frac{10}{6}e^{-t/30}$. Rearranging, we obtain $0.3 = \frac{1}{e^{t/30}}$, or $e^{t/30} = 3.3$.

Thus, $t = 30\ln(3.3) = 35.8$ s.

(e) The parallel LC combination will sinusoidally resonate at its natural frequency. The frequency can be found by writing Kirchhoff's law for the loop as follows:

* This general rule is derived from the general expression for current in this type of circuit, $I = \frac{V}{R}e^{-t/RC}$. For $t = 5RC$, the exponential term is nearly zero.

$$0 = \frac{1}{C}\int I dt + L\frac{dI}{dt}.$$

Taking the derivative of both sides, we obtain $0 = \frac{d^2I}{d^2t} + \frac{1}{LC}I.$

The natural frequency is the square root of the coefficient of the I term and is given by $\omega_n = \sqrt{\frac{1}{LC}}$ with a value of about 0.3 rad/s, corresponding to $f = \omega / 2\pi = 0.045$ Hz.

Alternatively, a sketch of a sine curve will show how the voltage will vary. Ideally, the frequency or period will be included.

3. (a)

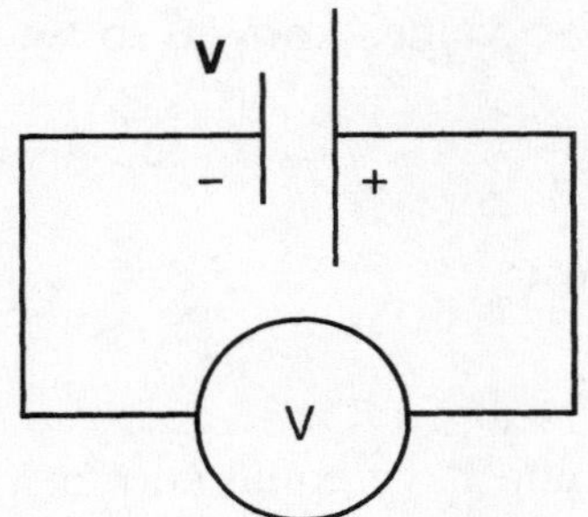

(b)

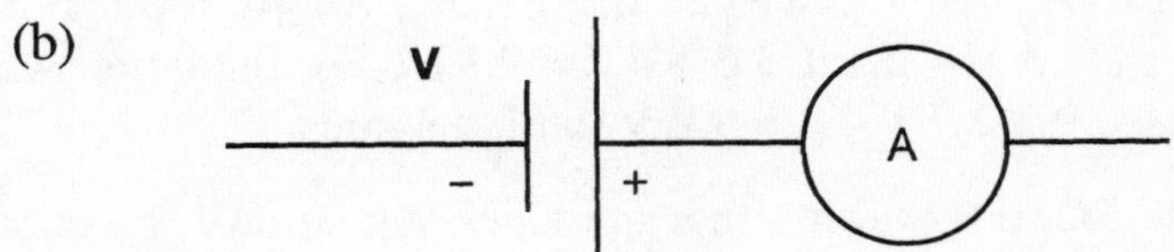

(c) R_1 and R_3, because they both have the total battery current passing through them, irrespective of their values.

(d) Disconnecting one end of the resistor will interrupt the current flow. Either end is okay.

Alternatively, a switch could be installed in series with the resistor and put into the open position.

(e)

Resistor ID	Volt Drop (V)	Current (mA)	Resistance (kΩ)
R_1	**2.1**	2.1	1.0
R_2	3.6	**1.2**	**3.0**
R_3	4.2	**2.1**	**2.0**
R_4	**0.9**	0.45	2.0
R_5	**0.9**	0.45	**2.0**
R_6	2.7	**0.9**	3.0

Battery voltage = **9.9 V**

The values are obtained by successive use of $V = IR$ and Kirchhoff's laws for summing currents into a junction and voltage drops around a loop. (Unknown values are shown in **bold** for clarity.)

R_1, R_4, and R_6 all have two values known, so by using $V = IR$, we find

$$V_1 = (2.1)(1) = 2.1 \text{ V}$$

$$V_4 = (0.45)(2.0) = 0.9 \text{ V}$$

$$I_6 = (2.7)/3 = 0.9 \text{ mA}$$

R_4 and R_5 are in parallel and have equal currents, so they must have the same resistance value and voltage drop.

Battery voltage can be found by adding up the voltage drops around the R_1, R_2, R_3 loop or the R_1, R_4, R_6, R_3 loop. For the former, we get $V = 2.1 + 3.6 + 4.2 = 9.9$ V. For the latter, we get $V = 2.1 + 0.9 + 2.7 + 4.2 = 9.9$ V, which agrees.

I_2 can be found by noting that the algebraic sum of the currents into the junction connecting R_1 and R_3 must be zero. Thus, $I_1 = I_2 + I_4 + I_5$. Substituting values, we obtain $2.1 = I_2 + 2(0.45)$. Thus, $I_2 = 1.2$ mA, and $R_2 = 3.6/1.2 = 3$ kΩ.

Finally, $I_3 = 2.1$ mA by inspection, because the return battery current must be the same as the outgoing battery current, I_1. Thus, $R_3 = 4.2/2.1 = 2.0$ kΩ.

AP PHYSICS C

Test 4

AP PHYSICS C
Test 4: Mechanics

Section I

Time: 45 Minutes
35 Questions

DIRECTIONS: Each of the questions or incomplete statements below is followed by five answer choices or completions. Choose the best answer to each question.

Refer to the vector diagram for questions 1, 2, and 3.

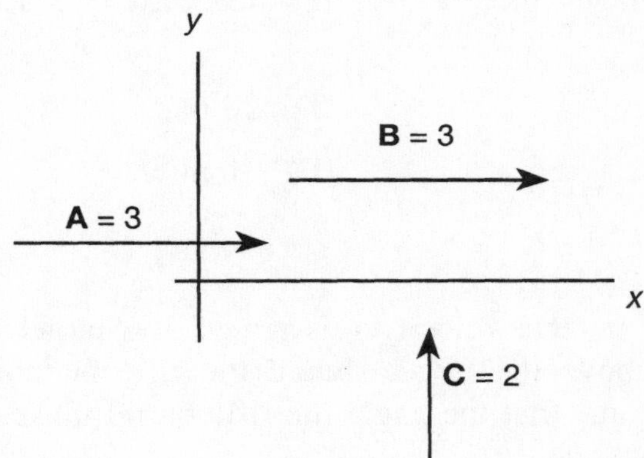

1. The magnitude of (**A** – **B** – **C**) is

(A) $2\sqrt{3}$.
(B) $4\sqrt{2}$.
(C) 8.
(D) 2.
(E) 1.

2. The direction of (**A** – **B** – **C**) is

(A) to the right and parallel to the x-axis.
(B) to the left and parallel to the x-axis.
(C) up and parallel to the y-axis.

(D) down and parallel to the y-axis.

(E) 45 degrees measured counterclockwise from the positive x-axis.

3. The vector cross-product **C** × **B** is

(A) a zero-magnitude vector.

(B) a vector of magnitude 6 pointing perpendicular into the paper.

(C) a vector of magnitude 6 pointing perpendicular out of the paper.

(D) a vector of magnitude 6 pointing parallel to the paper and to the right.

(E) a vector of magnitude 6 pointing parallel to the paper and to the left.

4. The position in meters of an object is given by $x = 3t^2 - 2t$. The object's average velocity over the interval $t = 2$ seconds to $t = 5$ seconds is

(A) 15 m/s.

(B) 28 m/s.

(C) 19 m/s.

(D) 18 m/s.

(E) 10 m/s.

5. A rifle with muzzle velocity v is aimed at a target r meters away. How high above the target should the rifle be pointed to hit its center? (Assume that the angle the rifle barrel makes with the horizontal is small.)

(A) $\sqrt{2g/r^2v}$

(B) $2v^2/gr^2$

(C) gr/v^2

(D) $5gr^2/2v$

(E) $gr^2/2v^2$

6. Which of the following statements about free-falling bodies in air is (are) true?

I – Acceleration is constant throughout the trajectory.

II – Terminal velocity depends only on the mass of the object falling.

III – Terminal velocity depends on both the mass and shape of the object falling.

(A) III only
(B) II only
(C) I and II
(D) I and III
(E) None of these

7. A 5-kg block is pushed up a frictionless plane by horizontal force F. The block accelerates at 5 m/s^2. The magnitude of F is nearest

(A) 50 N.
(B) 70 N.
(C) 35 N.
(D) 90 N.
(E) 125 N.

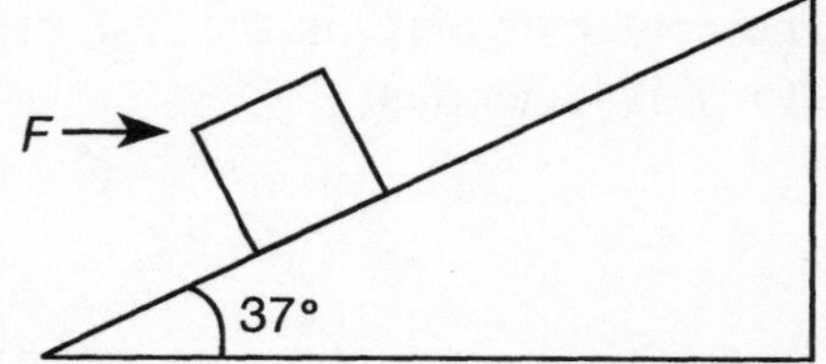

8. Three chain links that hang vertically are accelerated upward at 3 m/s^2 by a single vertical force applied to the topmost link. If the mass of a single link is 1 gram, the contact force between the top link and the middle link is nearly

(A) 0.075 N.
(B) 0.035 N.
(C) 0.045 N.
(D) 0.013 N.
(E) 0.026 N.

9. An object is moving in a straight line on a horizontal frictionless surface. A force applied to the object varies as shown in the figure. The total work done is about

(A) 1120 J.
(B) 400 J.
(C) 820 J.
(D) 320 J.
(E) 560 J.

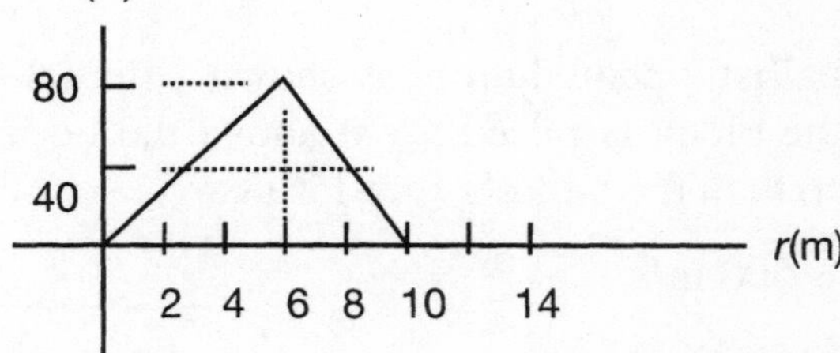

10. The power developed by a certain engine is given by $P = 6t^2 - 7t + 4$, where t is the time after initiation of power. At what time is the engine power a minimum?

    (A) 1 s
    (B) 3/4 s
    (C) 1/12 s
    (D) 7/12 s
    (E) 5/12 s

11. The center of mass in the X-Y plane for a wire of length 8ℓ bent as shown is located at

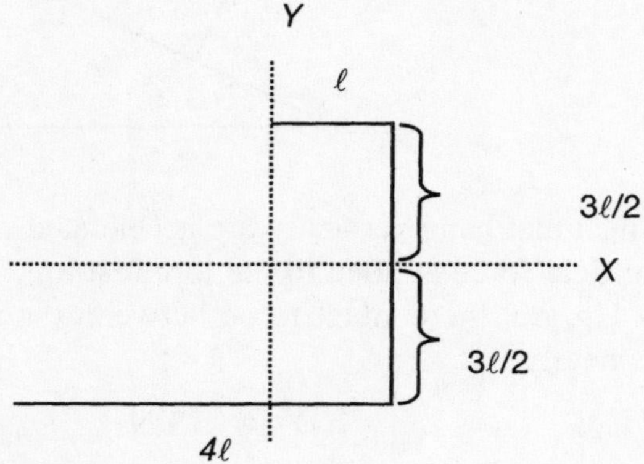

    (A) $\overline{X} = (-5/16)\ell, \overline{Y} = (-11/16)\ell$
    (B) $\overline{X} = (-1/16)\ell, \overline{Y} = (-9/16)\ell$
    (C) $\overline{X} = (-7/16)\ell, \overline{Y} = (-9/16)\ell$
    (D) $\overline{X} = (-7/16)\ell, \overline{Y} = (9/16)\ell$
    (E) $\overline{X} = (-3/16)\ell, \overline{Y} = (9/16)\ell$

12. A ballistic pendulum is as shown with a 1-gram bullet approaching. If the block is raised 5 cm above the horizontal by the bullet's impact, then the bullet's speed is nearly

    (A) 500 m/s.
    (B) 5000 m/s.
    (C) 800 m/s.
    (D) 2000 m/s.
    (E) 1000 m/s.

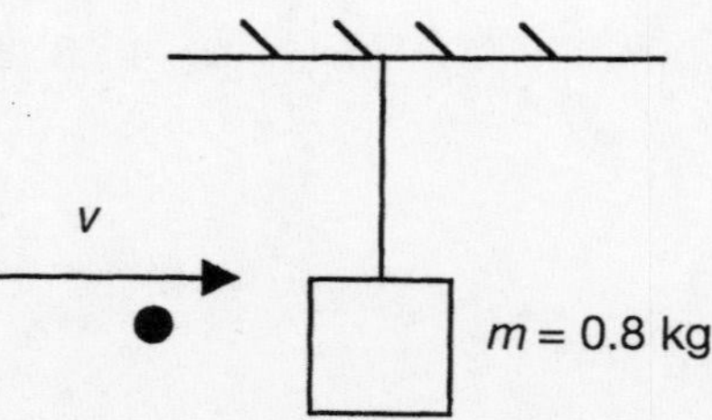

13. Which of the following statements about rotational moment of inertia is (are) correct?

    I – It is defined only for systems of discrete particles.

    II – It is the same for all axes.

    III – Both mass and its distribution relative to a given axis determine the value of the moment of inertia.

    (A) I and III
    (B) I and II
    (C) I only
    (D) III only
    (E) II only

14. The angular speed for a bus traveling at 72 km/hr going around a circular curve with radius 100 m is about

    (A) 0.1 rad/s.
    (B) 0.2 rad/s.
    (C) 0.4 rad/s.
    (D) 0.6 rad/s.
    (E) 0.8 rad/s.

15. The objects shown have velocities and masses as indicated. All vectors lie in the plane of the page and both velocities are perpendicular to the radius vectors. The magnitude of the total angular momentum about a perpendicular axis through *O* is nearly

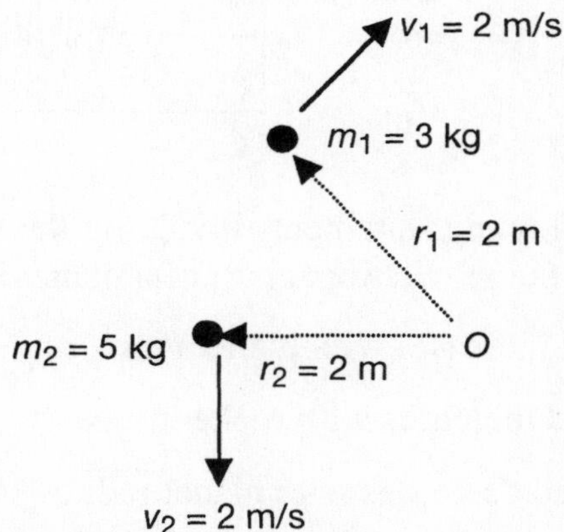

    (A) 32 kgm²/s.
    (B) 0 kgm²/s.
    (C) 16 kgm²/s.
    (D) 20 kgm²/s.
    (E) 8 kgm²/s.

16. An Atwood machine is shown. The mass of m_1 is 5 kg and m_2 is 10 kg. The pulley has negligible friction and inertia, and the coefficient of friction on the surface is 0.2. The acceleration of the blocks is nearly

(A) 2 m/s^2.

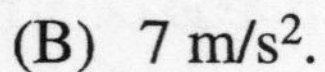
(B) 7 m/s^2.

(C) 3 m/s^2.

(D) 6 m/s^2.

(E) 1 m/s^2.

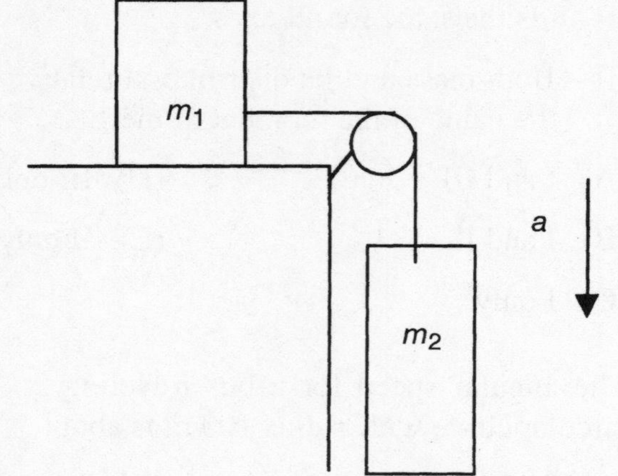

17. A mass-spring system is oscillating on a horizontal surface as shown. Friction is negligible. The frequency of oscillation is

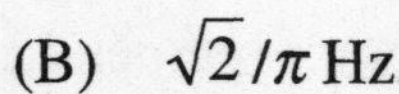
(A) $10\sqrt{2}/\pi$ Hz.

(B) $\sqrt{2}/\pi$ Hz.

(C) $\sqrt{2}/10$ Hz.

(D) $10\sqrt{2}$ Hz.

(E) $5\sqrt{2}/\pi$ Hz.

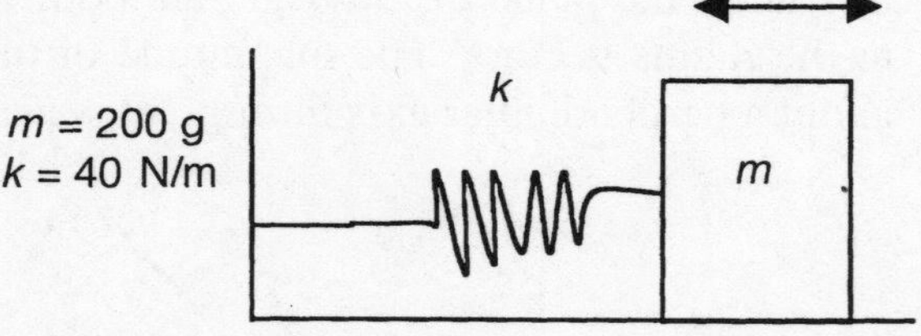

18. Which of the following statements involving the speed required for a rocket to escape the gravitational pull of a planet is (are) correct?

I – Escape speed increases with planet mass.

II – Escape speed increases with rocket mass.

III – Escape speed decreases with planet radius.

IV – Escape speed increases with planet radius.

(A) I and II

(B) I only

(C) I and III

(D) III only

(E) I and IV

19. A large spherical shell is made up of material of density ρ and has a volume V. A distant second mass m is r units away from the sphere center. The gravitational attractive force between both masses is given by

(A) $GV\rho m/r^2$.
(B) $G\rho m/r^2$.
(C) GVm/r^2.
(D) $GV\rho m/r$.
(E) $GV^2\rho m/r$.

20. Two point masses are r units apart. The force acting on m_1 is tripled when it is repositioned relative to the second mass m_2. If the second mass was halved just before repositioning, the new separation distance is

(A) $r/6$.
(B) $r/\sqrt{6}$.
(C) $r/\sqrt{3}$.
(D) $r/3$.
(E) $r/2$.

21. A canoe is paddled against the current in a river for 10 minutes while moving 600 meters of distance as measured on shore. If the river current is 0.5 m/s, the canoe's speed, when paddling with the current, will be nearly

(A) 0.5 m/s.
(B) 1.0 m/s.
(C) 1.5 m/s.
(D) 2.0 m/s.
(E) 2.5 m/s.

22. A 5-g mass is attached to a fish line of length 1 m with tensile strength of 0.5 N. It is then swung in a circle lying in the vertical plane. The angular speed at which the line will break is nearest

(A) 9.3 rad/s.
(B) 7.5 rad/s.
(C) 5.2 rad/s.
(D) 2.1 rad/s.
(E) 4.1 rad/s.

23. Two balls of unequal mass experience a glancing elastic collision as shown. If m_1's velocity is 7 m/s at an angle 30 degrees from its original direction after the collision, m_2's velocity magnitude after the collision is nearly

(A) 6 m/s.

(B) 8 m/s.

(C) 10 m/s.

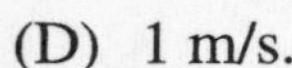
(D) 1 m/s.

(E) 2 m/s.

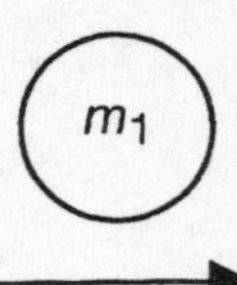

$v_1 = 10$ m/s $\quad v_2 = 0$ m/s

$m_1 = 20$ g $\quad m_2 = 10$ g

24. The potential energy for a particle moving in one dimension is given by $U(x) = 6x^2 - 3x + 4$. The magnitude of the force acting on the particle when $x = 0.5$ m is

(A) 6 N.

(B) 7 N.

(C) 3 N.

(D) 4 N.

(E) 5 N.

25. The drag coefficient for a free-falling body in air is 0.2 Ns/m. If the mass of the falling body is 50 g, the terminal velocity is nearest

(A) 22 m/s.

(B) 6.2 m/s.

(C) 2.5 m/s.

(D) 9.8 m/s.

(E) 4.9 m/s.

26. A body initially at rest experiences an acceleration as shown. After 3 seconds the velocity magnitude is

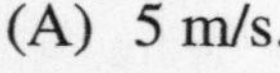
(A) 5 m/s.

(B) 2 m/s.

(C) 1 m/s.

(D) 4 m/s.

(E) 3 m/s.

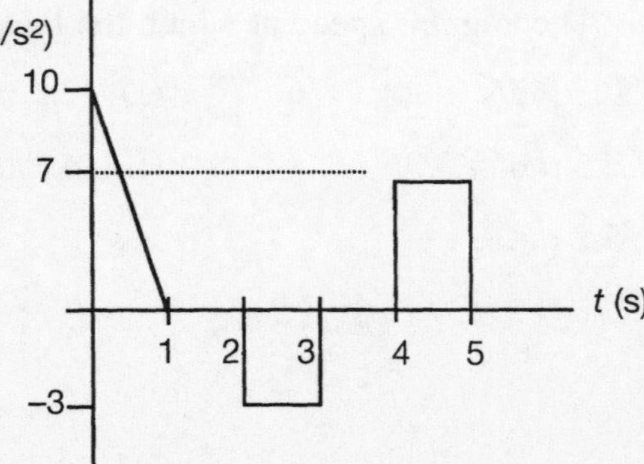

27. Which of the following statements as applied to collisions is (are) INCORRECT?

I – Momentum is always conserved.

II – Kinetic energy is not always conserved as kinetic energy.

III – Inelastic collisions never involve a joining of the colliding masses.

(A) I only
(B) III only
(C) II and III
(D) I and III
(E) I and II

28. A wheel is rotating at an angular speed of 120 rev/min. It is then uniformly braked to rest over a period of 10 seconds by a braking torque of 50 Nm. The moment of inertia of the wheel is about

(A) 200 m^2kg.
(B) 125 m^2kg.
(C) 300 m^2kg.
(D) 350 m^2kg.
(E) 80 m^2kg.

29. The frequency of an oscillating body is 5000 Hz. The corresponding period is

(A) 0.4 ms.
(B) 0.6 ms.
(C) 1.2 ms.
(D) 0.1 ms.
(E) 0.2 ms.

30. A block with mass *m* slides down a 37° plane at constant speed. The coefficient of friction between the block and plane is nearly

(A) 0.30.
(B) 0.50.
(C) 0.75.
(D) 0.40.
(E) 0.10.

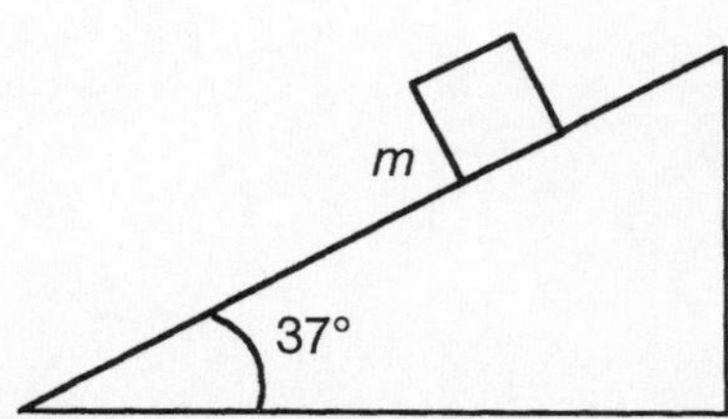

31. Which of the following statements about the coefficient of friction is (are) true?

I – The coefficient of friction is a dimensionless quantity.

II – The numerical value of the coefficient of friction is always greater than one.

III – The coefficient of friction is inversely proportional to the normal force.

(A) I and II
(B) II and III
(C) I only
(D) I and III
(E) II only

32. The acceleration due to gravity on planet X is 4 times that on Earth (i.e., it is $4g$). If planet Y is three times as massive as planet X and has a radius 3 times larger than planet X, its acceleration of gravity is

(A) $4g$.
(B) $(4/3)g$.
(C) $(3/4)g$.
(D) $(4/9)g$.
(E) g.

33. A nonlinear spring has a characteristic of $F = 9x^{3/2}$, where F is the force in newtons and x is the elongation of the spring in meters. The work done to stretch the spring from $x = a$ to $x = b$ is

(A) $\frac{18}{5}(b^{5/2} - a^{5/2})$.
(B) $\frac{18}{5}(b^{3/2} - a^{3/2})$.
(C) $\frac{12}{5}(a^{3/2} - b^{3/2})$.
(D) $\frac{12}{5}b^{3/2}$.
(E) $\frac{18}{5}b^{5/2}$.

34. A hoop of mass m and radius r starts from rest and rolls down an inclined plane of height h. The thickness of the hoop is small in comparison with r. The initial elevation $h = 0.5$ m, $r = 0.1$ m and $m = 1$ kg. The angular speed of the hoop when it reaches the bottom is nearest

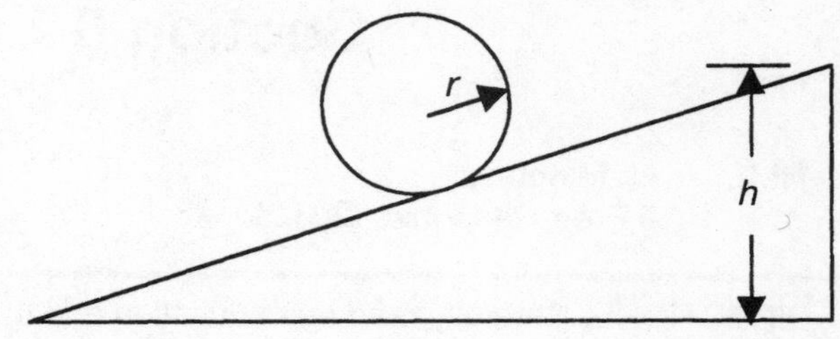

(A) 150 rad/s.

(B) 120 rad/s.

(C) 30 rad/s.

(D) 20 rad/s.

(E) 10 rad/s.

35. A ball of mass 20 g travels at speed v and impacts and then compresses a spring by 10 cm. If the spring constant is 400 N/m and friction is negligible, the speed of the ball is nearly

(A) 10 m/s.

(B) 14 m/s.

(C) 28 m/s.

(D) 40 m/s.

(E) 36 m/s.

AP PHYSICS C
Test 4: Mechanics

Section II

TIME: 45 Minutes
3 Free-Response Questions

DIRECTIONS: Carefully read each question and then make sure to answer *each part* of the question. You must show your work. Crossed out work will not be graded. You will lose credit for incorrect work that is not crossed out.

1. A cannonball is shot at an angle 30 degrees above the horizontal, as shown. The cannon stands at the edge of a vertical drop of 20 m to a flat surface that is inclined 30 degrees below the horizontal. The maximum height of the ball's trajectory is 30 m above horizontal *AB* shown in the figure. (Assume that air friction is negligible.)

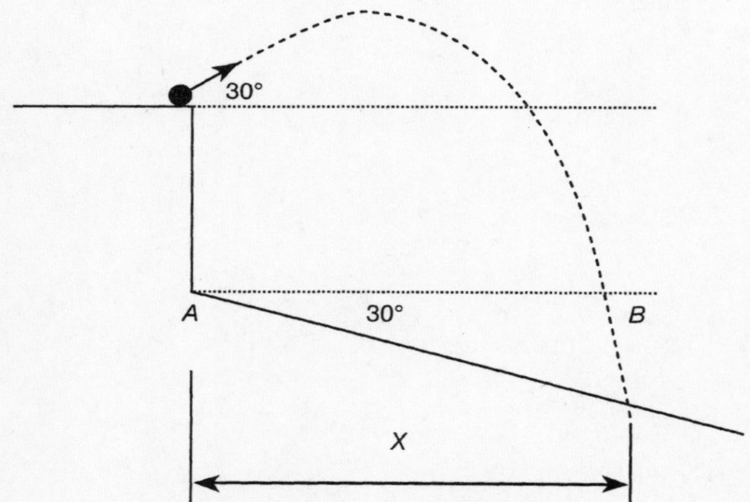

(a) Draw a free-body diagram of the ball at the highest point of its trajectory. Show all force, velocity, and acceleration vectors.

(b) Find the initial velocity of the ball in m/s.

(c) What is the range X of the ball?

(d) How much time does the ball spend in the air before impact?

2. A wheel with nonnegligible inertia rotates about a perpendicular axis through O. It has mass M, radius R, density ρ, and thickness t, with two masses m_1 and m_2 attached to a string wound around the wheel one half turn. There is no slippage, and frictional effects are negligible. (Assume that $m_2 > m_1$.)

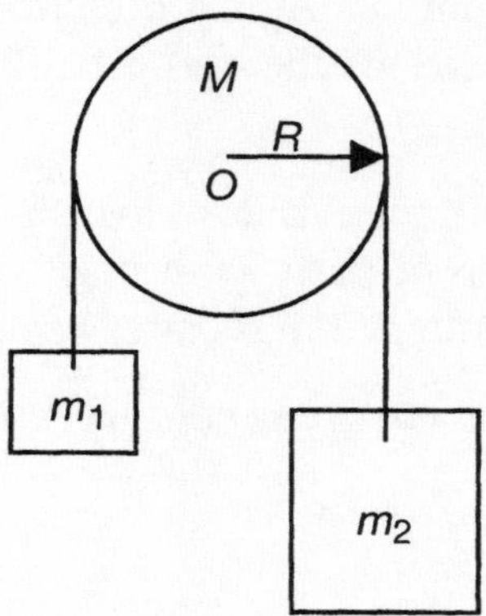

(a) Draw free-body diagrams for all three bodies, showing all external forces acting on each.

(b) Find moment of inertia of the wheel, utilizing r, ρ, and t. Show calculations that lead to the final result.

(c) Set up the equations in terms of mass and external forces required to solve for the angular acceleration α of M. Do *not* solve for the acceleration.

(d) Solve the equations in part (c) numerically for angular acceleration α, using $m_1 = 1$ kg, $m_2 = 3$ kg, $M = 5$ kg, and $R = 0.2$ m.

(e) Calculate how far m_2 falls in 1 s, if it starts from rest.

3. A ball is struck by another object, imparting a force as shown in the accompanying plot. The mass of the ball is 200 g. (Neglect air frictional effect.)

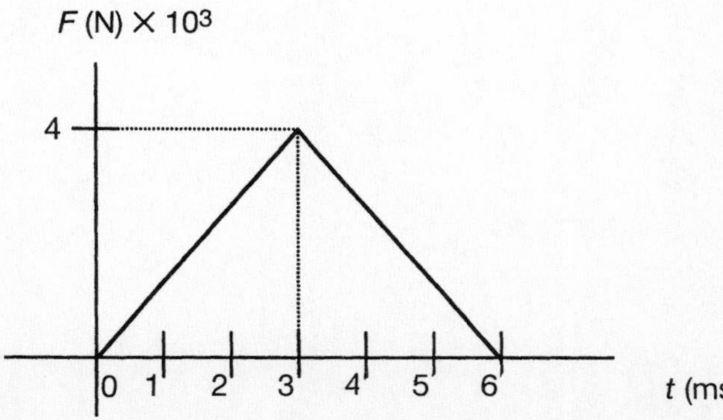

(a) What is the total impulse on the ball?

(b) What is the velocity of the ball immediately after impact?

(c) After acquiring its velocity, the ball elastically impacts a stationary ball of mass 400 g. If the 200-g ball caroms off at an angle of 30 degrees from its original direction with a speed of 35 m/s, what is the velocity of the 400-g ball? (Determine both magnitude and direction.)

(d) Assume that the situation described in part (c) instead involved a stationary lump of putty with mass of 300 g. Find the kinetic energy of the combined mass after impact.

(e) Explain how total energy is conserved in an inelastic collision.

AP PHYSICS C
TEST 4

Section I

ANSWER KEY

1.	(D)	10.	(D)	19.	(A)	28.	(A)
2.	(D)	11.	(B)	20.	(B)	29.	(E)
3.	(B)	12.	(C)	21.	(D)	30.	(C)
4.	(C)	13.	(D)	22.	(A)	31.	(D)
5.	(E)	14.	(B)	23.	(C)	32.	(B)
6.	(A)	15.	(E)	24.	(C)	33.	(A)
7.	(C)	16.	(D)	25.	(C)	34.	(D)
8.	(E)	17.	(E)	26.	(B)	35.	(B)
9.	(E)	18.	(C)	27.	(B)		

DETAILED EXPLANATIONS OF ANSWERS

TEST 4
Section I

1. **(D)** Vectors **A** and **B** cancel one another in the subtraction, leaving only **C** with magnitude 2.

2. **(D)** Similarly, the direction of the resultant is the direction of –**C**, since the two other vectors have canceled each other out.

3. **(B)** By definition, the cross-product magnitude is equal to the product of each vector's magnitude and the sine of the angle between them. In this case the angle is 90 degrees, so the sine is 1. Therefore, $2 \times 3 \times 1 = 6$. The direction is given by the right-hand rule as perpendicular to the paper and into it.

4. **(C)** The definition of average velocity is $\Delta x/\Delta t$, where the numerator is the change in displacement, x, during the time given in the denominator. For this problem, $\Delta x = x_5 - x_2$, where the first term represents the displacement at $t = 5$ seconds and the second the displacement at $t = 2$ seconds. Evaluating, we get $x_5 = 3(5)^2 - 2(5) = 65$ and $x_2 = 3(2)^2 - 2(2) = 8$. Thus, average velocity is $v = (65 - 8)/(5 - 2) = 57/3 = 19$ m/s.

5. **(E)** The bullet must be elevated above the horizontal by angle θ and aimed high by distance h in order to hit the target center (tc) as indicated in the sketch. As shown, the bullet takes a parabolic path.

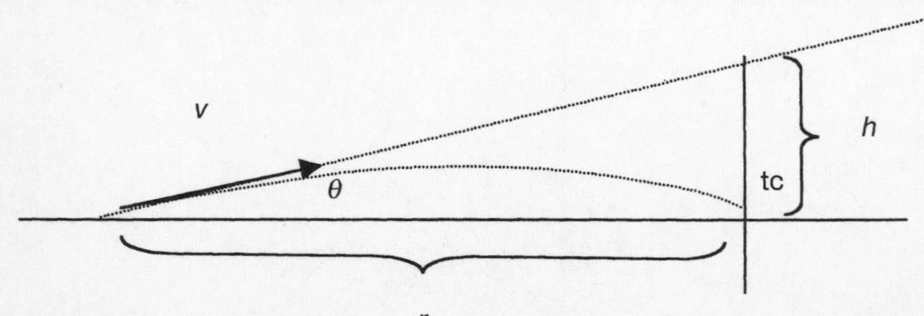

We start by noting that $\tan \theta = h/r$. Thus, to find h in terms of r, g, and v, we will need to develop an expression for $\tan \theta$. Starting with $x = (v \cos \theta)t$ and $y = (v \sin \theta)t - \frac{1}{2}gt^2$, we can apply these at the time when $x = r$ and $y = 0$. The first equation becomes $r = (v \cos \theta)T$ and the second becomes $0 = (v \sin \theta)T - \frac{1}{2}gT^2$, or $v \sin \theta = \frac{1}{2}gT$ after canceling out a T on both sides. (T is the time at which the bullet impacts the target.) Eliminating T from the equations, we arrive at $0 = v^2(\sin \theta)(\cos \theta) - (gr/2)$. But since θ is small, this equation can be approximated as $0 \approx v^2 \tan \theta - (gr/2)$. Solving, $\tan \theta = \frac{gr}{2v^2}$. Therefore, $h = \frac{gr^2}{2v^2}$.

6. **(A)** If we write $F = ma$ for a free-falling body that has reached terminal velocity v_T, we obtain $mg - kv_T = 0$, where the first term is the weight and the second is the drag force at v_T (where k, drag, is a function of shape or area). The right side is zero, because acceleration is zero after the terminal speed is reached, thereby ruling out I. Solving for v_T, we get $v_T = mg/k$. We see that the terminal velocity depends on both m and k. Thus, II is ruled out, and the answer is given by III.

7. **(C)** Applying $F = ma$ along the plane, we obtain $F \cos 37° = (5)(5) = 25$. Solving for F, we obtain 31.3 N.

8. **(E)** Free-body diagrams are shown for the two bottom links. Note that the bottom link has two forces acting on it (the contact force between the middle and bottom links and its weight), whereas the middle link has three (contact force with the top link in the upward direction, its weight, and the contact force with bottom link, the last two acting in the opposite direction). Note that the contact forces are equal and opposite, as required by Newton's third law of action/reaction.

The objective is to find F_{tm}, which is the contact force between the top and middle link. The approach is to first find F_{mb} and then use it to find F_{tm}.

Applying Newton's second law to the bottom link, we obtain $F = F_{mb} - mg = ma$. Solving for F_{mb}, we get $F_{mb} = mg + ma = (0.001)(9.8) + (0.001)(3) = 0.013$ N. Applying Newton's second law to the middle link, we get $F_{tm} - F_{mb} - mg = 3m$. Solving for F_{tm}, we obtain $F_{tm} = F_{mb} + mg + 3m = 0.013 + 0.01 + 0.003 = 0.026$ N.

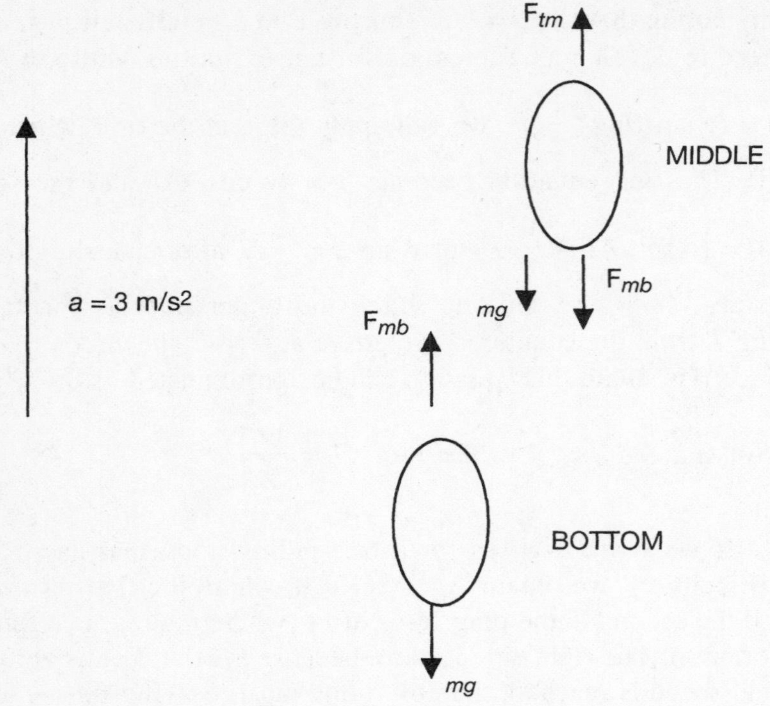

9. **(E)** Work is, by definition, $\int F \cos \theta dr$, where $F \cos \theta$ is the component of total force in the direction of displacement r. Since displacement and force lie along the same straight line for this problem, $F \cos \theta = F$. Thus, to obtain total work, we need to evaluate $\int_0^{14} F dr$, where the limits have been obtained from the problem statement. This means taking the area under the F versus distance curve over the stated interval. Since the area is seen to consist of a triangle and a rectangle, it is a simple matter to sum these as follows: $W = (0.5)(10)(80) + (40)(14 - 10) = 560$ J.

10. **(D)** This problem can be approached by means of trial and error or by using differential calculus. If the former is used, then direct substitution of values given, along with simplifying estimation values, can point to the answer. However, the latter approach is simpler, as maximums and minimums occur when the slope of the function is zero. Taking the derivative (slope) of the given function yields $12t - 7$. Equating this to zero and solving for t gives the result $t = 7/12$ s.

11. **(B)** The approach is to sum moments of the bent wire about each axis and equate them to the moment produced by the entire mass of the bent wire at the center-of-mass coordinates.

For the Y-coordinate, we sum moments about the X-axis, writing the expression $8\ell\overline{Y} = (3\ell/2)\ell - (3\ell/2)4\ell$. Here all the mass is taken to be 8ℓ and the Y-coordinate for center of mass is $\overline{Y}$. The two terms on the right are moments due to, respectively, the ℓ and 4ℓ sections, each $3\ell/2$ units away from the X-axis. (There is a zero moment for the 31 section due to its symmetry.) Solving, we obtain $\overline{Y} = (-9/16)\ell$.

For the X-coordinate, we sum moments about the Y-axis, writing the expression $8\ell\overline{X} = \ell(\ell/2) + 3\ell(\ell) + \ell(\ell/2) - 3\ell(3\ell/2)$. Again, all the mass is taken to be 8ℓ and the X-coordinate for center of mass is $\overline{X}$. The four terms on the right are moments due to the three sections of the bent wire. The first term is the moment due to the ℓ section with all its mass considered to be lumped at $\ell/2$. The second term is the moment due to the 3ℓ section at a moment distance of ℓ. The third and fourth terms are the moments due to the 4ℓ section with the third term being subsection ℓ considered to be acting at distance $\ell/2$, and the fourth term for subsection 3ℓ considered to be acting at distance $3\ell/2$. Solving, we obtain $\overline{X} = (-1/16)\ell$.

12. **(C)** The problem is solved in two parts. First, use the conservation of energy to obtain the block speed immediately after impact. Then, use conservation of momentum to find the bullet speed.

By conservation of energy, the potential energy of the block at its high point must equal its kinetic energy at the low point, i.e., immediately after bullet impact. In equation form, we write $mgh = (1/2)mv^2$. The block m's cancel out, and solving for v we obtain $v = \sqrt{2gh} = \sqrt{2(9.8)(0.05)}$, which is nearly 1 m/s. Then, using conservation of momentum, we can write $m_b v_b = m_{blk} v_{blk}$, where the subscripts b and blk refer, respectively, to bullet and block, and m and v are the usual symbols for mass and velocity. The term on the left side is the momentum before impact, and the term on the right is the momentum after impact. (Note that the bullet mass does not appear in the right-hand side because its mass is so small relative to the mass of the block that it can safely be neglected.) Solving for v_b, we obtain $v_b = (m_{blk}/m_b)v_{blk}$. The ratio of masses is 800 and the block velocity from above is about 1 m/s, leading to a bullet velocity of nearly 800 m/s.

13. **(D)** The moment of inertia is defined as $I = \int r^2 dm$, where r is the radial distance from the axis of rotation to mass element dm. Nothing in this definition rules out continuous mass systems such as wheels or discs, so I is eliminated. The axis choice for I is arbitrary (i.e., one can pick any convenient point to obtain a value), so II is ruled out because it is clear that a rod, for example, will have a much smaller moment of inertia about

its long axis than an axis perpendicular to the long axis. Because both mass and radial distance from an axis appear in the definition, only III is correct.

14. **(B)** Angular speed is given by $\omega = v/r$, where v is speed in m/s and r is the radius of curvature. In this problem v = (72 km/hr)(1000 m/km)(1 hr/3600 s) = 20 m/s, and r = 100 m. Therefore, ω = 20/100 = 0.2 rad/s.

15. **(E)** The angular momentum of a system is the vector sum of its parts. For this system we can write $L = \Sigma\, m_1v_1r_1 + m_2v_2r_2$ with m, v, and r being, respectively, the mass, velocity, and radial distance from axis O for both masses. Note that for each term, this is equivalent to the cross-product expression of $\mathbf{L} = \mathbf{r} \times \mathbf{p} = \mathbf{r} \times m\mathbf{v}$. Applying it to either yields for magnitude $L = mvr \sin (90) = mvr$. Applying the right-hand rule to both objects yields L-vectors whose directions are perpendicular to the page that have opposite sense. Thus, L is given by $L = 3(2)(2) - 5(2)(2) = 12 - 20 = -8$ kgm^2/s. Note that the magnitude is 8 with the sign assignment for sense being arbitrary.

16. **(D)** Free-body diagrams are shown for each block.

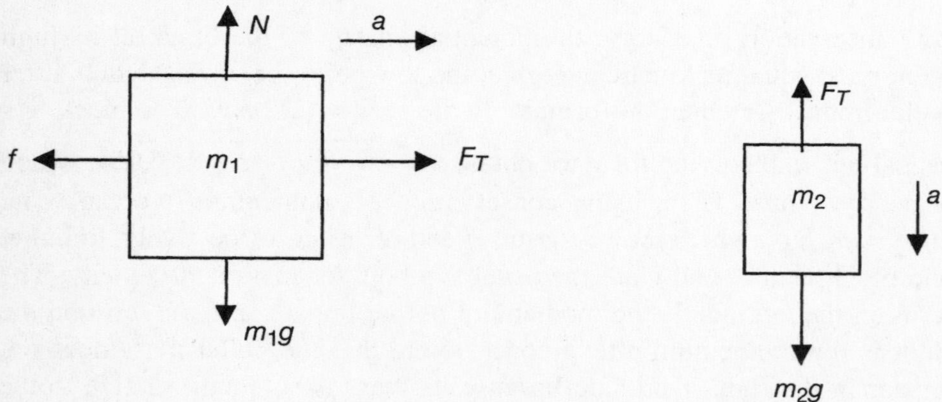

We apply Newton's second law to each block. For the block moving horizontally, we write $F_T - f = m_1a$, where f is the frictional force and F_T is the string tension. For the block moving vertically, we write $m_2g - F_T = m_2a$. Eliminating F_T from these equations, we write $m_2g - f = a(m_1 + m_2)$. But $f = \mu N = \mu m_1 g$, where μ is the coefficient of friction and N is the normal force. Substituting into the previous result and solving for a, we obtain $a = (m_2g - \mu\, m_1g)/(m_1 + m_2) = g(10 - 1)/(10 + 5) = (3/5)g$, or about 6 m/s^2.

17. **(E)** The angular frequency of a mass-spring system is given by $\omega = \sqrt{k/m}$, where k is the spring constant and m is the mass. Also, $\omega = 2\pi f$, where f is the frequency. Solving, we get $f = (1/2\pi)\sqrt{k/m} = (1/2\pi)\sqrt{40/0.2} = (1/2\pi)(10\sqrt{2}) = 5\sqrt{2}/\pi$ Hz.

18. **(C)** Escape speed v is given by $\sqrt{2GM/R}$, where G is the universal gravitational constant, M is planetary mass, and R is planetary radius. Rocket mass does not appear, so any answer involving II is ruled out. Escape speed increases directly with planetary mass and decreases inversely with planetary radius, so IV is ruled out, and I and III are correct.

19. **(A)** The spherical shell can be treated as a point mass, and then Newton's universal law of gravitation is used. The spherical shell has a mass of ρV. Considered as a point mass at distance r, the attractive force acting on both masses is given by $F = Gm(\rho V)/r^2$.

20. **(B)** The gravitational force F between the two point masses before repositioning is given by $F_b = \frac{Gm_1m_2}{r^2}$, where m is the symbol for mass and r is the original distance. After repositioning, we can write $F_a = 3F_b = \frac{Gm_1(m_2/2)}{x^2}$, where x is the new separation distance, and subscripts a and b denote "after" and "before," respectively. Dividing the F_b equation by the F_a equation, we obtain $\frac{1}{3} = \frac{2x^2}{r^2}$, the force, gravitational, and mass symbols all canceling. Solving, we get $x = r/\sqrt{6}$.

21. **(D)** The distance covered by the canoe in the problem statement is equal to its velocity relative to the shore multiplied by the time. Mathematically, we can write $r = (v - 0.5)t$, where the term in the parentheses is the relative speed and t is time. The v is the speed of the canoe in still water and 0.5 is the river current in m/s. Plugging values into the equation, we obtain $600 = (v - 0.5)(10)(60)$ with the 10 minutes converted to seconds by the factor 60. Solving for v, we get 1.5 m/s. To find how fast it would travel with the current, we add the current's velocity, 0.5 m/s, arriving at 2.0 m/s.

22. **(A)** The maximum tension in the fish line occurs when the mass is at the low point of the circle. The free-body diagram shows the forces involved, with F_T representing the tension in the line and mg the weight. Also shown is the tangential velocity v and the centripetal acceleration a.

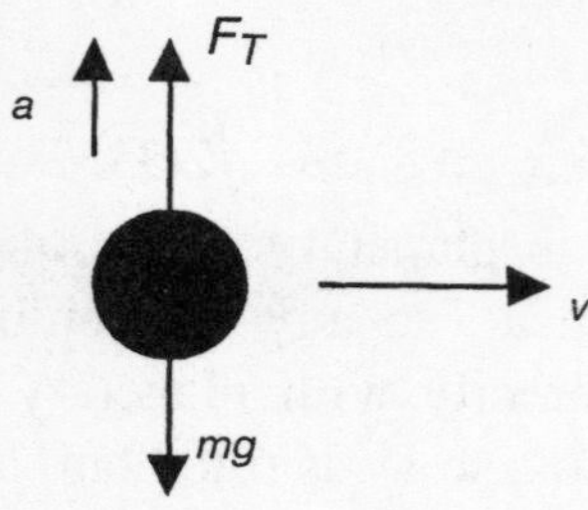

Applying Newton's second law in the radial direction, we can write $F_T - mg = ma$. But, $a = r\omega^2$, and substituting this, we obtain $F_T - mg = mrw^2$. Solving, we obtain $\omega = \sqrt{(F_T - mg)/mr} = \sqrt{(0.5 - 0.005)/0.005} \approx \sqrt{0.5/0.005} = \sqrt{100} = 10$ rad/s. The nearest answer is 9.3 rad/s and it is smaller, as it should be if the simplifying approximation is not made.

23. **(C)** This is a problem involving conservation of momentum. Since momentum is a vector quantity, the problem must be solved taking both magnitude and direction into account. A vector diagram illustrating momentum conservation is shown below, with $\alpha = 30°$.

As indicated, all the momentum before the collision is represented by a single vector. After the collision, each ball has momentum, so their momentum vectors must add together in head-to-tail fashion to equal the "before" momentum. From this point, we can use components or the law of cosines; the latter is much easier.

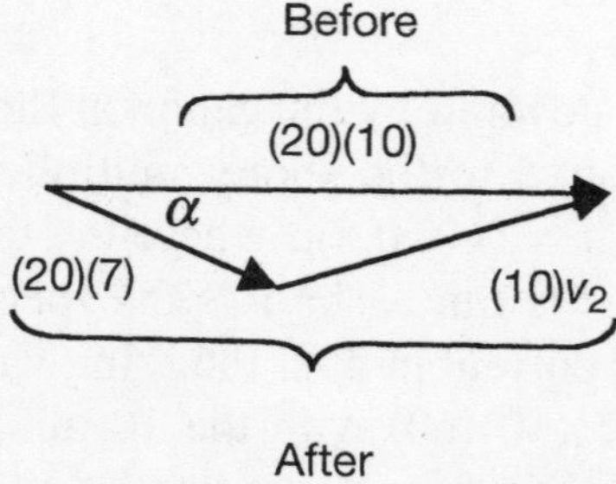

To begin, each vector magnitude (triangle side) can be divided by 10 to simplify the math. This results in a similar triangle with lengths of 14, 20, and v_2. Applying the law of cosines, we obtain $v_2^2 = 14^2 + 20^2 - 2(14)(20)\frac{\sqrt{3}}{2}$ $= 196 + 400 - 560(0.87) \approx 100$. Therefore, v_2 is nearest to 10 m/s. Note that for problems of this type, we need not convert the grams into kilograms, because when terms with common units appear in every term of an equation, the units cancel.

24. **(C)** By definition, $F = -dU/dx$, where U is the potential energy function. Disregarding the negative sign and taking the derivative, we obtain $F = 12x - 3$. For $x = 0.5$ m, $F = 6 - 3 = 3$ N.

25. **(C)** Applying $F = ma$ after reaching terminal velocity, we obtain $mg - kv_t = 0$. Here, the right side is zero because acceleration is zero. The first term on the left side is the weight, and the second is the equal and opposite drag force. The drag force itself is the product of the drag coefficient k and the velocity. Solving for v_t, we get $mg/k = (0.05)(10)/(0.2) \approx$ 2.5 m/s.

26. **(B)** Velocity v is related to acceleration as follows. $v = v_0 + \int a dt$, where v_0 is the initial velocity, a is the acceleration, and t is time. For this problem, v_0 is zero, so evaluation of the integral is all that is required. Evaluation involves finding the area under the a-t curve for the 0-to-3 second interval. Thus, $v = (1/2)(10)(1) - (3)(3 - 2) = 5 - 3 = 2$ m/s. Note: It is important to bear in mind that areas below the t-axis are considered to be negative (decelerations), whereas areas above the axis are positive (accelerations).

27. **(B)** This question has to do with the nature of collisions. Perfectly elastic collisions always conserve both momentum and kinetic energy. Perfectly inelastic collisions always conserve momentum, but not kinetic energy. Thus I is always true and any answer containing it can be eliminated. II is true, so any answer containing it can also be eliminated. This leaves only III, which incorrectly reverses the usual situation for inelastic collisions, where colliding bodies do stick together.

28. **(A)** The approach here is to use $\tau = I\alpha$ and $\omega = \omega_0 + {}^1/_2\alpha t^2$. The former equation relates torque τ, moment of inertia I, and angular acceleration α. The latter relates initial angular velocity ω_0 and final angular velocity ω with α and time t.

To obtain α, we work with the second equation, writing $0 = (120)(2\pi)/60 - {}^1/_2\alpha(100)$. (Note that 0 was used for the left-hand side because that was the velocity corresponding to $t = 10$ s.) Solving, we obtain $\alpha = (4.8\pi)/60 \approx 0.25$ rad/s^2. Plugging this into the first equation and solving for I, we obtain $I = 50/0.25$ or about 200 m^{2}kg.

29. **(E)** By definition, the period T is the reciprocal of the frequency f, or $T = 1/f$. For this problem, $T = 1/5000$ Hz. Thus, the answer is 2×10^{-4} s or 0.2 ms.

30. **(C)** By definition, the coefficient of friction is the ratio of friction force to normal force, or $\mu = f/N$, where f is the friction force and N is the normal force. For this problem, the normal force N is $mg \cos \theta$, and the friction force is $mg \sin \theta$, because the block is in equilibrium, with no acceleration along the plane. Forming the ratio, we get $\mu = (mg \sin \theta)/(mg \cos \theta) = \tan \theta = \tan 37° = 0.75$.

31. **(D)** By definition, the coefficient of friction is the ratio of friction force to normal force, or $\mu = f/N$, where f is the friction force and N is the normal force. Since the ratio is of like quantities, units cancel; so any answer containing I is a candidate answer. The numerical value is always less than 1, so any answer involving II can be ruled out. For a given f, μ is inversely proportional to N, so both I and III are correct.

32. **(B)** The approach here is to use Newton's universal law of gravitation and $F = ma$ to form a ratio of accelerations.

On planet X, the force acting on any object of mass m is $F_X = \dfrac{GmM_X}{r_X{}^2}$, with G the universal gravitational constant, M_X the mass of planet X, and r_X as its radius. For planet Y, we can write $F_Y = \dfrac{Gm3M_Y}{9r_Y{}^2}$. Forming the ratio of F_Y to F_X yields $^1/_3$, after cancellations. Using $F = ma = mg$, we see that ratio of accelerations are the same as the ratio of forces. Finally, since planet X's acceleration of gravity is $4g$, the acceleration of gravity on planet Y is $(4/3)g$.

33. **(A)** By definition, the total work done is $W = \int_{r_1}^{r_2} F dr$, where F is the force and r is the displacement from position 1 to position 2. For this problem, we can write $W = \int_a^b 9r^{3/2} dr = \dfrac{18}{5}(b^{5/2} - a^{5/2})$.

34. **(D)** The approach used on this problem is that of conservation of energy. The energy of the hoop at the top of the inclined plane is all potential, becoming all kinetic at the bottom. Mathematically, we write $mgh = \frac{1}{2}mv^2 + \frac{1}{2}I\omega^2$ with the left side representing the potential energy and the right side the kinetic. Note that the kinetic energy takes two forms: translational (first term) and rotational (second term). We now substitute for $I = r^2m$ and $v = r\omega$ and solve for ω, arriving at $\omega = \frac{\sqrt{gh}}{r} = \frac{\sqrt{(9.8)(0.5)}}{0.1} = 22$ rad/s.

35. **(B)** This is a conservation of energy problem with the ball's kinetic energy being completely converted to potential energy in the compressed spring. To find v, we set the potential energy equal to the kinetic energy, $\frac{1}{2}kx^2 = \frac{1}{2}mv^2$, and solve for v, obtaining $v = \sqrt{\frac{k}{m}}x = \sqrt{\frac{400}{0.02}}(0.1) = 14$ m/s.

DETAILED EXPLANATIONS OF ANSWERS

TEST 4
Section II

1. (a)

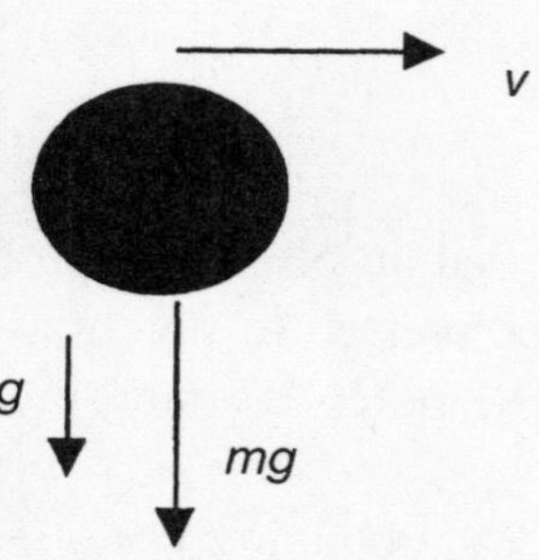

Note that at the highest point the velocity vector is parallel to the horizontal. The weight mg is perpendicular and down, and the acceleration due to gravity is also perpendicular and down.

(b) Use conservation of energy to equate the change in the potential energy to the kinetic energy lost. Mathematically, we can write $mg\Delta h = \frac{1}{2}mv^2$, where the left-hand side is the change in potential energy and the right-hand side is the kinetic energy lost. However, the velocity v appearing in this equation is not the total v, as only the y-component of velocity contributes to increasing the potential energy. Thus, after canceling out the m's, the above equation is modified to $g\Delta h = {}^1/_2(v \sin \theta)^2$. Plugging in the values given, we obtain $(9.8)(30 - 20) = (9.8)(10) = \frac{1}{2}v^2\frac{1}{4}$. Thus, $v = 28$ m/s. Note that $(30 - 20)$ is the Δh associated with the change in potential energy.

(c) This problem is most easily solved by using a graphing calculator and finding where the parabolic curve describing the trajectory intersects the straight line formed by the sloping bottom of the canyon. Alternatively, the two equations from (b) can be set equal to one another, and the resulting quadratic equation solved. The following solution was done with a graphing calculator.

We choose an origin for the x- and y-axes at the location of the cannon. The equation for the straight line representing the inclined flat surface is then $y = -20 - (\tan 30°)x = -20 - (0.58)x$.

The equation for the parabola is derived from $x = (v \cos \theta)t$ and $y = (v \sin \theta)t - {}^1/_2 gt^2$ by plugging in the values given and then eliminating t. For the x-equation, $x = 28\frac{\sqrt{3}}{2}t$. For the y-equation, $y = 28{}^1/_2 t - (4.9)t^2 = 14t - 4.9t^2$.

Solving for t in terms of x in the first equation and plugging that into the second equation, we obtain $y = (14)\frac{x}{24.2} - (4.9)\left(\frac{x}{24.2}\right)^2 = 0.58x - 0.0084x^2$.

The solution of this equation is where it and the equation of the straight line intersect, which is about $x \approx 154$ m.

(d) Since we know the horizontal range of the ball, it can be set equal to the horizontal velocity times the time in the air, and then we can solve for time. In equation form, we write $x = (v \cos \theta)t$. Solving for t, we get $t = (154)/(28)(0.86) = 6.4$ s.

2. (a)

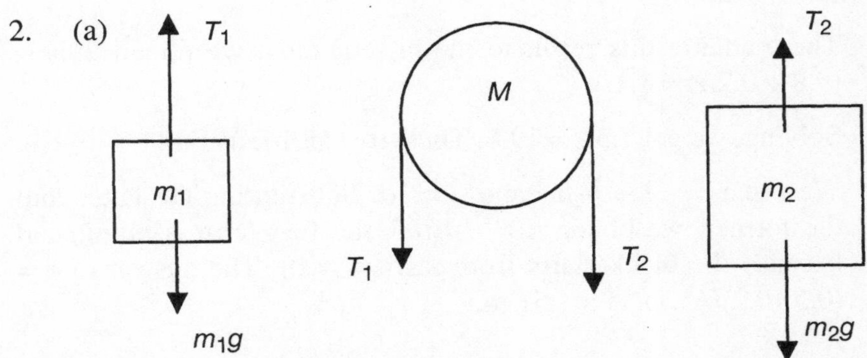

Note that because of the nonnegligible inertia of the wheel, the tension in the string is *not* the same on both sides.

(b) The definition of the moment of inertia is $I = \int r^2 dm$, where the integration is carried out for each differential mass dm at distance r from the axis of rotation. For this problem, the axis of rotation is through point O. Consider a concentric ring of material with $dm = (2\pi r dr)\rho w$.

Then we can write $dI = r^2 dm = 2\pi\rho w r^3 dr$. Thus, $I = \int_0^R 2\pi\rho w r^3 dr$.

Evaluating, we obtain $\frac{1}{2}(\pi R^2 \rho w)R^2 = \frac{1}{2}MR^2$, the terms inside the parentheses being the mass M of the wheel.

(c) For the two masses, we utilize $F = ma$, and for the wheel, we utilize $\tau = I\alpha$. The former is Newton's second law for straight-line motion and the latter is the same law for rotation.

For m_1, we write $T_1 - m_1 g = m_1 a = m_1 R\alpha$. Here, in addition to Newton's second law, we make use of the equation $a = R\alpha$, which relates linear to rotational acceleration. Similarly, for m_2, we write $m_2 g - T_2 = m_2 a = m_2 R\alpha$. For M, we write $\tau = (T_2 - T_1)R = I\alpha = (\frac{1}{2}MR^2)\alpha$. These three equations contain three unknowns: two tensions and the angular acceleration.

(d) Substituting the values given, we obtain the following: for m_1, $T_1 - (9.8) = a = (0.2)\alpha$, or $T_1 - 9.8 = (0.2)\alpha$; for m_2, $3(9.8) - T_2 = 3a = 3(0.2)\alpha$, or $29.4 - T_2 = (0.6)\alpha$; and for M, $(T_2 - T_1)(0.2) = \frac{1}{2}(5)(0.04)\alpha$, or $T_2 - T_1 = (0.5)\alpha$.

There are various ways to solve this system of equations for α. In the method used here, we eliminate T_1 by solving for it in the m_1 equation and substituting into the M equation, obtaining $T_2 - (9.8 + 0.2\alpha) = 0.5\alpha$.

Then, adding this result to the m_2 equation, we obtain $29.4 - (9.8 + 0.2\alpha) = 1.1\alpha$.

Solving, we get $1.3\alpha = 19.6$. Thus, $\alpha = 15.1$ rad/s^2.

(e) We use $x = v_0 t + \frac{1}{2}at^2$ and $a = r\alpha$. Substituting the latter into the former, we obtain $x = \frac{1}{2}R\alpha t^2$; the first term is eliminated because the block starts from rest ($v_0 = 0$). The answer is $x = (0.5)(0.2)(15.1)(1) = 1.51$ m.

3. (a) Impulse is defined as $\mathbf{J} = \int \mathbf{F}dt = \Delta\mathbf{p}$. Equivalently, the change in momentum is equal to the area under the force-time curve. For this problem, the area is $(\frac{1}{2})(4000)(0.006)$Ns = 12 Ns.

(b) By the above definition, the change in momentum must be equal to 12 Ns. The initial momentum was zero, so the change is equal to the final momentum. Thus, $mv = 12$, or $(0.2)v = 12$, so $v = 60$ m/s.

(c) This is a conservation of momentum problem with the total momentum before collision having to equal the total momentum afterwards. Since momentum is a vector, both magnitude and direction must be taken into account when working this type of problem.

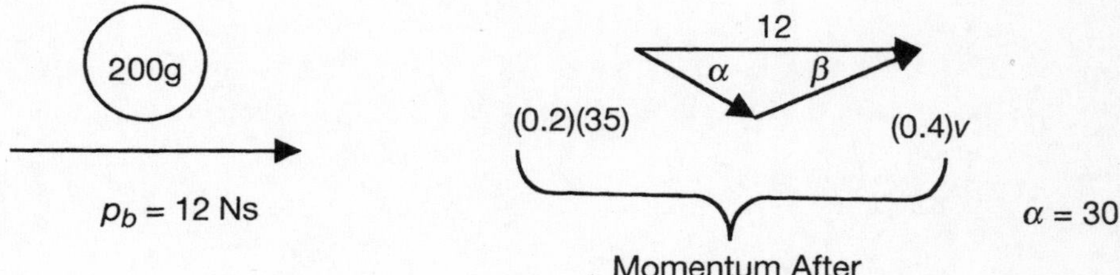

The situation before impact is shown on the left in the diagram above. After the collision, the two vectors shown on the right in the diagram above must equal 12 when added in head-to-tail fashion. To solve for the velocity v of the 0.4-kg ball, we utilize the law of cosines: $(0.4v)^2 = 144 + 49 - 2(12)(7) \cos 30° = 53$. Solving, $v = 18.2$ m/s.

To obtain the direction, we find the angle β using the law of sines.

We write $(\sin 30°)/(0.4)(18.2) = (\sin \beta)/7$. Solving, $\sin \beta = 0.48$ and $\beta = 29°$.

(d) By conservation of momentum, $12 = (0.2 + 0.3)v$, where v is the velocity of the combined mass after impact. Thus $v = 24$ m/s. The kinetic energy is $K = \frac{1}{2} mv^2$, which is about $(0.5)(0.5)(576) = 144$ J. Note that since the original kinetic energy was $(0.5)(0.2)(3600) = 360$ J, much energy has been "lost."

(e) The energy is not all converted into kinetic energy. Whatever is not conserved in this way is converted into heat. Thus, energy is always conserved but not always in its original form.

ANSWER SHEETS

AP PHYSICS B – TEST 1

1. Ⓐ Ⓑ Ⓒ Ⓓ Ⓔ
2. Ⓐ Ⓑ Ⓒ Ⓓ Ⓔ
3. Ⓐ Ⓑ Ⓒ Ⓓ Ⓔ
4. Ⓐ Ⓑ Ⓒ Ⓓ Ⓔ
5. Ⓐ Ⓑ Ⓒ Ⓓ Ⓔ
6. Ⓐ Ⓑ Ⓒ Ⓓ Ⓔ
7. Ⓐ Ⓑ Ⓒ Ⓓ Ⓔ
8. Ⓐ Ⓑ Ⓒ Ⓓ Ⓔ
9. Ⓐ Ⓑ Ⓒ Ⓓ Ⓔ
10. Ⓐ Ⓑ Ⓒ Ⓓ Ⓔ
11. Ⓐ Ⓑ Ⓒ Ⓓ Ⓔ
12. Ⓐ Ⓑ Ⓒ Ⓓ Ⓔ
13. Ⓐ Ⓑ Ⓒ Ⓓ Ⓔ
14. Ⓐ Ⓑ Ⓒ Ⓓ Ⓔ
15. Ⓐ Ⓑ Ⓒ Ⓓ Ⓔ
16. Ⓐ Ⓑ Ⓒ Ⓓ Ⓔ
17. Ⓐ Ⓑ Ⓒ Ⓓ Ⓔ
18. Ⓐ Ⓑ Ⓒ Ⓓ Ⓔ
19. Ⓐ Ⓑ Ⓒ Ⓓ Ⓔ
20. Ⓐ Ⓑ Ⓒ Ⓓ Ⓔ
21. Ⓐ Ⓑ Ⓒ Ⓓ Ⓔ
22. Ⓐ Ⓑ Ⓒ Ⓓ Ⓔ
23. Ⓐ Ⓑ Ⓒ Ⓓ Ⓔ
24. Ⓐ Ⓑ Ⓒ Ⓓ Ⓔ
25. Ⓐ Ⓑ Ⓒ Ⓓ Ⓔ
26. Ⓐ Ⓑ Ⓒ Ⓓ Ⓔ
27. Ⓐ Ⓑ Ⓒ Ⓓ Ⓔ
28. Ⓐ Ⓑ Ⓒ Ⓓ Ⓔ
29. Ⓐ Ⓑ Ⓒ Ⓓ Ⓔ
30. Ⓐ Ⓑ Ⓒ Ⓓ Ⓔ
31. Ⓐ Ⓑ Ⓒ Ⓓ Ⓔ
32. Ⓐ Ⓑ Ⓒ Ⓓ Ⓔ
33. Ⓐ Ⓑ Ⓒ Ⓓ Ⓔ
34. Ⓐ Ⓑ Ⓒ Ⓓ Ⓔ
35. Ⓐ Ⓑ Ⓒ Ⓓ Ⓔ
36. Ⓐ Ⓑ Ⓒ Ⓓ Ⓔ
37. Ⓐ Ⓑ Ⓒ Ⓓ Ⓔ
38. Ⓐ Ⓑ Ⓒ Ⓓ Ⓔ
39. Ⓐ Ⓑ Ⓒ Ⓓ Ⓔ
40. Ⓐ Ⓑ Ⓒ Ⓓ Ⓔ
41. Ⓐ Ⓑ Ⓒ Ⓓ Ⓔ
42. Ⓐ Ⓑ Ⓒ Ⓓ Ⓔ
43. Ⓐ Ⓑ Ⓒ Ⓓ Ⓔ
44. Ⓐ Ⓑ Ⓒ Ⓓ Ⓔ
45. Ⓐ Ⓑ Ⓒ Ⓓ Ⓔ
46. Ⓐ Ⓑ Ⓒ Ⓓ Ⓔ
47. Ⓐ Ⓑ Ⓒ Ⓓ Ⓔ
48. Ⓐ Ⓑ Ⓒ Ⓓ Ⓔ
49. Ⓐ Ⓑ Ⓒ Ⓓ Ⓔ
50. Ⓐ Ⓑ Ⓒ Ⓓ Ⓔ
51. Ⓐ Ⓑ Ⓒ Ⓓ Ⓔ
52. Ⓐ Ⓑ Ⓒ Ⓓ Ⓔ
53. Ⓐ Ⓑ Ⓒ Ⓓ Ⓔ
54. Ⓐ Ⓑ Ⓒ Ⓓ Ⓔ
55. Ⓐ Ⓑ Ⓒ Ⓓ Ⓔ
56. Ⓐ Ⓑ Ⓒ Ⓓ Ⓔ
57. Ⓐ Ⓑ Ⓒ Ⓓ Ⓔ
58. Ⓐ Ⓑ Ⓒ Ⓓ Ⓔ
59. Ⓐ Ⓑ Ⓒ Ⓓ Ⓔ
60. Ⓐ Ⓑ Ⓒ Ⓓ Ⓔ
61. Ⓐ Ⓑ Ⓒ Ⓓ Ⓔ
62. Ⓐ Ⓑ Ⓒ Ⓓ Ⓔ
63. Ⓐ Ⓑ Ⓒ Ⓓ Ⓔ
64. Ⓐ Ⓑ Ⓒ Ⓓ Ⓔ
65. Ⓐ Ⓑ Ⓒ Ⓓ Ⓔ
66. Ⓐ Ⓑ Ⓒ Ⓓ Ⓔ
67. Ⓐ Ⓑ Ⓒ Ⓓ Ⓔ
68. Ⓐ Ⓑ Ⓒ Ⓓ Ⓔ
69. Ⓐ Ⓑ Ⓒ Ⓓ Ⓔ
70. Ⓐ Ⓑ Ⓒ Ⓓ Ⓔ

AP PHYSICS B – TEST 2

1. Ⓐ Ⓑ Ⓒ Ⓓ Ⓔ
2. Ⓐ Ⓑ Ⓒ Ⓓ Ⓔ
3. Ⓐ Ⓑ Ⓒ Ⓓ Ⓔ
4. Ⓐ Ⓑ Ⓒ Ⓓ Ⓔ
5. Ⓐ Ⓑ Ⓒ Ⓓ Ⓔ
6. Ⓐ Ⓑ Ⓒ Ⓓ Ⓔ
7. Ⓐ Ⓑ Ⓒ Ⓓ Ⓔ
8. Ⓐ Ⓑ Ⓒ Ⓓ Ⓔ
9. Ⓐ Ⓑ Ⓒ Ⓓ Ⓔ
10. Ⓐ Ⓑ Ⓒ Ⓓ Ⓔ
11. Ⓐ Ⓑ Ⓒ Ⓓ Ⓔ
12. Ⓐ Ⓑ Ⓒ Ⓓ Ⓔ
13. Ⓐ Ⓑ Ⓒ Ⓓ Ⓔ
14. Ⓐ Ⓑ Ⓒ Ⓓ Ⓔ
15. Ⓐ Ⓑ Ⓒ Ⓓ Ⓔ
16. Ⓐ Ⓑ Ⓒ Ⓓ Ⓔ
17. Ⓐ Ⓑ Ⓒ Ⓓ Ⓔ
18. Ⓐ Ⓑ Ⓒ Ⓓ Ⓔ
19. Ⓐ Ⓑ Ⓒ Ⓓ Ⓔ
20. Ⓐ Ⓑ Ⓒ Ⓓ Ⓔ
21. Ⓐ Ⓑ Ⓒ Ⓓ Ⓔ
22. Ⓐ Ⓑ Ⓒ Ⓓ Ⓔ
23. Ⓐ Ⓑ Ⓒ Ⓓ Ⓔ
24. Ⓐ Ⓑ Ⓒ Ⓓ Ⓔ
25. Ⓐ Ⓑ Ⓒ Ⓓ Ⓔ
26. Ⓐ Ⓑ Ⓒ Ⓓ Ⓔ
27. Ⓐ Ⓑ Ⓒ Ⓓ Ⓔ
28. Ⓐ Ⓑ Ⓒ Ⓓ Ⓔ
29. Ⓐ Ⓑ Ⓒ Ⓓ Ⓔ
30. Ⓐ Ⓑ Ⓒ Ⓓ Ⓔ
31. Ⓐ Ⓑ Ⓒ Ⓓ Ⓔ
32. Ⓐ Ⓑ Ⓒ Ⓓ Ⓔ
33. Ⓐ Ⓑ Ⓒ Ⓓ Ⓔ
34. Ⓐ Ⓑ Ⓒ Ⓓ Ⓔ
35. Ⓐ Ⓑ Ⓒ Ⓓ Ⓔ
36. Ⓐ Ⓑ Ⓒ Ⓓ Ⓔ
37. Ⓐ Ⓑ Ⓒ Ⓓ Ⓔ
38. Ⓐ Ⓑ Ⓒ Ⓓ Ⓔ
39. Ⓐ Ⓑ Ⓒ Ⓓ Ⓔ
40. Ⓐ Ⓑ Ⓒ Ⓓ Ⓔ
41. Ⓐ Ⓑ Ⓒ Ⓓ Ⓔ
42. Ⓐ Ⓑ Ⓒ Ⓓ Ⓔ
43. Ⓐ Ⓑ Ⓒ Ⓓ Ⓔ
44. Ⓐ Ⓑ Ⓒ Ⓓ Ⓔ
45. Ⓐ Ⓑ Ⓒ Ⓓ Ⓔ
46. Ⓐ Ⓑ Ⓒ Ⓓ Ⓔ
47. Ⓐ Ⓑ Ⓒ Ⓓ Ⓔ
48. Ⓐ Ⓑ Ⓒ Ⓓ Ⓔ
49. Ⓐ Ⓑ Ⓒ Ⓓ Ⓔ
50. Ⓐ Ⓑ Ⓒ Ⓓ Ⓔ
51. Ⓐ Ⓑ Ⓒ Ⓓ Ⓔ
52. Ⓐ Ⓑ Ⓒ Ⓓ Ⓔ
53. Ⓐ Ⓑ Ⓒ Ⓓ Ⓔ
54. Ⓐ Ⓑ Ⓒ Ⓓ Ⓔ
55. Ⓐ Ⓑ Ⓒ Ⓓ Ⓔ
56. Ⓐ Ⓑ Ⓒ Ⓓ Ⓔ
57. Ⓐ Ⓑ Ⓒ Ⓓ Ⓔ
58. Ⓐ Ⓑ Ⓒ Ⓓ Ⓔ
59. Ⓐ Ⓑ Ⓒ Ⓓ Ⓔ
60. Ⓐ Ⓑ Ⓒ Ⓓ Ⓔ
61. Ⓐ Ⓑ Ⓒ Ⓓ Ⓔ
62. Ⓐ Ⓑ Ⓒ Ⓓ Ⓔ
63. Ⓐ Ⓑ Ⓒ Ⓓ Ⓔ
64. Ⓐ Ⓑ Ⓒ Ⓓ Ⓔ
65. Ⓐ Ⓑ Ⓒ Ⓓ Ⓔ
66. Ⓐ Ⓑ Ⓒ Ⓓ Ⓔ
67. Ⓐ Ⓑ Ⓒ Ⓓ Ⓔ
68. Ⓐ Ⓑ Ⓒ Ⓓ Ⓔ
69. Ⓐ Ⓑ Ⓒ Ⓓ Ⓔ
70. Ⓐ Ⓑ Ⓒ Ⓓ Ⓔ

AP PHYSICS C – TEST 3

1. Ⓐ Ⓑ Ⓒ Ⓓ Ⓔ
2. Ⓐ Ⓑ Ⓒ Ⓓ Ⓔ
3. Ⓐ Ⓑ Ⓒ Ⓓ Ⓔ
4. Ⓐ Ⓑ Ⓒ Ⓓ Ⓔ
5. Ⓐ Ⓑ Ⓒ Ⓓ Ⓔ
6. Ⓐ Ⓑ Ⓒ Ⓓ Ⓔ
7. Ⓐ Ⓑ Ⓒ Ⓓ Ⓔ
8. Ⓐ Ⓑ Ⓒ Ⓓ Ⓔ
9. Ⓐ Ⓑ Ⓒ Ⓓ Ⓔ
10. Ⓐ Ⓑ Ⓒ Ⓓ Ⓔ
11. Ⓐ Ⓑ Ⓒ Ⓓ Ⓔ
12. Ⓐ Ⓑ Ⓒ Ⓓ Ⓔ
13. Ⓐ Ⓑ Ⓒ Ⓓ Ⓔ
14. Ⓐ Ⓑ Ⓒ Ⓓ Ⓔ
15. Ⓐ Ⓑ Ⓒ Ⓓ Ⓔ
16. Ⓐ Ⓑ Ⓒ Ⓓ Ⓔ
17. Ⓐ Ⓑ Ⓒ Ⓓ Ⓔ
18. Ⓐ Ⓑ Ⓒ Ⓓ Ⓔ
19. Ⓐ Ⓑ Ⓒ Ⓓ Ⓔ
20. Ⓐ Ⓑ Ⓒ Ⓓ Ⓔ
21. Ⓐ Ⓑ Ⓒ Ⓓ Ⓔ
22. Ⓐ Ⓑ Ⓒ Ⓓ Ⓔ
23. Ⓐ Ⓑ Ⓒ Ⓓ Ⓔ
24. Ⓐ Ⓑ Ⓒ Ⓓ Ⓔ
25. Ⓐ Ⓑ Ⓒ Ⓓ Ⓔ
26. Ⓐ Ⓑ Ⓒ Ⓓ Ⓔ
27. Ⓐ Ⓑ Ⓒ Ⓓ Ⓔ
28. Ⓐ Ⓑ Ⓒ Ⓓ Ⓔ
29. Ⓐ Ⓑ Ⓒ Ⓓ Ⓔ
30. Ⓐ Ⓑ Ⓒ Ⓓ Ⓔ
31. Ⓐ Ⓑ Ⓒ Ⓓ Ⓔ
32. Ⓐ Ⓑ Ⓒ Ⓓ Ⓔ
33. Ⓐ Ⓑ Ⓒ Ⓓ Ⓔ
34. Ⓐ Ⓑ Ⓒ Ⓓ Ⓔ
35. Ⓐ Ⓑ Ⓒ Ⓓ Ⓔ

AP PHYSICS C – TEST 4

1. Ⓐ Ⓑ Ⓒ Ⓓ Ⓔ
2. Ⓐ Ⓑ Ⓒ Ⓓ Ⓔ
3. Ⓐ Ⓑ Ⓒ Ⓓ Ⓔ
4. Ⓐ Ⓑ Ⓒ Ⓓ Ⓔ
5. Ⓐ Ⓑ Ⓒ Ⓓ Ⓔ
6. Ⓐ Ⓑ Ⓒ Ⓓ Ⓔ
7. Ⓐ Ⓑ Ⓒ Ⓓ Ⓔ
8. Ⓐ Ⓑ Ⓒ Ⓓ Ⓔ
9. Ⓐ Ⓑ Ⓒ Ⓓ Ⓔ
10. Ⓐ Ⓑ Ⓒ Ⓓ Ⓔ
11. Ⓐ Ⓑ Ⓒ Ⓓ Ⓔ
12. Ⓐ Ⓑ Ⓒ Ⓓ Ⓔ
13. Ⓐ Ⓑ Ⓒ Ⓓ Ⓔ
14. Ⓐ Ⓑ Ⓒ Ⓓ Ⓔ
15. Ⓐ Ⓑ Ⓒ Ⓓ Ⓔ
16. Ⓐ Ⓑ Ⓒ Ⓓ Ⓔ
17. Ⓐ Ⓑ Ⓒ Ⓓ Ⓔ
18. Ⓐ Ⓑ Ⓒ Ⓓ Ⓔ
19. Ⓐ Ⓑ Ⓒ Ⓓ Ⓔ
20. Ⓐ Ⓑ Ⓒ Ⓓ Ⓔ
21. Ⓐ Ⓑ Ⓒ Ⓓ Ⓔ
22. Ⓐ Ⓑ Ⓒ Ⓓ Ⓔ
23. Ⓐ Ⓑ Ⓒ Ⓓ Ⓔ
24. Ⓐ Ⓑ Ⓒ Ⓓ Ⓔ
25. Ⓐ Ⓑ Ⓒ Ⓓ Ⓔ
26. Ⓐ Ⓑ Ⓒ Ⓓ Ⓔ
27. Ⓐ Ⓑ Ⓒ Ⓓ Ⓔ
28. Ⓐ Ⓑ Ⓒ Ⓓ Ⓔ
29. Ⓐ Ⓑ Ⓒ Ⓓ Ⓔ
30. Ⓐ Ⓑ Ⓒ Ⓓ Ⓔ
31. Ⓐ Ⓑ Ⓒ Ⓓ Ⓔ
32. Ⓐ Ⓑ Ⓒ Ⓓ Ⓔ
33. Ⓐ Ⓑ Ⓒ Ⓓ Ⓔ
34. Ⓐ Ⓑ Ⓒ Ⓓ Ⓔ
35. Ⓐ Ⓑ Ⓒ Ⓓ Ⓔ

INDEX

A

B

C

D

E

F

G

M

N

O

U

V

W

X